CORRUPTION

Ethics and Power in Florence, 1600–1770

JEAN-CLAUDE WAQUET

Translated by
Linda McCall

The Pennsylvania State University Press
University Park, Pennsylvania

First published as *De la corruption: Morale et pouvoir à Florence aux XVIIe et XVIIIe siècles*
© 1984 Librairie Arthème Fayard

This English translation © 1991 Polity Press

First published in the United States of America in 1992 by The Pennsylvania State University Press, Suite C, 820 North University Drive, University Park, PA 16802

ISBN 0–271–00810–5

Library of Congress Cataloging in Publication Data
A CIP catalogue record for this book is available from the Library of Congress.

Typeset in 11 on 13 pt Baskerville by Wearside Tradespools, Fulwell, Sunderland
Printed in Great Britain by Billing and Sons Ltd., Worcester

It is the policy of The Pennsylvania State University Press to use acid-free paper for the first printing of all clothbound books. Publications on uncoated stock satisfy minimum requirements of American National Standard for Information Sciences—Permanence of Paper for Printed Library Materials, ANSI Z239.48–1984.

CONTENTS

Introduction   The history of corruption: false   1
problems and real questions

Part I   The Smell of Money

Introduction   19
1   The grand embezzlement from the 'Abbondanza'   23
2   Just one of many cases of embezzlement   38

Part II   Dissolute Morals

Introduction   59
3   Appropriating the state   64
4   The misfortunes of virtue   85

Is there a universal model?   97

Part III   Consciences at Peace

Introduction   101
5   On the strength of lies   104
6   Saved by reason   119

Part IV   The Justice of the Lord

Introduction   145
7   The grandeur of clemency   149

Contents

8   The good of punishment   168

The fragility of the state   190

Notes   197
Index   218

INTRODUCTION
THE HISTORY OF CORRUPTION:
FALSE PROBLEMS AND REAL QUESTIONS

Open either volume of Professor Mousnier's classic, albeit recent work *Les Institutions de la France sous la Monarchie absolue*.[1] Leaf through the 1,200 pages of this study and then look in the index for the heading 'corruption' to see if you can find the passages indicating the extent to which the *ancien régime* was crippled by this scourge. You will have searched in vain: there is no such heading.

Does that mean that formerly corruption was unknown? The answer is not at all. In fact, *La vénalité des offices sous Henri IV et sous Louis XIII* by the same author describes how, during the first half of the seventeenth century, candidates for posts in government offices not only purchased their positions but, if necessary, bribed anyone likely to have a positive influence on their appointment.[2] Likewise, in south-west France, members of the nobility who found it quite natural to bribe the taxman were as common as taxmen who used to take bribes.[3] A century later, the magistrates of the Parlement of Paris were openly criticized for allowing themselves to be swayed by gifts or by the irresistible charms of young female litigants.[4] Even the king's privy council had its black sheep[5] and every now and again an embarrassing affair would cause a stir in the ranks of the *Grands maîtres des eaux et forêts*.[6] As for the shrewder ministers, they knew full well how to exploit the theme of corruption and the corresponding myth of integrity for political ends. Colbert, apparently, was an expert on the matter.[7]

The above examples were not chosen at random. On the one hand they illustrate the extent to which corruption had penetrated the *ancien régime*, and on the other hand they prove that, today, historians are fully aware of the phenomenon, since it is from their works that the examples were drawn. This sheds a new light on my observation concerning *Les Institutions de la France*. If indeed in the index of this major work there is no heading 'corruption', it is by no means owing to lack of facts. On the contrary, the facts are stated quite clearly. Neither is it through lack of documentation since, as we have just seen, there is adequate information on the subject. The silence seems to me to have deeper roots. It reflects a historiographic perspective which, although it recognizes the existence of corruption, does not make an issue of it. It is not that anyone denies the historically verifiable facts, but that nobody considers it necessary to take the matter further or to carry out more research on the subject, for which a few paragraphs tucked away in some thesis seem to suffice. As a result, the theme of corruption is difficult to classify. We cannot say that it has yet to be discovered since everyone is aware of and recognizes its existence. But, at the same time, the chances of it benefiting from deeper analysis are slim because nobody takes the subject seriously enough.[8] Consequently, as far as historical research in France is concerned, the scientific future of this theme is somewhat limited. It will no doubt continue to appear on history's stage, but it is unlikely to become a leading figure.

The perspective changes completely when we depart from an exclusive French context. In other countries there are a number of historians who have examined the theme of corruption, and the fruits of their work now form quite an impressive mass of material. It is their output and not French publications that should serve as a starting point to reinstate corruption in the position it deserves in historical research. In fact, the work of historians in other countries presents as a historical problem what in France has been treated in a merely anecdotal manner.

It thus lays the foundations of a scientific approach to corruption. That does not mean, however, that we should follow their conclusions blindly. On the contrary, once we have familiarized ourselves with their work, we must proceed to a critical appraisal. Only then can we set some problems concerning corruption in early modern Europe.

* * *

It is not easy to get to grips with foreign literature dealing with corruption. The difficulties arise firstly from the diversity of languages in which it is written and more profoundly from the variety of situations described, examples being taken from all historical periods and referring to countries throughout the world. But the difficulties can be explained above all by the great diversity of the authors themselves: some are historians, others sociologists or political scientists. Some, such as Van Klaveren, deal in abstractions which can sometimes be rather dangerous. Others, such as Chabod, stick firmly to concrete facts, which they illustrate to perfection without, however, really defining the aim of their analysis. The situation therefore calls for clarification. Such is the aim of the following presentation which, although unavoidably simplified in parts, is a necessary step towards a true analysis of the problem.

The study on which most historians base their work is a long article written by Jakob Van Klaveren[9] and published in the late 1950s in a German periodical. According to this author, corruption is quite simply the exploitation of public office in accordance with the rules of the market. When it occurs, the public office becomes a kind of private enterprise, the product being the public service, and the public being the customer. Judges market sentences, customs officers trade in import licences and court dignitaries sell posts in government offices. This *'fraude érigée en système'** is, for Van Klaveren, part and parcel of a particular stage in the development of a constitutional order. It cannot occur without two conditions being

* Translator's note: in French in Van Klaveren's text.

fulfilled: firstly, an administration which allows its officials a
wide margin of autonomy; and secondly, a moral code which
does not impose any kind of standard of probity on state
functionaries. This kind of context can be found in oligarchic
republics and in limited monarchies. On the contrary, the
establishment of a despotic order or the triumph of democracy
would bring the schemes of corrupt officials to an end. In both
cases the constitutional order would be doubly modified:
autonomies would give way to rigorous centralization; vague
standards would fade away before a demanding formulation of
a code of ethics concerning integrity. Civil servants would then
be obliged to become paragons of honesty and corruption
would from then on occur only in the form of regrettable
incidents put down to cupidity, judged in court and – according
to Van Klaveren – of no importance to historians.

Three features can be clearly outlined in the ideas of Van
Klaveren. He provides an economic – and therefore amoral –
definition of corruption. Having thus defined it, he associates it
with the absence of centralization and of moral rigour which
would have reigned in certain types of organization: oligarchic
republics and limited monarchies. He nevertheless believes it to
be incompatible with democratic or despotic forms of government in which functionaries are kept under control by new
regulations coupled with threats of penalties. Thus, in Van
Klaveren's view, the civil servant appears firstly as a *homo
oeconomicus* who, devoid of any moral conscience, is naturally
led to turn his office into an industry; he then becomes a
malleable being who, when kept under control by a coercive
regime, bows without defence to the rules and values that are
imposed on him from above.

Many of the Anglo-Saxon authors who have tackled the
question of corruption are sociologists, political scientists or
anthropologists. Their works are somewhat influenced by the
writings of Max Weber. They are also less inclined to adopt an
economic definition of the phenomenon.

The *social scientists* often base their theories on the distinction
between rational bureaucracies and pre-bureaucratic systems.
Rational bureaucracies, as everybody knows, are centralized

and hierarchical organizations based on wide-scale regulation determining the precise attributes and duties of each office and of each official. Authority is exercised in a rigorously impersonal way by salaried experts who have no way of becoming the owners of their means of production. Through discipline and control, rational bureaucracy thus guarantees, or is supposed to guarantee, an effective, permanent, rapid and discreet administration with no internal conflicts. It is opposed to previous forms of organization described as pre-bureaucratic. In the latter, hierarchy is far less rigid, and centralization is weak. Officials are given a great deal of autonomy and their functions are empirically defined. Employees are in general prominent citizens and usually own their offices. Such organizations lack formal structure and control and are thus subject to frequent authority clashes. According to the German sociologist, their relative inefficiency makes them bound to be replaced by rational bureaucracies, that is to say, the kind of organizations that characterize the major administrations of contemporary States.[10]

Secondly, these authors do not necessarily base their studies on an economic definition of corruption. They often prefer an approach founded on the notion of general interest or on that of integrity. Corruption, from that point of view, seems less an amoral quest for personal gain (Van Klaveren) than an attack on the general well-being or as failure to adhere to moral values. Thus, James Scott, opting for the second approach, defines corruption as 'a behaviour which deviates from the formal duties of a public role because of private regarding wealth or status gains; or violates rules against the exercise of certain types of private regarding influence.'[11]

In reuniting these two characteristics – Weberian inspiration and a definition linked to the idea of duty – the theory of the *social scientists* departs from that of Van Klaveren in two ways. Firstly, it ceases to consider corruption in relation to political constitutions in order to examine it in relation to the various forms of bureaucratic organization. The problem at this stage is no longer to ascertain whether or not corruption is intrinsically linked to limited monarchies or oligarchies, but to define the specific place it should occupy both in pre-bureaucratic systems and in rational bureaucracies. The second difference lies in the definition of corruption itself. Instead of being seen in an economic light, it is now based on the concept of integrity.

This new perspective, when applied to the early modern European states, leads to interpretations that differ greatly from Van Klaveren's idea. The case of the Stuarts in England is, in this respect, very enlightening.

The English monarchy of the first half of the seventeenth century was, for Van Klaveren, a good example of a corrupt regime in that it combined almost complete freedom of action for its public servants with very open permissiveness. Under these conditions, the sovereign's servants could run their offices as if they were grocery shops. Corruption was widespread. As for Scott, he does not deny the practices described by Van Klaveren. But he points out that these practices, far from being condemned by the law, 'often occurred openly and legally.'[12] In this context, the definition of corruption given above cannot be applied. As a result, Scott concludes that it is impossible to apply the term 'corrupt' to England during the first half of the seventeenth century, not because the practices we now consider to be corrupt did not occur, but because the English of that time were not conscious of the illicit nature of their practices.[13] The relationship between His Majesty's subjects and corruption was, therefore, rather like those between Monsieur Jourdain and prose writing*: they did it without knowing they were doing so and, according to Scott, if they did not know they were committing corrupt practices then their acts were not corrupt.

Compared with Van Klaveren, this is a radical reversal of ideas. What was once a paragon of corruption is now a model of innocence. Despite this difference of opinion, the two writers do actually agree on one fundamental point. Both rule out the possibility that traditional organizations – pre-bureaucratic systems for Scott, limited monarchies and oligarchies for Van Klaveren – could have regarded the problem of corruption

---

* Translator's note: Monsieur Jourdain, a character in Molière's 'Le Bourgeois Gentilhomme', was fascinated to discover that he had been writing prose for years without knowing it.

from an ethical point of view. On the contrary, these two political systems would have been completely indifferent to the idea of integrity. Moreover, they would not have been able to eliminate practices which were nonetheless very widespread within their institutions. They could not, therefore, have culpabilized corruption.

The works examined so far have led me to emphasize one aspect of the scientific analysis of corruption: the fact that it was impossible for traditional organizations to culpabilize corruption because they were unable to develop a concept of it. The question that must now be tackled is completely different: what role does corruption play in modern forms of organization, rational bureaucracies?

The problem of the relationship between corruption and rational bureaucracy arises with particular acuity in the development phase of these new organizations. The modernization of structures, as in fact some authors underline, is accompanied by a rigorous formulation of a moral code concerning the integrity of its civil servants. This does not necessarily mean that officials used to greater freedom were necessarily able to assimilate immediately that notion of integrity. Thus, new organizations are often faced with a corruption which is all the more conspicuous in that it had previously been forbidden. What is more, this corruption is stimulated by a new political demand, arising from groups who are at a disadvantage owing to the growth of a new political order and who try to regain lost ground by acting indirectly on civil servants. Paradoxically, therefore, modernization seems to go with a corruption which can be stamped out only at the cost of a long task of political stabilization and moral education.[14]

In rational bureaucracies, corruption would therefore often be linked to cultural inadaptation which, although it does not explain corruption entirely, helps us to understand more clearly how it broke out. This was the case particularly in the United States and in several third world countries. Van Klaveren states quite firmly that the recrudescence of corruption at the beginning of the twentieth century in the country of George Washington resulted largely from the arrival of immig-

rants from several Latin and Slavonic countries. These were
countries in which 'the French Revolution had had little effect,
and in which there was no large cultivated bourgeoisie and
where the corruption of the old regime had never ceased to
exist.'[15] Benson, for his part, places the stress more on the
particular sensibility of Irish emigrants, who were to a considerable extent responsible for municipal corruption in the United
States. He explains how, 'from years of subjection in Ireland,
they had developed a sovereign disdain for the forms of
democracy under which they had been ruled by the Anglo-
Protestant minority.' This disdain in its turn turned into an
'equal contempt for the law and for government.'[16]

Cultural maladaptation does not concern only new arrivals.
In some American public offices, managers have difficulty in
making values concerning integrity accepted by minor officials.
The sociologists Thomas Barker and Julian Roebuck observed
that, within the police force, the rules imposed by the upper
echelons of the hierarchy are not always taken seriously by
subordinates. In some cases, the more scrupulous officials are,
the more deviant they are seen to be by their colleagues. The
system of values expressed in the regulations which oppose
integrity to corruption is replaced by another, more subtle code
which distinguishes between *clean money* and *dirty money**, money
that comes from honest people and money obtained from the
underworld; if the latter poses a problem, there is occasionally
no shame in accepting the former.[17]

In third world countries, where rational bureaucratic structures have been brutally implanted in a ground that was not
necessarily ready to receive them, the discrepancies between
Western values systems and the culture of the colonies or
ex-colonies had far-reaching consequences. The phenomenon
in Nigeria was analysed very clearly by two British experts in
the 1960s. The order installed by the British was far from
assimilated in the mentality of the local people, for whom tribal
obligations remained the absolute priority. 'The tribal loyalty is
immensely strong,' remarked Ronald Wraith and Edgar Simp-

---

* Translator's note: in English in Waquet's text.

kins, 'stronger by far among the mass of people than loyalty to Region or Federation.' Thus, Nigerians, who were fully aware of the meaning of honesty, a virtue that they applied fully in their tribal 'unions', found it difficult to conceive that integrity could be applied in the same way in public service. On the contrary, 'to put your fingers in the till of the local authority will not unduly burden your conscience, and people may well think you are a smart fellow and envy you your opportunities. To steal the funds of the unions would offend public conscience and ostracize you from society. The ethic is there, but it has not yet been transferred from the seat of natural loyalty, which is the clan or tribe, to the new seat of loyalty which is the State.'[18]

Almost twenty years later, Hyacinthe Sarassoro, a lawyer from the Ivory coast, published a very similar etiology of corruption in Ghana, Zaïre, the Ivory Coast and Mali. According to him, the African civil servant today is still subject to three types of pressure: one from the public, opposed to a new, oppressive and inefficient administration that is poorly adapted to local customs; another which is produced by the Western consumer model and powerfully motivated by the traditional tendency towards ostentation; and the third which comes from the African social and psychological structures. As a member of a family full of parasites, of a tribe that imposes nepotism and favouritism on him, the civil servant in young republics finds it difficult to make his own, let alone put into practice, the moral duty of integrity. He soon rallies with those who believe that, all things considered, 'robbing the State is not thieving.'[19]

We are thus faced with a second idea which, instead of focusing on the innocence of traditional organizations, stresses the problems arising from the survival of attitudes and sentiments from previous systems into emerging rational bureaucracies. In this case, corruption is condemned by public authority, but the reasons for the condemnation are not understood by officials. The result is that the officials are not conscious of the real nature of their actions. They are not therefore really guilty, save in the eyes of a law whose foundations they have not assimilated and which they feel is unjust. Even when taken to court, the corrupt official has no sense of guilt. In his heart, he feels innocent. Scholars thus have come to an interpretation of corruption in rational bureaucracies which is as 'deculpabilizing' as the other we summarized in the first stage of the analysis and which deals with pre-bureaucratic systems. In both cases, the official is justified.

In as much as we consider that rational bureaucracies developed only in the nineteenth century, the cultural inadaptation explanation of corruption seems, at first sight, to be of only limited interest to early modern historians, who study periods prior to this date. If, however, we admit that modernization did not just suddenly appear but developed very gradually over a long time, commencing from the end of the Middle Ages, this theory is of more interest. It provides the tool for interpreting the various forms of corruption that can be observed from the beginnings of the modern age.

The case of Ferrante Gonzaga, who was studied by the historian Federico Chabod, can be taken as an example. Gonzaga was governor of Milan at the time of Charles V. He was a faithful subject who had no qualms about selling the family silver to serve his prince better. But, at the same time, he flouted all the laws taken or approved by the same sovereign by committing an endless series of fraudulent acts. Whence Chabod's conclusion that 'these were the consequences of the particular sensibility of these great personages who had no attachment through the "duty of his function" to an impersonal state, but were nonetheless linked by an individual feeling of loyalty to the physical person of the sovereign: the dying but powerful remains of the spirit of feudalism and chivalry.'[20] Whether or not Gonzaga was a loyal subject or a traitor, guilty or innocent, depends on what point of view has been adopted. Another variance of this type can be observed two centuries later, this time in the context of the local administration in the State of Milan under Maria Theresa and Joseph II. Cesare Mozzarelli based his analysis on the results of surveys ordered by the emperor and clearly demonstrated that the ideal of public service unceasingly advocated by the Austrian monarch still remained quite foreign to the Lombard officials.[21] The situation would not have been very different in England, where

it was not until the nineteenth century with its *Victorian attitude*[*],
itself a derivative of puritan morality, that a stronger sense of
public service and responsibility became imperative in civil
servants.[22]

The previous pages outline two ideas: the first is that of the
innocence of pre-bureaucratic systems which, although drenched in corruption, would apparently have been unaware of
the fact; the second, that of the survival of practices which,
stubbornly defended by benighted officials, had withstood the
modernization of the political systems. Taken separately, these
two affirmations can be applied to the early modern age.
According to the first theory, European countries did not reach
a level of rational organization before the nineteenth century,
and, remaining at a pre-bureaucratic stage of development,
practised and simultaneously ignored a corruption that they
were unable to recognize as such. According to the second
hypothesis, which relies on the assumption that modernization
began at the end of the Middle Ages, the Europe of the *ancien
régime* did, in fact, condemn corruption. It must, however, be
pointed out that those who continued to commit corrupt
practices had not assimilated the new system's values and were
not actually aware of the criminal nature of their acts. Thus, the
men of the *ancien régime*, although guilty, would always have
been innocent.

*　　*　　*

A great deal of caution is called for before any conclusions can
be drawn on the innocence of the *ancien régime*, whether they be
based on the fact that no rules existed or that, if the rules did
exist, they had not been assimilated by the elite classes.

First of all, it is advisable to dismiss Van Klaveren's idea that
there is some kind of link between corruption and the constitution of states. Contrary to his affirmations, neither democracies
nor despotisms are free from such abuse. He himself had
become aware of it with regard to American democracy[23] well

---

[*] Translator's note: in English in Waquet's text.

before Arnold Heidenheimer underlined the idea that the incompatibility between corruption and democracy was 'empirically refutable'.[24] But the criticism could be extended to the despotic states, and it is certain, on this subject, that Van Klaveren fell into the trap that the flatterers contemporary with Ernest Lavisse kindly held out for him and was far too optimistic about the administration of Louis XIV. It appears that there is no relationship between the constitution of a state and corruption. The latter, in reality, affects more or less all types of political systems: tyrannies and monarchies, oligarchies and democracies, socialist dictatorships and military governments. To express an opinion to the contrary is tantamount to accepting verbal terrorism of despotic governments, or by those principles that are loudly proclaimed by democratic constitutions without necessarily being willing or able to put them into practice.

Corruption has been condemned for a very long time. The hackneyed idea that the *ancien régime* was an innocent society in which happy officials were engaged in corrupt acts which were not actually corrupt because no law considered them as criminal, seems to me excessively optimistic, indeed far from reality. It does not take into account the fact that moral rules concerning integrity had been established very early on. As early as the reign of Charles V, the biennial officers of the State of Milan swore the following oath before taking up office: 'You shall swear by the Holy Gospels (on pain [in the event of a breach] of a fine of 500 *scudi* to be paid to the Imperial Chamber, with perpetual exile from the State of Milan and a more serious corporal punishment to be determined by the Senate) [you shall swear] to tell the truth regarding payment or promise of payment you would have offered to anyone in view of applying for or obtaining this post, either directly or indirectly, in person or through a middle-man.'[25] Equally significant are the instructions given by Philip II to Don Luis de Castillo, who was sent to Milan in 1582 in order to inspect the public services of the state: the job of the *visitador* was, among other things, to find out if 'the president [of the Senate of Milan], or a senator or any other officers have abused their authority by committing fraud or other crimes; if they have been in collusion with third parties, offering or promising them something, or threatening to use their authority against them, should they speak ill of them in this inspection; if they have either talked or sent any letters to lower-ranking judges in favour of somebody in view of persuading these magistrates to judge the affair according to their wishes; if they have issued writs in an attempt to impede the marriage of the girls from the most important families in order to have them marry members of their own family or other people whom they have tried to favour by this method.'[26]

Furthermore, it must not be forgotten that it was not rare for lawyers to treat the misbehaviour of judges and accountants as crimes of lese-majesty.[27] Neither must we overlook the measures taken by Charles V in 1539 to reduce the number of illicit acts practised by ministers in the Kindom of Naples.[28] Nor should we fail to mention French legislation on embezzlement[29] or imagine that Francis Bacon, John Beaumont and Lionel Cranfield were impeached in the absence of any law in England authorizing their punishment.[30] In reality, corruption among judges, dishonesty among accountants and fraudulent bailiffs were all considered by public authorities to be shocking and reprehensible well before the Age of Enlightenment. Throughout the *ancien régime*, laws stormed down on officials as they do today on African civil servants, imposing the utmost respect of their duties. There is no doubt, therefore, that it has been erroneous to state that in traditional Western societies 'the norms governing public office holders [were] not clearly articulated or [were] non existent.'[31]

We have shown that the duty of integrity was a current notion in the administrative systems of the *ancien régime*. The question that remains to be answered is whether or not the extent of this affirmation should be limited by admitting that the new concept had never been fully understood by officials who were incapable of assimilating it.

I do not wish to deny any value to the explanation by cultural inadaptation. On the contrary, I feel it would be dangerous to underestimate the lessons that we owe here, for instance, to Chabod or Mozzarelli. Nevertheless, I refuse to believe that *all*

officials were incapable of understanding the language of the
state, and that this lack of understanding lasted from the reign
of Charles V to that of Louis XIV and was still present under
Maria Theresa. We do, in fact, possess proof to the contrary.

Here, for example, is the case of Baron Pfütschner, who until
his death in 1765 was one of the closest advisers to the Emperor
Francis Stephen. Pfütschner must have been aware that, at the
court of Vienna, there were rascals who accepted bribes,
euphemistically called 'treats', 'pins', 'coifs' or 'hats'. But he
considered that 'even the most elegant of names cannot change
the real nature of these acts and described these fraudulent
deviations severely and without mincing his words as the poison
of justice and of probity.'[32] He was therefore certainly not
indifferent to the notion of integrity. What is more, his attitude
was not original. A number of officials and dignitaries in the
service of Emperors Joseph I and Charles VI were of the same
opinion at the turn of the century. Or at least that is what was
observed by the ambassador sent by Cosimo III, Grand Duke of
Tuscany, to negotiate with the imperial government on the
military contributions to be paid following the European wars
of the beginning of the eighteenth century. Count Lamberg,
the emperor's favourite, or Baron Slich, a Milanese army
commissioner, were not incorruptible, explained this diplomat.
But there were also a number of officials who observed the
utmost respect of their duty, such as Prince Eugene, Prince of
Salm, Count Wratislaw and the Marquis of Prié. Finally, they
were offered no bribes.[33]

We can now abandon these paragons of virtue to turn to the
Kingdom of Naples, where, at the beginning of the seventeenth
century, the auditor of Lucera, a judge named Campana, was
completely corrupt. Should we infer from his misbehaviour
that he was simply a good savage, incapable of understanding
not only his duty but the very notion of integrity? The answer
is no, for this very same magistrate was also the author of *De
requisitis ad commendabilem judicum creationem*, in other words, an
essay on the virtues of the perfect judge.[34] Just as enlightening
is the case of a Spaniard named Lope de Soria who *in articulo
mortis* bequeathed to Charles V the sum of 3,000 *scudi* 'which he

said he owed since he had not kept perfect account of the funds entrusted to him.'[35] There is no doubt that he had deviated from the line of duty. Nonetheless, he had internalized his orders sufficiently well to be able, on his deathbed, to recall the language of virtue.

The call for integrity launched by the sovereign was backed up by Holy Scripture, from which lawyers drew no end of moral quotations.[36] This religious reinforcement will perhaps appear to be of no importance to those who, like Van Klaveren, make no distinction between the man of the *ancien régime* and the *homo oeconomicus* of the nineteenth-century economics. Its importance becomes clear, however, when we consider that the officials we are talking about were also Christians, in other words, men who confessed, performed their Easter duties, thought over their wills, were admonished by their priests, treated harshly by their preachers and feared hell. The denunciation of corruption was therefore not intended only for the prince's subjects, but also for the tormented soul of early modern man, assailed by sin.[37]

In this context, there is no reason to disregard a figure who is *also* at the centre of corruption: that of a man who has fully assimilated the duties assigned to him through his office, who is aware of the religious implications of the interdictions imposed on him, and who, for all that, violates day after day the precepts whose value he nevertheless recognizes. Of course, this figure is not specific to *ancien régime* Europe. He can still be found today throughout the whole world, just as he existed before in the streets of Naples or Milan, so that Sarassoro invented for him a new denomination, that of the 'morally sick'.[38] These 'sick' people also pose a problem. They turn the study of corruption into the very human story of remorse and accommodation with conscience. '*Tout comprendre, c'est quelque chose pardonner*'*, observed Wraith and Simpkins[39] in a plea to their compatriots not to analyse the behaviour of Nigerian functionaries on the basis of Victorian criteria. A few years later, Joël Hurstfield echoed the plea by declaring: 'We have, as historians, been too

---

* Translator's note: 'To understand everything is to forgive someone for something'. This passage appears in French in the original text.

ready to look back on the past with Victorian eyes – to fall victim to the anachronism of judging one age by the standards of another.'[40] These manifestations of common sense are praiseworthy, but we must also realize that if we were to pardon everything we would end up by understanding nothing. I would conclude then, for my part, that corruption, in the sense of failure to adhere to ethical standards of integrity, existed in the organizations of the *ancien régime* – whether they were rational or pre-bureaucratic – in the same way that it exists today in most parts of the world. The laws on corruption were not necessarily less precise or perfect than they are today, and many to whom these laws were addressed were not only aware of them, but also had a moral conscience enabling them to distinguish between good and bad, vice and virtue. The story of corruption in the early modern age is therefore more than just the adventures of the 'Ingénu in the land of Integrity'. It is, or is also, one of the pages in the long history of moral conscience.

*   *   *

With the above critique, I differ from those theoretical approaches which tend to exculpate corruption. It leads me to formulate the problem of corruption in terms which are slightly different from those used by historians up till now.

I believe that the first question to be asked is *why* these practices, which were denounced over and over again, stood the challenge of time and survived in practically all states till the end of the *ancien régime* only to be revived sometime later in new constitutions. If this is the case, could it not be said that what appears to be a 'dysfunction' is in fact a latent function? Is corruption a perturbation of the political body, in fact an essential factor in social stability? This first question can be most wisely answered by seeking inspiration, as far as is possible for an early modern historian, from the functional method of analysis, as applied by Robert Merton to one of the most remarkable manifestations of contemporary corruption: 'machine politics' in major American cities.[41] This will perhaps enable us to discover the *reason* for what would otherwise seem to be inexplicable.

The next question to be examined is *how*, in a society that was not very permissive, civil servants succeeded in reconciling their infringement of the law with the legal and religious precepts they tried to instill in them. What *justification*, to use deliberately a term which evokes Judgement Day, could the guilty provide or invent when faced with their prince, their God or their own consciences? How did corruption function?

The whys and the wherefores are just two of the aspects I shall explore in this book. As a case example, I have chosen a central Italian state at the end of the early modern period: the Grand Duchy of Tuscany.

In 1737 Tuscany changed masters. The Medici family, who had governed since 1532, ceded their place to the House of Lorraine in the person of Francis Stephen, husband of Maria Theresa of Austria, who was soon to be crowned Holy Roman Emperor. The new regent for the sovereign, Count Richecourt, was shocked by the situation he found upon his arrival in Florence:

> Theft is everywhere in the military and civil administration, in the finances; there is no tribunal, no receivership where the prince is not deceived and the people oppressed. The general officer, the governor, the *provveditore* and the minister all *eat*, to use the local term, they eat off everything, off the vilest things, off the most miserable people. The evil is so widespread and so strongly canonized that, rather than censure such activity, it is commonly said of such a man that he is smart and knows a thing or two about business. . . .[42]

The conclusion of this philippic would certainly have pleased Van Klaveren. It is, however, no more than a controversial simplification by a man who described his new citizens as follows: 'Florentines are generally quick-witted and have a great deal of insight. They are cunning and self-interested. They are proud, presumptuous and also vile, base and insidious.' Besides this, 'few of them are moved by honour; only two things can make them act: profit and fear. One must either

give in to their greediness or threaten them with punishment.
The latter is the safest solution, because a Florentine that you
have paid can never be trusted, whereas a Florentine in whom
you have put fear, trembles.'[43]

Although Count Richecourt's caricatured outrage cannot
necessarily be trusted, it cannot be denied that his letter to
Francis of Lorraine is significant for two reasons. First, it draws
attention to the corruption that was consuming the grand
duchy at the end of the Medici era. Secondly, it implies that the
activities which had been tolerated in the past were not likely to
be admitted under the Lorraines. It thus sums up two characteristics which, when combined in the Tuscan state, turn this
political system into a reservoir of experiments for the historian: widespread illicit practices on the one hand, and, on the
other, a political change which was to cause a revealing wave of
repression.

The plan of this study reflects the questions set forth above.
Firstly, I shall examine the problem from the 'functional'
perspective to show how the manifest 'dysfunctions' produced
by corrupt business corresponded more profoundly to latent
functions that could account for their social utility. Once this
first stage of explanation has been completed, I shall note that
there was an age-old contradiction between actions and precepts. I shall then analyse the functioning of corruption by
exploring the ways in which individuals in their hearts, and the
princes in dispensing justice, were able to overcome the difficulty with which they were faced.

Part I

THE SMELL OF MONEY

Introduction

To study corruption is first and foremost to render an account
of the 'affairs' and assess to what extent these irregularities
disrupted the smooth running of the state and the well-being of
its citizens. It also means being aware of the fact that these
affairs served powerful interests and procured considerable
gains for those who engaged in such practices and who thereby
consolidated their social, economic or political status. Let us
imagine, for example, a country in which civil servants agree,
for a fee, to allow a foreign minority which is legally banned
from international trade to run its contraband business. The
adverse effects of this venality would be obvious, both for the
treasury, which would lose its income, and for national firms,
which would simply vegetate. The positive outcome would be
just as clear: firstly, for the foreign minority, which would
prosper, but also for the civil servants, who would use the
bribes to climb rapidly up the social ladder. Corruption would,
in this case, be perfectly ambivalent: it would be detrimental to
public finance and hinder the development of the national
economy, while at the same time favouring the integration or
social mobility of groups which would otherwise be ostracized

or underprivileged and could become centres of political or
social unrest.

In an analysis of corruption two goals must be set. The first is
to examine the adverse effects of incriminated practices, and
the second to show the positive effects of those same practices,
which, although they can be condemned from a moral point of
view, may contribute to the stability of a given social and
political organization. Seen in this light, the study of corruption
gains by the use of the functional method of analysis.

Fundamental to this type of analysis is the concept of
function. It is based on vital or organic processes, so called for
the very reason that they contribute to the maintenance or
adjustment of a given social system. Dysfunctions, on the other
hand, are processes having the opposite effect to the detriment
of the adjustment of the system. Functions and dysfunctions
may be manifest: in this case, they are recognized and intended
by the members of the organization; they may also be latent, in
which case they are unrecognized and unintended.

The theoretical basis of functional analysis is that behaviour
observed in social life 'allows for a given item having diverse
consequences, functional and dysfunctional', with patterns per-
sisting only to the extent that they have 'a net balance of
functional consequences'. This leads us to a type of analysis
which goes much further than a superficial examination of just
a few functions – or dysfunctions – fulfilled by a given type of
behaviour. It takes into account the entire set of its implications, functional, latent or manifest. What at first sight seems
inexplicable, indeed irrational, then becomes clear. This intellectual process has been illustrated by Robert Merton with
regard to American machine politics.[1]

Machine politics have long been a typical characteristic of
local administration in the United States, where they reached a
climax at the turn of the century. They were the instruments
used by local 'bosses' to control local power and its economic
benefits. These untouchable politicians were anxious to preserve the loyalty of their voters. They could do this by two
methods: gaining votes through acts of generosity, or using
more or less violent pressure to discourage citizens from voting

for opponents. To attain these goals, the 'bosses' had two tools at their disposal. The first was the local administration which was totally biased, and the second a network of personal relations in the 'right' places: owners of saloons, captains of the fire-brigade and so forth. The effectiveness of these relations was proportional to the amount of resources made available to them. As a result, corruption was widely practised to fund the machine. This corruption took various forms: bribes offered when making contracts, the sale of offices in local administration to the highest bidder, or protection provided for the activities of the underworld: bootleggers, casinos and brothels. These practices enabled machine politics to satisfy the needs of its voters and thereby keep their favour. However, the very nature of this income meant, as a consequence, a bad administration. In the grips of less scrupulous entrepreneurs, contracts for public works were not fully carried out; as the offices were sold to the highest bidder, the administration was deficient; protected by the authorities, organized crime thrived.[2]

From the facts given in this description, it is difficult to understand why the Americans did not systematically remove their oppressors. Robert Merton's merit lies in the fact that he showed how the survival of machine politics can be explained by the numerous latent functions they fulfilled. In effect, if we abandon moral indignation, it becomes clear that they made up for a number of 'the functional deficiencies of the official structure.' In an institutional organization where power was very divided, they introduced an effective centralization of authority. In a strongly bureaucratic world, they reintegrated 'quasi-feudal relationships' and thereby 'fulfilled the important social function of humanizing and personalizing all manner of assistance to those in need.' In a keenly competitive economy, they offered businesses the way to 'avoid the chaos of uncontrolled competition' by guaranteeing, in exchange for bribes, monopolistic positions. In a society drenched in the myth of individual success, they provided avenues for personal advancement for those who otherwise would not even have been able to dream of it. Finally, in a repressive legislative system, they enabled the entrepreneurs of vice and of the

'racket' to carry out their business in peace. Thus, Robert
Merton reached the conclusion that the political machine
'fulfils some functions for these diverse subgroups which are
not adequately fulfilled by culturally approved or more conven-
tional structures.'[3]

It remains to be seen to what extent this method of analysis
can be applied to the corruption observed during the *ancien
régime*. The first two parts in this work attempt to provide an
affirmative, answer to this question. The use of functional
analysis, and in particular the notion of latent function, allows a
very subtle interpretation of practices which would otherwise
be incomprehensible. It also makes it possible to avoid falling
into the trap of oversimplifying explanations, and in particular
of attributing to the protagonists of corruption intentions they
never had. I shall therefore begin by rendering an account of a
number of affairs which, as already indicated, have been taken
from the Grand Duchy of Tuscany, while calling attention to
the 'dysfunctional' aspects of these cases. In part II, I shall
examine the question of the manifest or latent functions
fulfilled by corruption. I will then attempt to show that it is
precisely because these functions were latent that corruption
was able to survive on a long-term basis. This will lead me to
conclude that, contrary to first impressions, the function of
repressive laws was not only to eliminate corruption, but also to
render it tolerable.

1

THE GRAND EMBEZZLEMENT FROM THE 'ABBONDANZA'

Night had already fallen on 21 December 1731 when Tommaso Buonaventuri, a Florentine senator and patrician, took leave of Mormorai, one of the Grand Duke's closest advisers. The streets into which he ventured were so dark that, despite the lantern held by his valet, he did not notice that he was being followed by a stranger. At first, his pursuer kept his distance. Then, just as Buonaventuri and his servant were crossing one of the most deserted parts of the town, the stranger suddenly caught up with them and shot the senator with a pistol. The unfortunate Buonaventuri collapsed to the ground and, asking for a confessor, prayed to the Lord for forgiveness of his sins. A moment of silence followed and within a few moments he was dead. As for the assassin, he examined the body without the slightest trace of emotion, walked away from the scene of the crime and faded into the darkness. He was never found.

The murder of Tommaso Buonaventuri did not leave Florentine society indifferent. For one thing, the senator occupied a high position in the state. He was on good terms with the court and could boast of privileged relations with the powerful Corsini family, to which the recently elected pope Clement XII belonged. In the world of finance, he held several important posts, one of which was that of *provveditore* of the 'Monte redimibile', a major credit institution. He was also famous for having inspired the last debt conversion which had made interest rates fall and which earned him the enmity of share-holders. More generally, he was despised by the public at large who criticized him for his harsh, contemptuous and biased behaviour. On the other hand, he was admired in literary circles. In fact, as director of the grand ducal printing press, secretary to the Florentine Academy, member of the 'Crusca' Academy and Arcadian poet, Tommaso Buonaventuri played an important role in the world of letters. What is more, he had published a great number of literary works, notably the first Florentine edition of the works of a man whose fame was still great, despite the fact that he had been persecuted during his lifetime: Galileo Galilei.

There was inevitably a great deal of gossip. And since it was common knowledge that the late senator, following the example of many a Florentine patrician, had been a defender of Florentine republican traditions, he was believed to have been murdered on political grounds. Well-informed people held that the assassination had been carried out on the order of the emperor, in order to punish Buonaventuri's contestation of the court of Vienna's feudal claim to Florence. Other experts, possessing equally reliable information on cabinet secrets, claimed that the hand of the assassin was armed by the King of Spain, who was supposedly irritated by the fact that Buonaventuri had argued that a Spanish succession would not have benefited the Grand Duchy. Nobody, however, suspected that this fishy affair was on the verge of turning into a financial scandal.

Some days after the death of Buonaventuri, rumour spread in Florence that more than 13,000 *scudi* had been found missing from the coffer of the 'Monte redimibile', of which Buonaventuri, until his death, had been in charge. This was quite a considerable sum and the way in which it had been misappropriated opened up just two hypotheses: the first incriminated the senator, and the second his closest collabor-ator, a certain Benini who was *sotto-cancelliere* of the 'Monte'. Benini was thrown into prison and charged not only with embezzlement, but also with the murder of his superior, which he was alleged to have committed in the aim of covering up his crime by imputing to Buonaventuri the fraud for which he himself was guilty. In his defence, the *sotto-cancelliere* revealed certain facts: he claimed that, several years earlier, Buonaventuri had appropriated 800 *scudi*. He said that his former employer had illicitly taken a cut of the proceeds of taxes levied on meat. In addition, he stated that the senator had abandoned the trial against an employee of the 'Monte', who was accused of embezzling several thousand *scudi*. Benini stressed, above all, the fact that Buonaventuri had been in such dire financial straits from 1714 onwards that his debts had to be taken into hand by the magistrates court. The *provveditore*'s fortune, added the perfidious Benini, had not sufficed to pay off his debtors, who were still owed approximately 11,500 *scudi*.

Buonaventuri's heirs also had their turn to speak in court. According to their portrait of Benini, the *sotto-cancelliere* was a frequent buyer of lottery tickets in Genoa, Milan and Naples. He also betted in Florentine gambling houses, apparently playing like a madman, placing outrageous sums. He lost money as soon as he placed it, and built up debts so as to be able to continue playing. He would lose again, and borrow in order to keep playing and losing over and over again. There was no doubt about it: he was the one who had dipped his fingers in the till, while the senator, a paragon of virtue, who had sacrificed all his worldly goods to pay off the debts left by his brother, would have been incapable of such a crime.

A compromise was reached by the court. Benini was not charged with the murder of the senator, but was nevertheless found guilty of embezzlement and condemned to the galleys for the rest of his days. The Grand Duke then commuted this sentence to life imprisonment in the dungeons of a fortress. Benini, however, never confessed, and even resisted seven hours' torture inflicted on him to make him talk. As for Buonaventuri, rumour spread, a few years later, that it was the Grand Duke who had ordered his murder, under the pretext that the *provveditore* was in secret correspondence with the emperor.[1]

There are several ways in which Buonaventuri's fate could be interpreted. One chronicler, Squarcialupi, a rather narrow-minded Florentine aristocrat, considered that, 'in substance, it was his intriguing nature that lead to his morbid death.'[2] The Grand Duke, Gian Gastone, on the other hand, declared ironically that 'he deserved all he got because he thought he could change the world, and such is the fate of people like him.'[3] However, it could also be said of the Buonaventuri affair that it is in many ways revealing and that it shows that matters of corruption should be treated with great caution. Firstly, it is a reminder that Florentine administration was subject to scandal. It also suggests that aristocrats, and in particular penniless aristocrats, could be involved in unpleasant affairs. It then leads us to suspect that the authorities were perhaps not completely impartial. It would thus induce a superficial observer to conclude that there was a link between corruption, the way public affairs were handled by the aristocracy and the selective nature of repression. In fact, the Buonaventuri affair seems above all to show that scepticism and effort are needed: scepticism, because in these matters it is difficult to establish the truth; effort, because only a very thorough examination of the records makes it possible to confirm or invalidate the impression obtained after a superficial examination.

The history of corruption must therefore begin with a micro-history. Hence, I begin with a very careful study of a huge scandal: the grand embezzlement from the 'Abbondanza'[4] in Florence, which dates back to 1747. It is not, however, sufficient to examine just one case, which is why, in chapter 2, I demonstrate the fact that the 'Abbondanza' affair was just one of many cases of embezzlement.

*   *   *

In the eighteenth century, travellers arriving from Pisa could enter the Tuscan capital through the San Frediano gate in the ramparts on the south bank of the Arno. From here, the road followed the river, and just as the silhouette of the Ponte Vecchio and Palazzo della Signoria began to sharpen they would reach a large square bordered on one side by the embankment and on two others by the convent and the church of San Frediano. Opposite the convent buildings there was a massive, austere construction whose walls, pierced with large windows and typically Florentine protruding roofs, attracted the attention of visitors. According to the guide books, this was the public corn house of Florence, built by the architect Foggini and commissioned by the late Grand Duke, Cosimo III.[5] Employees of the corn house called it the 'Palco nuovo dell'Uccello', designating by that the storehouses of the 'Abbondanza' provisioning magistracy which assured the supply of grain for the urban population.

In Florence, as in all Western countries, the public authorities used to buy up grain stocks because they knew that they would sooner or later be needed to feed a starving population.[6] Agents of the 'Abbondanza' bought cheap grain when harvests were good, thereby building up considerable reserves which in times of shortage were supplemented with emergency purchases from the international market, that is, from Leghorn. Sales of grain were mainly held during periods of shortage. Grain was then sold retail on the Piazza del Grano, just behind the Palazzo della Signoria. Besides this, the 'Abbondanza' released to bakers half or even the total amount of flour they needed. When the shortage was over, it continued selling its stocks, obliging bakers to purchase at a price that was set slightly higher than the grain prices currently being quoted on the market. In this case, the aim of the 'Abbondanza' was not to counteract the shortage, but to compensate its own previous losses incurred by having to sell off a part of its stocks at a reduced price.

The operation of the 'Abbondanza' made it possible to build up considerable stocks, both monetary and material. The grain sales, on the one hand, which were supplemented by some fiscal, parafiscal and patrimonial revenues, fed a cache of ready money which was kept by a *camerlengo* and had always to be available in order to pay for new supplies. Purchases of grain, on the other hand, led to the constitution of impressive provisions kept in the storehouses of San Frediano square and in the connecting silos. The value of these stocks was counted in tens of thousands of *scudi*. It was therefore important to place them in the hands of honest agents whose loyalty was a guarantee of the prince's interests and of public well-being.

*   *   *

Not far from the Ponte Vecchio, about half way between the San Frediano storehouses and the Piazza del Grano, was Via Degli SS. Apostoli, a narrow and winding road, lined on both sides with buildings whose protruding roofs blocked out the daylight. This was where knight Borgherini, *provveditore* – that is, director – of the 'Uccello' storehouse since 1716, resided with his wife. The interior of the *palazzo* was far from frugal: fine paintings signed by Vasari, Santi di Tito, l'Empoli, Allori and Dandini adorned the walls, and in the ground floor *sala* this decoration was enriched by handsome furniture and by a dozen statues.[7] One of the busts represented senator Pier Francesco, the father of Vincenzo Gaspero Borgherini, and was an indication of the patriciate origins of a family allied to some of the most important households in Florence. Vincenzo Vaspero, for all that, had much in common with several of the town's aristocrats: noble birth, possession of a *palazzo* in the town centre, a villa in Fiesole, land in the country, a post in a government office, the cross of the knights of *Santo Stefano,* an order founded by the Grand Duke Cosimo I, and, last but not least, a wife who, as daughter of the senator Francesco Gaetani, came from one of the most noble families of Florence.

Apart from being Vincenzo Gaspero Borgherini's father-in-law, senator Gaetani was also *provveditore*, not just of the storehouses, but of the entire administration of the 'Abbondanza'. A member, like his son-in-law, of the Florentine patriciate, he could boast of belonging to the 'very ancient and very noble Gaetani family of Florence, the same family as the Gaetanis of Pisa, Naples, Rome, Anagni, Gaeta, Syracusa and Palermo.' According to genealogists, the family descended directly from Hugo, Baron of the Empire, son of Ducibolo and second Duke of Gaeta, who lived during the tenth century. The family was also proud of having given two pontiffs to Christianity: Gelasius II and Boniface VIII.[8] In 1733, Gaetani had succeeded another nobleman, the Marquis Torrigiani, whose son-in-law, the senator and knight Braccio Degli Alberti, was, in 1747, still a member of the board of *protettori* of the 'Abbondanza', the trustees and eminent supervisors of the provisioning magistracy. Gaetani's deputy, the *sotto-provveditore* Libri, was also on the board of trustees and likewise belonged to the Florentine patriciate.

Among the lower ranks of the 'Abbondanza' there were far fewer aristocrats. These posts were generally held by men of more modest extraction, such as the *cancelliere* Vivai, responsible for the registry, the accountant Bechi, who kept the books, or Lorenzo Rossi, who, under the direction of Borgherini, was the *custode* of the 'Uccello' storehouse. According to his contemporaries, Lorenzo Rossi was the incarnation of the banality typical of talentless subordinates with neither fortune nor future. He was said to have 'a good reputation. . . . He has no particular vice, never spent a penny, is timid, complaisant and narrow-minded.'[9] He was a barber's son who lodged stingily with his sister, herself a widow, and in whose house he had retired following the death of his own wife. His functions at the storehouse, where he arrived every day never dressed in anything but black, and the Barnabite education of his two children seemed to be the only two preoccupations of the dismal existence he had led for years. No vice could be attributed to him, the food served at his table was mediocre, he kept very few servants and rarely indulged in any form of entertainment. Nothing, in short, could have led one to imagine that one day his career would be brought to an end by a death sentence.

*   *   *

During the night of the 24 to 25 August 1747, the town of Florence became the theatre for a very strange spectacle. About a hundred soldiers from the fortress received orders from the garrison colonel to go to the town centre, where the chief of police was waiting with his officers, who were carrying four

long ladders. The group then divided up into four teams, and
each team, equipped with a ladder, penetrated into the darkness of the night. A few minutes later, *cavaliere* Borgherini,
who was sleeping peacefully in his bed, was woken by the noise
of a ladder being propped against his window. Before he had
realized what was happening, the policemen had already
broken into his room and were accompanying him to the
fortress of Saint John the Baptist, the 'fortezza da basso' as it
was known as in Florence. There he discovered his father-in-
law, Gaetani, the *provveditore* of the 'Abbondanza', and his two
colleagues, the *protettore* Alberti and the *sotto-provveditore* Libri.
All four had been arrested in connection with an affair which
had set tongues wagging all over Florence: the grand embezzlement from the 'Abbondanza'.[10]

It had all begun one and a half months earlier, on 9 July to be
precise, with the sudden disappearance of Lorenzo Rossi who,
instead of returning home after his day's work had left the
Grand Duchy for an unknown destination. This distressing
news had soon been followed by two even more sensational
events. Firstly, it was discovered that the provisions of the
'Abbondanza' reported on the balance sheets at more than
73,000 *staia** had been stolen, and that only 1,685 *staia* were left.
As for the silos, they were completely empty. This first discovery was quickly followed by another even more remarkable
revelation. Before leaving, Lorenzo Rossi had left a note
denouncing the men responsible for the crime. This note,
which had ended up in the State Prosecutor's Office, accused
the principle directors of the 'Abbondanza': Gaetani, Borgherini, Alberti and Libri. The note rang all the more true in that
Gaetani and Libri had shown unusual eagerness to restore the
quantities Rossi claimed they owed. The behaviour of Borgherini and of his father-in-law in the hours following the departure
of Rossi raised suspicions even more; not only had Gaetani
waited no less than two days after Rossi's departure before
informing the government of his disappearance, but Borgherini, even more imprudently, had rushed to his former collabor-

* A *staia* was worth 24.36 litres.

ator, demanding to be left alone in the office where the department records were kept, and had then left with several documents under his arm.

*   *   *

The law soon learned that Galli, the clerk in charge of bringing to the 'Uccello' the money gained from the sales of grain on the public square, had not always returned to the office by the most direct and quickest road. On the contrary, he often made a little detour by one or other of the many tax offices in Florence. There he used the money received from the public to pay off the taxes personally owed by his master, knight Borgherini. Galli, of course, handed the remaining money to his superior Rossi, the *custode* of the 'Uccello'. Rossi in turn took his cut of the funds collected on the public square in order to reimburse the debts of the all-powerful *provveditore*. All Borgherini's debtors had come to the 'Palco' to claim their due, and Rossi, whether he liked it or not, had settled accounts with his cook, his fishmonger, his shoemaker, his tailor, his tanner and his chaplain, and had paid 4,000 *scudi* owed from the purchase of a villa in Fiesole. Borgherini, for all that, had not been content just to obtain money indirectly from the 'Abbondanza'. He had even come in person to the storehouse to get cash. Thus Borgherini, who only came sporadically to work at the 'Palco', had been seen bursting into the premises, shutting himself away with Rossi and leaving a short while later, his pockets stuffed full.

According to Lorenzo Rossi, the cost to the 'Abbondanza' totalled 9,411 *scudi*. The law claimed the sum to be 8,500 *scudi*, which although lower than Rossi's estimate was nevertheless equivalent to 17,000 *staia* of grain. Borgherini had therefore been very successful in appropriating the money gained from sales. He outdid by far Gaetani, who obtained only 60 *scudi*, and Alberti, who had to be content with the 600 *scudi* he received from Rossi. Borgherini's method was not, however, the only one used to defraud the 'Abbondanza' and in fact, in other fields, the excellent knight was beaten by his colleague, senator Alberti.

A cruder, but no less effective way of sapping the storehouse consisted quite simply in removing grain from the provisions, either personally or using an intermediary. One could, by doing so, satisfy one's personal needs as well as those of friends. None of the men accused of corruption in this affair had been able to resist the temptation of this method. *Sotto-provveditore* Libri had arranged for four *staia* to be delivered to the Saint Apollinaris convent in Florence, the accountant Bechi had given his peasants 127 *staia* for sowing, and Borgherini took 68 *staia* from the 'Abbondanza' in 1728. Worse still, *provveditore* Gaetani had fallen into the bad habit of sending one of his servants to the 'Palco' every time he needed grain in his house. By doing so, he had appropriated 700 *staia*. The most brazen in the matter, however, was beyond doubt senator Alberti. The former *sotto-provveditore* had in fact obtained for his own use 5,544 *staia* using the names of three Florentine bakers: Torricelli, Berretti and Fossi.

The methods mentioned above were by no means particularly subtle. The same cannot however be said of another, far more sophisticated technique, that of the *mandati a vuoto*, or false money orders.

Money orders constituted an important part of the job of Lorenzo Rossi. They were delivered to anyone who had deposited grain in the silos of the 'Uccello'. With Rossi's signature on it, the money order authorized the cash clerk of the 'Abbondanza', the *camerlengo* Donnini, to pay the owner of the grain a sum corresponding to the quantity deposited. The operation was simple: the grain seller, or his representative, presented himself at the 'Uccello'. He deposited his grain, in exchange for which he received a money order. He then proceeded to the pay desk where the *camerlengo* examined the money order and paid for the grain sold to the 'Abbondanza'. The *camerlengo*, of course, was not in a position to judge the authenticity of the situation to which the money order referred. He did not know, and had no means of knowing, whether or not the grain had been deposited. In his eyes, Rossi's signature was guarantee enough of the validity of the paper presented to him.

The only difficulty was to convince Rossi to deliver the money orders without any grain having been deposited. The *mandati a vuoto* seemed as authentic as any others, the *camerlengo* paid up without batting an eyelid and the receiver obtained the cash. All it cost him, in fact, was a small effort of persuasion to convince the *custode* of the 'Uccello'.

Among the three culprits who had used this ingenious technique, Libri was the least persevering – or the least persuasive. He obtained only 1,400 *staia*. Borgherini, on the other hand, and to a greater extent Alberti, put the technique to full use. The former managed to gain 6,546 *staia* and the latter 12,350. Both men used false names so as not to arouse the suspicion of the cash clerk. Borgherini began using the technique around 1720, and managed to obtain money orders in the name of the bailiff of his estates, a certain Giovanni Nencini, or else in the names of his servants, Giuseppe Virgili and Girolamo Pieri, or indeed in the name of the doorman of the 'Accademia dei Nobili', Antonio Dell'Agata. Alberti's secretary, a certain Ciacchi, thought up an even more complex system, two versions of which, Rossi's and that of the main witness, were described to the court. According to Rossi, Ciacchi had had money orders drawn up in the names of various landowners of Florence: Pier Antonio Gabbrielli, *cavaliere* Serselli, *cavaliere* Del Caccia, the Strozzi family, the nuns of Saint Martha and of Fuligno. He then sought out the business attorneys of these individuals and the procurers of these convents, persuading them to go to the 'Uccello' and claim reimbursement for the false money orders and to hand the cash over to him. For example, 'if [the money orders] were made out in the name of the nuns, he sought out their procurers and the procurers claimed reimbursement from the *camerlengo* of the 'Uccello'; they then brought to Ciacchi the money received and Ciacchi handed it to senator Alberti.'[11]

When it was Ciacchi's turn to be questioned, he presented a slightly different version of the story. He explained that Rossi wrote out money orders in the name of invented persons. He gave these money orders to Ciacchi, who immediately gave them to Alberti. Alberti then handed them to a third party. The last-named presented himself at the pay desk, where he claimed to be the beneficiary – the imaginary one – of the money order, or his business attorney. This accomplice collected the cash and delivered it to the senator who used it for his personal needs.

It is difficult to ascertain which is the correct version. Both no doubt reflect the care taken by its author to limit his share of the responsibility, and yet they have one point in common: both attest to the existence of a sophisticated organization which was also very effective, since it worked for twenty-five years.

* * *

In fact, theft among the 'Abbondanza' staff went on for years. The books were altered with such expertise, however, that nobody, in the office or elsewhere, was aware of the precise extent to which the provisions were being drained. Nobody that is, except a well-informed confederate: the unfortunate Lorenzo Rossi, signatory of all those money orders for which he did not pocket a penny and distributor of amounts of grain he would have done better to keep and of money of which he should have been the faithful trustee. He knew full well that the silos were empty. In fact, around the year 1745, the provisions were so depleted that his conscience began to bother him and he became anxious to put things right.

Rossi did all he could to encourage the *protettori* to purchase grain. The market, unfortunately, did not react, for the prices of the 'Abbondanza' were not advantageous. He then considered the credit made available to him to cover the costs of storage and conservation of the grain in the silos. He had never needed to break into these funds since the silos were almost empty. He could not, however, admit this fact since it would have meant revealing what he wanted to hide. The money was there, and available, but had no destination. Rossi, of course, did not hesitate in creating one and used it to offer an 'unofficial' bonus to the people who brought grain to the 'Abbondanza'. Grain was then paid for in two stages. Firstly the official price was paid by the *camerlengo*, and secondly a bonus was paid by Rossi, who urged the beneficiaries to keep the matter secret. The happy, though somewhat surprised, grain dealers pocketed the cash and spread the word among their colleagues. They did not disclose any information to the public, who knew nothing of the story until the scandal blew up and the law revealed Rossi's dealings.

The artfulness of the 'Uccello's' custodian nevertheless had little effect on the depleted provisions which the directors of the 'Abbondanza' had been blindly draining for twenty-five years. As a result, at the beginning of July 1747, when the threat of a shortage loomed and with it the increasingly intense pressure on stocks from individuals and bakers, Rossi had no choice but to run away. He fled, leaving behind him a pitiful letter addressed to his deputy, Galli, 'I will go begging for a little bread for myself and for my poor innocent children, and if I should die, I do not know who will come to their aid. Maybe it was my excessive complaisance that caused my downfall.'[12]

*   *   *

Was Lorenzo Rossi just a rather naive subordinate exploited by his less scrupulous but more intelligent superiors? In any case, that is the theory he used when he returned to Tuscany, having pressed for and obtained a safe-conduct, in order to convince the judges of his innocence. His witnesses heaped accusations on the managers of the 'Abbondanza' and their evidence led the magistrates to charge the five men with the misappropriation of up to 49,163 *staia* of grain. The largest amounts were attributed to Borgherini, with 24,608 *staia*, and to Alberti, with 22,184 *staia*. However, the judges remained slightly perplexed by the fact that the 'Abbondanza' had in fact been robbed of 99,944 *staia* and not 71,315 as had originally been believed. Rossi had no convincing explanation for the whereabouts of the remaining 50,000 or so *staia* which had still to be accounted for.

For want of a better solution, it was the *custode* of the 'Uccello' who was held responsible for the disappearance of this huge quantity. He was accused, for example, of having sold the grain from the 'Abbondanza' as retail without the permission of his superiors, and also of having made the mistake of granting credit to the buyers, without ever having managed to obtain the payment of the sums owed to him. He was also accused of having made cash advances to individuals with funds from the till in exchange for the promise of compensation of these advances by deliveries of grain which, of course, never arrived. Lastly, he was accused of embezzlement, considering that at one time or another he must surely have obtained his share of the spoils. Thus Lorenzo Rossi was again forced to flee, this time leaving a letter addressed to a Barnabite relation. In this letter he declares his innocence for the last time: 'not having at my disposal the justifications and documents needed to prove what I must prove, I take leave . . . and yet I know the state of my conscience.'[13]

As is the case for all affairs of corruption, not all the mysteries of the 'Abbondanza' were solved. No one will ever know for sure where half of the stolen capital went. All that can be said is that Lorenzo Rossi did not apparently have the strength, the intelligence or the vice needed to misappropriate such a large sum.

*　　*　　*

Apart from causing a legal stir, the 'Abbondanza' scandal left Florence without resources right at a time when, following a catastrophic season, bakers had only a week's stock left. It seemed inevitable, after the departure of Lorenzo Rossi, that a shortage was about to hit the city.

Count Richecourt, the omnipotent regent for the emperor in Florence, made efforts to avert the danger. He sent a trustworthy man to Leghorn with the instructions to buy quantities of grain, rapidly, secretly and at the best price, equal to the amount of the depleted provisions. He also worked out a plan to thwart the speculation that was likely to break out in Florence, where news of the shortage was spreadingly rapidly, creating the danger of artificial price rises.

The threat of hoarding and speculation was the most urgent problem. Richecourt decreed special measures. He sent the police and their chiefs to the bakeries, the convents and the farms in the area with orders to make an inventory of all existing stocks. He called upon all the bakers in Florence to grind all the grain they had and demanded that the convents come to aid if need be. He thereby succeeded, in just a few days, in bringing the provisions of the 'Abbondanza' up to 24,000 *staia*. He calmed the speculation by announcing the acquisition from Leghorn of more than 100,000 *staia*. Florence was not on the point of starvation.[14]

The affair was a harsh blow to the 'Abbondanza'. It was forced to borrow 457,374 Tuscan *lire* from the grand ducal treasury in order to build up new stocks. In addition, it had to raise the price of bread by 12.61 per cent as from 28 July 1747.[15] More profoundly, the mechanism that guaranteed the supply of foodstuffs for the population of the capital and protected it from bread riots showed signs of fragility. Cheated by its own managers, the 'Abbondanza' had failed to fulfil its function of maintaining social equilibrium through the effective provision of grain. All that remains to be seen now is whether or not this unfortunate affair was simply an isolated one. Did it constitute an accident in the history of Florentine institutions? Or was it, on the contrary, just one of many manifestations of what was actually a widespread practice? The answer to this question may be found through research into other examples of corruption in the Grand Duchy of Tuscany, and the collected examples may then be used as a basis for a study of the function fulfilled by corruption.

2

JUST ONE OF MANY CASES OF
EMBEZZLEMENT

Suspects tended to disappear as soon as the law began examining their cases. Some, taken by surprise, took hasty refuge in churches or convents, which enjoyed ecclesiastical immunity. Others, who were more organized or more courageous, left the state and went to Lucca, Rome, Naples or, more often than not, Venice. They were all accused of embezzlement and they all preferred by far the bitterness of exile or voluntary retreat to the blinding light of a trial.

This crowd of fugitives was markedly uniform: from Alessandro Degli Alessandri, *sotto-provveditore* of the 'Dogana', or customs station at Leghorn, who withdrew into a church in 1716 after having made the port's quarantine camp bankrupt, to Antonio Malegonelle, who, in 1717, fled to Venice leaving the Florentine customs station almost completely depleted, and Luigi Mercianti, who 'under the pretext of being called to Naples on important business' suddenly abandoned his position of *camerlengo* at the 'Monte Pio' pawn office in Leghorn, from which he had stolen 900 piasters.[1] The repetitive nature of this succession is proof that embezzlement was, in fact, a frequent occurrence in Tuscan institutions. The 'Abbondanza' affair can thus be placed in its true context.

*   *   *

It would be impossible to make a complete list of all the cases of embezzlement committed in the Grand Duchy, even in a lifetime of work sorting out the maze of Tuscan archives. The fifty or so examples that I have gleaned, therefore, constitute just an initial sampling, incomparably inferior to the results that could be obtained by exhaustive research, were it possible in practice. The advantage of these particular examples, however, is twofold. Firstly, they show the repetitive nature of embezzlement in Tuscan institutions and, secondly, they attest to the great diversity found in this type of administrative corruption.

The affairs I have researched concern the seventeenth and the eighteenth centuries. With the exception of one or two cases, they occurred between 1630 and 1760. They are distributed irregularly over this period, being less frequent before 1700 (twenty-one cases), more recurrent after this date (thirty cases) and reaching their most intense frequency during the periods 1713 to 1720 (nine cases), 1728 to 1731 (seven cases) and 1738 to 1751 (eleven cases). Should it be concluded that there was a trend of corruption in the Grand Duchy? And could it be implied that this phenomenon occurred with the greatest acuity at the end of the Medici dynasty – a period in which there was little monarchic authority – only to be brought to light on a large scale at the beginning of the more repressive Lorraine era? It is tempting to analyse the situation from this point of view. However, such an analysis would not take into account the fact that some periods are better documented than others. It is true, for example, that the eighteenth century, in which an important number of cases of embezzlement are recorded, coincides with the end of the Medici regime and the arrival of the Lorraines. But it is also the era for which the archives are most accessible and therefore more fruitful. Therefore caution is advisable, for it must be recognized that, at the present time, no sure statistical base exists which enables an unequivocable conclusion to be reached stating that there were more cases of embezzlement during a particular period than another.

Nevertheless, the number of examples is proof alone that the

'Abbondanza' affair was more than merely an isolated incident. The period from 1679 to 1682, for instance, begins with the fraud committed by a certain Catignani who had appropriated 1,286 *scudi* from the small 'Dogana' in Pietrasanta, in the north-west of the state, where he was employed as *camerlengo*. This affair faded into the background in 1680 when the two Zampogni, both accountants from Scarperia, north of the capital, became the debtors of the 'Abbondanza' in Florence and of the Fortresses office for the sum of 1,611 *scudi*. The same year, it was discovered that a so-called Ghezzi, employed at the 'Monte Pio' pawn-office in Siena, was unable to account for the paltry sum of 8,055 *scudi*. Then, in 1681, it was the turn of the treasurer of the grand ducal household, a certain Ambrogi, to be charged with appropriating 1,596 *scudi*, a mere trifle compared with the 4,730 *scudi* that 'disappeared' from the till of the capital's 'Zecca' or mint, for which Chiavani, the master of the mint, was held responsible.

A new, even more intense series began in the second decade of the eighteenth century. A blow by blow account runs as follows: the two Teri brothers, patricians from Florence, left the Pisa customs station and the 'Abbondanza' of Florence, respectively, depleted by considerable sums: some 10,000 *scudi* for the first and 6,500 for the second. An inexplicable discrepancy appeared the following year in the books kept by the *camerlengo* of the 'Monte Comune' in Florence, the most ancient of all public credit organizations: another patrician, Tommaso Del Pugliese, was implicated in this affair which was soon superseded by that of Francesco Matteo Bindi, in charge in Florence of the 'Magona', the monopoly for the production of iron, and of Alessandro Degli Alessandri, *sotto-provveditore* of the Leghorn customs station; the sums involved were 2,229 and some 7,000 *scudi* respectively. Another upsurge occurred in 1718, when the *sotto-provveditore* of the Fortress of Pisa, Giovanni Battista Pandolfini – yet another patrician – died, leaving behind him a debt of 2,194 *scudi*, which, in fact, was nothing compared with 17,000 artfully and consciously appropriated at the same time from the Florentine customs station by the *camerlengo* Anton Malegonelle, again a patrician. The following year, 1719, was marked by the crimes of Lorenzo Rustici, patrician and *camerlengo* of the 'Monte Pio' in Siena. This affair took more than forty years to settle. Last but not least, in 1720, Antonio Maria Gherardini, *camerlengo* of the 'Gabella', or salt tax office, was found guilty of embezzling 7,543 *scudi*. Here again, one of the noblest families of Florence was put to shame.

The end of the 1720s coincided with the outbreak of a new series of scandals. Francesco Maria Malegonelle, brother of Antonio who, as we have already seen, was forced to flee from Florence, died leaving a sum of 24,772 *scudi* missing from the military bank of which he was treasurer. This case of embezzlement was soon followed by others, the authors of which were his subordinates: Raffaello Amiconi, *camerlengo* of the military bank at Leghorn, and Filippo Bussotti, also *camerlengo*, but at Portoferraio on the island of Elba: 9,951 *scudi* appropriated by the former and around 3,500 by the latter. Other provincial towns were hit by the dishonesty of their accountants, in particular, Borgo San Sepolcro, in the Appenine hills, where a certain Jacopo Grifoni is said to have appropriated some 10,000 *scudi*, and Prato, where the governor of the flour tax office, a certain Bettazzi, had to shoulder an outstanding debt of 4,500 *scudi*. The year 1730 is apparently marked by a pause, whereas 1731 saw the downfall of the *camerlengo* Capei, charged with having stolen 1,000 *scudi* from the 'Decime ecclesiastiche', the tax paid on ecclesiastic property. It was in the same year, as we have already seen, that the Buonaventuri affair broke out: a dead body without an assassin and the disappearance without trace of 13,500 scudi.

The Lorraine government had only just come into office when it was faced with two Portoferraio cases: that of Giovanni Paolo Mearelli, employed at the 'Abbondanza' to which he owed 1,360 *scudi*; and that of Carlo Del Feo, who, having administered various coffers of the island for ten years or so, absconded with 3,020 *scudi*. Del Feo was a close relative of Zanobi Paoli, master of the mint at Florence. That brought the number of cases of fraud within the same family to two, since Paoli, recently dismissed from office, was forced to seek sanctuary in a church to avoid the judicial consequences of having helped himself to at least 2,700 *scudi* from the capital's mint. In the meantime, Orazio Maria Mancini, a Florentine patriciate, had left his job of *cassiere generale* of the 'Depositeria general' – the central treasury of the Grand Duchy – with 5,615 *scudi* missing from the accounts. Although this was quite a considerable sum, it was overshadowed by the 13,000 *scudi* appropriated by his former assistant, Lorenzo Bonsi-Bucetti, also of patriciate origins. As for the Siena *depositario*, the patrician Venturi-Gallerani was responsible for the disappearance in 1744 of 1,000 *scudi*.

The embezzlement from the 'Abbondanza' which, as we have already seen, occurred in 1747 was therefore far from an isolated case. Neither did it bring the series to an end, for the following year Luigi Del Turco, *camerlengo* of the 'Monte di Pieta' in Florence, made a sudden departure to Venice. Then, in 1754, it was the turn of Bernardino Fioravanti, cash clerk of the Treasury of Pistoia, and of Enrico Maria Cremoni, *camerlengo* at the 'Monte Pio' in Leghorn, to cause a stir. The latter, who pocketed the sum of 17,523 *scudi*, merely carried out a repetition, though on a larger scale, of what thirteen years earlier his colleague Bartolommeo Chiti had done when he appropriated 13,447 *scudi* over eleven years of office. Lastly, 1758 saw the fraud committed by Lorenzo de'Luigi, *camerlengo* of the 'Grascia', a magistracy that worked in parallel to the 'Abbondanza'. He misappropriated 4,717 *scudi*, to which must be added the sum of 5,667 *scudi*, for which, a year later, Giovanni Bati, *camerlengo* of the 'Decime ecclesiastiche', was required to answer. It is therefore quite safe to say that cases of embezzlement were everyday news in Florence.[2]

*   *   *

Among the fifty-one examples I have studied, about ten occurred within the 'Monti', or public credit institutions, eight in the 'Abbondanza', five in the military bank and another five in the 'Dogana', or customs stations. Over half of these cases, therefore, concern the four sectors of financial life in which the most considerable sums of cash were handled. This does not, however, imply that dishonesty among accountants was limited to just one part of Tuscan administration. The phenomenon was actually very widespread, as can be seen from the other half of the examples I have collected. These include two cases occurring in the 'Possessioni' or estates office, and as many in the mint, the grand ducal household and the 'Gabella dei Contratti', the office dealing with tax on notarized contracts. Three took place within the 'Magona', the privileged firm having the monopoly for the production of iron, and three within local communities. I should also add that I did not carry out systematic research on the balance sheets of local administrations. The few examples I came across on this subject do not fully reflect the real situation.

Although several affairs were taken from Florentine history, it would be wrong to believe that fraud took place only in the capital or was committed only by Florentines posted in the provinces by the Grand Duke. The case of Siena speaks for itself: apart from the Florentine Vittorio Nelli, the treasurer who, in 1666, because the author of a particularly sensational case of embezzlement, all the other men found guilty of corruption were natives of the town. The same applies to Leghorn, where, out of five cases, only one involved a Florentine: the patrician Alessandro Degli Alessandri.

Likewise, the misappropriation of public funds was not committed by members of just one particular social group. Raffaello Amiconi, *camerlengo* at the military bank of Leghorn, was quite simply a shopkeeper. However, the high percentage of defrauders from the aristocracy matched the huge proportion of administrative posts occupied by its members. A good half of the cases of embezzlement can thus be attributed to nobility. This figure remains as high even if we take only the most important affairs. Out of a dozen cases of embezzlement involving more than 10,000 *scudi*, just less than two-thirds involve Tuscan aristocrats. The proportion of Florentine patricians, in particular, is very high. The list includes, besides the authors of the 'Abbondanza' affair, the Teri brothers, the Malegonelle brothers, Antonio Maria Gherardini, Lorenzo Bonsi-Bucetti, Vittorio Nelli and so on.

Embezzlement seems, therefore, to have been well rooted in Tuscan institutions and society. It was not, however, the only form of corruption in Tuscany.

*   *   *

'December 8th 1746: one *scudo* and one lira given to Mr Fabbroni, of the 'Decime'*, in gratification for having dissimulated an outstanding payment of tax relating to our 'Nonziatina house.'[3] This short phrase is taken from the balance sheets of the convent of the Holy Spirit in Florence, which belonged to the congregation of Benedictines of Vallombrosa. It is typical of a whole society in which nuns realized they could not count only on divine assistance to settle their tax problems. Likewise, employees did not count on the generosity of the state to fill their pockets.

Bribery, which is even more difficult to track down than embezzlement, was integrated into the habits of Tuscan administration. It occurred even in the *Segreteria di Finanze*, one of the highest administrative authorities of the country. Among these secretaries was Tommaso Lucatelli, who felt justified in asking a candidate to pay the sum of 350 sequins in exchange for which Lucatelli promised him that he would obtain the post he required.[4] This scandal, which led to its author being banished, was not an isolated case in ministerial departments. In 1753, Lorenzo Mannucci, the custodian of the state secretariat, under suspicion of having drawn up false passports, was forced to leave the capital. The same charge led to the exile for three years of a certain Cozzini who was employed at the war department.[5]

Ministerial institutions were not the only ones to be affected by this type of misconduct. a *provveditore* such as the senator Uguccioni, governor of the 'Arte della Seta' or silk guild, also fell into the trap and was convicted in 1743 for accepting bribes from less scrupulous manufacturers, wishing to have sheets woven in a way that did not conform to regulations.[6] A few

* Direct property tax

years later, three employees from the 'Pupilli' magistracy, which functioned as a court of wards for children, were dragged from their beds and thrown into prison. These officials were in charge of auctioning movables belonging to these children. The grounds for arrest: suspicion of collusion with several antiques dealers to whom they had systematically accorded advantages.[7] Likewise, Giovanni Cammillo spinetti, *cancelliere* of a commune in lower Val d'Arno, was placed under arrest with nine charges against him. He was able to clear his name concerning two of the charges, but was found guilty of the remaining ones. He was charged with a series of illicit acts: acceptance of gifts, receiving undue payments, failure to disclose to the Florentine authorities the real nature of rented estates, and so on.[8]

Lastly, another form of corruption consisted in forcefully obliging less accommodating citizens to be more generous. In provincial towns, the police were sometimes guilty of this type of extortion. An example of this is corporal Benzoni who was sent to the galleys for extortion in the region of Lari, near Pisa, where he held office.[9] That is not to say that their Florentine colleagues did not behave any differently. It is reported that around 1680 the employees in charge of the food markets 'limited their rounds to one per day, just enough to collect tips from those who, owing to their jobs, were under their authority, and for those who refused to give tips a number of false denunciations were made.'[10]

* * *

It is very difficult to obtain the same quality of documentation on bribery and under-the-counter payments as that of the examples collected on embezzlement. Most transactions were carried out in secret and without any trace whatsoever being left. The result of this is that evidence is scarce, largely unsatisfactory and, indeed, rather dubious. Historians, who can only regret not being able to hear the confessions of public officials of the time, are wary of overestimating the importance of isolated events. We can be grateful for this reason to the

Florentines who, eager to record the events of their lives, kept journals of practically everything they did. Gratitude is also due to the archivists who have preserved these records carefully in the Uffizi palace. Two journals in particular are of specific interest to us: firstly, that of senator Francesco Gondi, and, secondly, the one kept by Prince Strozzi's business attorney.

Francesco Gondi, Florentine patrician and member of the family which, in France, lived on in the Cardinal of Retz, followed a rapid career worthy of a young man on good terms with the court. In 1719, at the age of twenty-five, he was named *provveditore* of the 'Gabella dei Contratti', the office that handled duties on notarized contracts. This was an important position in a town such as Florence, where death and dowry taxes were the nightmare of the aristocracy. Two years later he became senator, which, given his age and the fact that his father was also a senator, was an extremely honourable distinction. He thus enjoyed the highest favour of the court, and, as he proudly indicated in his journal, the Grand Duke Cosimo III granted him thirty-five audiences from 22 November 1719 to 16 August 1721, then thirty-nine from 28 August 1721 to 3 March 1723 and lastly six others from this date to the death of the sovereign a short time later.

Provveditore Gondi was also meticulous enough to keep a book of *ricordi* or 'memoires', in which, besides the important events of his life, he noted all his incomes and expenditures. In the chapter on incomes, he noted in particular the fruits of the gratuities paid to him as recompense for favours or for influencing the sovereign. He thereby kept a lasting trace of the perquisites of his high office in government administrations.

His entry for 30 November 1720 reads as follows: 'Francesco Berti sent me a gift of a glove box weighing two pounds, three ounces and five deniers, as recompense for having procured him subentry into the office of Giovanni Cortigiani, one of the custodians of the "Gabella dei Contratti".' 18 January 1721: 'The Abbot Francesco Dazzi sent me a gift of the following silverware: a chocolate bowl, a sugar bowl, four cups and four small spoons, weighing a total of three pounds and ten ounces, as recompense for having obtained for him a fixed monthly salary of nine *scudi*.' 30 November: 'Gaetano Cortigiani, son of the above-named Giovanni, sent me a gift of a silver ink pot with matching powder pot, the set weighing, all in all, ten ounces, as recompense for having procured him a post at the "Gabella" as substitute for Geri Artz, who is *custode* there.'

20 January 1722 is the turn of the tax payers to contribute to Gondi's income: 'Canon Giuseppe de'Nobili and his brother Francesco, son of Bernadino, accorded me a gift of some thirty-six *scudi*, as recompense for having obtained the permission of His Royal Highness to be relieved of one-third of the debt they had built up at the "Gabella dei Contratti".' With this money, Francesco Gondi treated himself to 'a small silver lamp bought from a shop on the Ponte Vecchio.'

Business continued, during the following April, with one of the employees of the office, Allegro Becattini, who was assistant to the *camerlengo*. Becattini had made a request to Cosimo III for a pay rise. Gondi was eager to express his support of that request to the Grand Duke. He pointed out that, since 1712, the office had not used the credit he obtained for the salary previously paid to a former employee. He proposed that the credit be used to augment Becattini's salary. This proposition was accepted and, to finish things off nicely, Gondi requested that the sums accumulated since 1712 be paid to the same Becattini. These sums, adds Gondi in his journal, 'amounting to 162 *scudi*, 2 *liras*, 13 *soldi* and 4 *denarii*, were given to me by the said Becattini as recompense for my having dealt with his case.'

In the month of July 1722 there was another gift, the expression of appreciation from Giovanni Fritelli, another of Gondi's subordinates: 'a well-crafted ebony tray framed in silver, with on it an ink pot, a powder pot, a pen holder, a little bell and a box for seal and wax, the whole set being in silver, as recompense for having obtained for him a rise of three *scudi* per month.' 'This gift', specified Gondi, 'considering the value of silver and the design, must have cost, according to the estimation of a trustworthy person, 37 *scudi* and two *liras*.'[11]

*   *   *

Unlike *provveditore* Gondi, Prince Strozzi was not employed by the Grand Duke's government. He lived in Rome, where he was known under the title of Prince of Foiano. His affairs in Florence, where he owned the famous palace of the via Tornabuoni, were handled by an attorney named Bellini. In 1722, Bellini had a particularly tricky problem to deal with concerning the death taxes to be paid by the prince following the death of a member of his family, Monsignor Leone Strozzi.

The amount to be paid to the 'Gabella dei Contratti' was likely to be overwhelming on account of the amount of goods inherited and the high rate – 7.75 per cent – of inheritance duties in Florence. The prince tried to think of the ways in which this amount could be reduced. His first idea was to reopen the file of an old affair: that of his ancestor Filippo, who long ago had taken up arms against the Grand Duke Cosimo I. Filippo had been defeated and had died in prison with all his worldly goods having been confiscated. Among these goods, supposed the Prince of Foiano, were a certain number of possessions belonging not to Filippo but to his family. These goods would have been wrongly confiscated, which meant that the Grand Duke therefore owed the Strozzi family the value of those possessions. That sum could quite opportunely be deducted from the duties owed after the death of Monsignor Leone.

Feeling very sure of his rights, the prince then contacted the highest Florentine magistrate, the first *auditore* of the 'Consulta', Giacomo Conti, who, far from discouraging the prince, transmitted the file to another judge called Landini. Being the good lawyer that he was, Landini asked Bellini for all the proof he could collect. Despite heroic research in the archives of the Strozzi family, all the evidence Bellini could find was rejected by the implacable lawyer. The recourse to legal proceedings was thus brought to an unfruitful end.

The prince abandoned his initial project and adopted a 'simpler, easier and shorter route, which consisted in dealing directly with the Grand Duke.' It was nevertheless still necessary to present a petition in proper form to the sovereign. The *auditore* Conti, the same man who had encouraged Prince

Strozzi in his fanciful projects and who had thereby made him realize how few rights he had, very kindly proposed to collaborate in the drawing up of this important document, which was then presented to the Grand Duke.

By chance, or perhaps as planned, Conti came back after a few days with the news that the Grand Duke had entrusted the handling of the file to himself. The outcome was therefore in the hands of the first *auditore* of the 'Consulta', who had previously proved the first project to be futile, had then been obliging enough to collaborate in the success of the second, and had now been designated arbitrator of the situation.

The excellent *auditore* could have settled the tricky matter rapidly in favour of Prince Strozzi in exchange for a juicy bribe. He preferred, on the contrary, to demonstrate his authority. He sought no kind of understanding or arrangement. Instead, he required the now terrified Bellini to provide him with a complete and detailed account of the inheritance. This news, communicated to Rome, brought the prince's anxiety to a climax. Nevertheless, the request was satisfied.

That as may be, Conti still had scruples. He engaged in the affair the agents of the 'Gabella dei Contratti', calling on their expertise several times. The representatives of the prince – Bellini, the procurator Vinci and *cavaliere* Manelli – were dragged into an endless series of meetings and confabs. Six months after the petitions had been handed to the Grand Duke, the matter had still not been settled. It was no earlier than 27 September 1722 that the sovereign signed an act which reduced the prince's death taxes by four-fifths, fixing it to 10,000 *scudi* instead of 50,000.

One can imagine Bellini's satisfaction at this 'inordinate and huge' act of mercy. It also becomes clear how skilful Conti had been in spending six months making the prince aware of the precariousness of his situation and then making him the beneficiary of an extremely clement decision that could only be put down to the influence the *auditore* had on the Grand Duke. The whole scenario was perfect from start to finish. It therefore comes as no surprise to learn that the *auditore* received from Prince Strozzi 'a generous gift proportional to his magnanimity and to the esteem and merit of the *auditore* himself'.

The *cancelliere* of the 'Gabella dei Contratti' also received around twenty gold pieces for the trouble to which he had been put. As for the grand ducal treasury, all it lost in the affair was a sum equal to one and a half year's income to the 'Gabella dei Contratti'.[12]

*   *   *

Like most Italian states, the Grand Duchy of Tuscany was literally swarming with public credit institutions, both small and large. Some of them, called 'Monti', drew savings on behalf of the state, by floating and managing loans. Others, called 'Monti di Pietà', also collected money from individuals, but in view of providing a charitable loan fund. The latter functioned as public pawnshops and their mission was to replace usurers.

These noble institutions handled considerable sums of cash. Another characteristic feature was their extremely complicated book-keeping system which was due to the multiplicity of creditors, their constant renewal, the rapid succession of payments to be made and collections to be carried out, and the daily accumulation of objects brought by individuals to be pledged. The complexity of the work meant that accountants had to be highly trained and skilful. At the same time it offered these accountants numerous opportunities to swindle the department. Indeed, more than any other institution, the 'Monti' were hit by corruption in all its forms.

Of all the different possible types of misbehaviour in this sector of activity, the most lucrative was undoubtedly the one which consisted in appropriating for one's personal use the revenue of credit institutions. This activity was made possible by an environment that had been made suitable through either tight complicity or a defective administrative organization. Without internal support, Bartolommeo Chiti, *camerlengo* of the 'Monte Pio' in Leghorn, could not have acted. His accomplice, Gabbrielli, the 'Monte's' copyist, prepared the way for his work by omitting to write in part of the sums paid into the 'Monte

Pio' in the form of rents, deposits or loans. All the *camerlengo* had to do then was to have the corresponding sums, which according to the books had never been paid, removed from the till. In this way, 13,447 *scudi* were made to change destination and all trace of the money was lost.[13]

The mysterious author of the embezzlement from the 'Monte redimibile' of Florence had made the most of an exceptionally favourable situation. Through an express directive of the Grand Duke, a certain quantity of securities had been with-drawn from the supervision of the 'Monte' and left to the disposal of the *provveditore* Tommaso Buonaventuri, assisted for this purpose by the *sotto-cancelliere* Benini. Buonaventuri could sell these securities on his own authority and without informing anyone else. He had, however, to hand the money collected to the *camerlengo* of the 'Monte'. The *provveditore* made full use of the capacity accorded to him and sold more than 120 securities, each one worth 100 *scudi*. Not a brass farthing of that money arrived in the till: a money-grabbing hand seized it half-way and thereby appropriated more than 12,000 *scudi*.[14]

The second way of getting rich out of the 'Monti' was to make them pay for imaginary expenditures using false documents. Bartolommeo Benini, the *sotto-cancelliere* of the 'Monte redimi-bile', was accused of having said to the *camerlengo* that a Florentine citizen Bartolommeo Archi had sold three securities to Giovanni Maria Fortunati, in other words, to the private account held by *provveditore* Buonaventuri. The *camerlengo* examined the documents, and paid the 312 *scudi* without hesitation. The sale, however, had never taken place and had never been considered by the unfortunate Archi, who was completely taken aback when approached on the matter. The money was never recovered.[15]

In Leghorn the *camerlengo* Chiti had achieved similar results by writing out interest payments that corresponded to nothing, but whose sums he pocketed himself. He relied once again on the complicity of his colleague Gabbrielli, who adjusted the books accordingly.[16] In fact, manipulating accounts was an essential part of this kind of operation. Everyone tried to work out the best way of doing it for his own purposes. The accountant Durazzi, who worked at the 'Monte di Pietà' in Florence, had various techniques up his sleeve. He managed to receive three payments for the same money order made out to the same accomplice, the archpriest Zeti of Prato. The same archpriest, thanks to Durazzi's trickery, also managed to receive interest payments on his securities six times a year instead of three.[17] If necessary, Durazzi also knew more subtle means. The following example illustrates his skill.

It was a well-known fact in Florence that the account books of the 'Monti' were full of *partite infognite*. These were accounts that had been opened in the past, had changed name several times over, and then had ceased to be used. The interest on the money in these accounts nevertheless continued to grow, and if the account holders claimed what was due to them they obtained the money owed. The only difficulty for the 'Monti' clerks was to identify the owners. For the owners, it was to trace the accounts which were sometimes not in their own name but in that, for instance, of a person who had made one of their distant ancestors beneficiary of their will. The highly skilled Durazzi made the most of this situation. He sent an accomplice to Father Masetti, a Dominican monk of Santa-Maria Novella, with the order to explain to this good monk that, among the *partite infognite* of the 'Monte di Pietà', there was one, well hidden, belonging to the Dominican monks of Pisa for whom Masetti was procurator. The accomplice then added that, if Masetti wished to know more, all he had to do was to promise to pay a third of the profits. Masetti promised and was taken to the 'Monte di Pietà' where Durazzi, after having pretended to carry out a little investigation, 'discovered' that indeed there was the *partita*, and handed a money order for 32 *scudi* in interest to the Dominican. He received 30 per cent of that sum through his accomplice. As for the *partita*, of course, it did not exist.[18]

Durazzi was suspected of having committed other small crimes of the same type. In this, he resembled the group of defrauders who, rather than wipe out the 'Monti' with thefts of huge sums, gradually drained them in small doses. Bronzuoli, a *stimatore* at the 'Monte di Pietà' in Florence, had become a master of this art. He was accused, for example, of having agreed, in exchange for a small reward, to receive from an indebted abbot and estimate as a diamond what in reality was a mere diamante. In general, he made it clear to his visitors that if they wished to obtain a higher estimation of the value of their objects, all they had to do was leave a small tip. The value of the overestimation would be proportional to that of the bribe left to him. Thus, for half a thaler, he brought the price of a gold necklace worth fifteen liras up to twenty-six liras. In exchange for three liras, a silver box whose real value was estimated at thirty-one liras soared up to eighty-four. Paintings jumped from seven to ten *scudi*, gemstones from 170 to 221 liras, and so on.[19] The mechanics of this system had only one defect: it cost the 'Monte' a great deal, since, on the basis of Bronzuoli's false expertise, it agreed to lend individuals sums of money much higher than the value of the pawned objects. This meant that, if borrowers were then unable to pay up, the sale of the pawned object did not bring in enough for the 'Monte' to recover its costs. The result of this is what in technical jargon is called a '*scapito di pegni*', or a loss on a pawned object. Further on, I will describe to what extent the repetition of these incidents damaged credit institutions.

The examples cited up till now concern only Florence and Leghorn. However, the 'Monti' were defrauded in all Tuscan towns. In Pistoia, for example, the 'Monte Pio' introduced a system of double records in an attempt to stamp out corrupt practices. Each time a loan was given in exchange for a pledged object, two documents were drawn up, one by the 'master' of the 'Monte' and the other by the 'copyist'. It was enough for the master, a certain Gherardi, to get hold of blank copies signed by his colleague for the machine to be derailed. Gherardi received pledges of low value, filled in the papers accordingly, and handed them to the copyist, who returned them in his own writing. He then threw away the first file and, using the blank papers, drew up a second in which he entered a higher sum, pocketing the difference.[20] Similar abuses of authority at the 'Monte Pio' in Colle, south of the Arno, had formerly led to he hanging of the person in charge of receiving pledges. This man was alleged to have delivered money orders corresponding to invented pawns in exchange for the sum of 788 liras.[21]

As if all these tricks were not enough, corrupt officials invented still more methods to obtain illicit profit from the 'Monti's' resources. Among these officials was doctor Roncalli, *cancelliere* of the 'Monte del Sale' in Florence. Roncalli had been encouraged by the earlier examples of two other employees of the 'Monte del Sale', Pitti and Vanni, as well as by the protection he enjoyed within the Tuscan administration. He engaged shamelessly in embezzlement which ended with his arrest in 1677. To start with, he had profited from a government campaign held from 1671 to 1676 to reimburse the state debt. The capital reimbursed to public securities-holders was placed at their disposal in the Ascanio Sanminiati bank in Florence, ready for them or their financial agents to collect. In many cases, however, and quite unexpectedly, it was an accomplice of Roncalli who presented himself at the bank and left with the money. 2,600 *scudi* were purloined in this way, at the expense of individuals from all social classes: aristocrats from Florence and elsewhere, ordinary folk, religious institutions and so forth.

Roncalli's second trick was to sell false securities to individuals and to use this money to pay off his own debts. With an audacity which in the end cost him dearly, he used this method to swindle a friend of one of the highest magistrates of Florence, the town representatives of Siena, the 'Estates' *camerlengo*, the French nurse of the reigning Grand Duchess, and the sovereign's own brother, Cardinal Francesco Maria dei Medici. His downfall was caused by the payment he made, with three completely counterfeit securities, for carpenty work carried out in his own home. The carpenter died shortly afterwards and the executor of his will, who was a little less naive about realities of financial dealings in Florence, immediately discovered the real nature of the documents that had been received from Roncalli. The *cancelliere* debated, resisted, procrastinated, and insisted he was innocent, but it was too late. He was soon arrested and thrown into prison. To his judges, the only explanation he was fit to give was: 'I made a mistake. Be patient with me. What can I say? I have been persecuted by everyone. I must pay the price. I give myself to the mercy of God. I did not have the time nor the means to pay back what I owed.'[22]

No other document shows the harmful effects of corruption as clearly as the balance sheet drawn up at the end of the financial year of 1758 for the 'Monte Pio' of Siena. This 'Monte', which was founded in 1570, had been able to commence operating by means of loans with no interest, most of them granted by local communities, brotherhoods, and the state hospitals of Siena. This initial capital had later been boosted by interest deposits from individuals, mostly natives of Siena. All these sums – initial capital and deposits from individuals – had been used to lend money against security in the form of pawned objects to the needy, at an interest rate that was slightly higher than that paid by the 'Monte' to the depositors. The difference between the two interest rates covered the administrative costs, or even went towards profits that could be used again to grant new loans. The situation of the 'Monte' at the end of 1758 was as shown in table 1:

Table 1   The situation of the 'Monte' at the end of 1758 (amounts in Tuscan liras, soldi and denari)

Liabilities		Assets	
Loans without interest		Cash	12,878.9.11
(initial capital):	207,173.9.3	Capital (and interest receivable) from loans against	
		security	363,907.8.10
		'Monte Pio' building	56,175.11.8
Loans with interest		Accounts receivable	
(deposits)		from employees	
capital:		having caused	
339,144.16.9		*scapiti di pegni*	109,384.18.5
interest payable		employees	
10,614.10.6	349,759.7.3	having committed	
Other interest payable	22,733.1.8	fraud	321,040.14.7
Income from 1570 to		other insolvent	
1758	315,163.4.8	debtors	31,442.15.9
	894,829.19.2		894,829.19.2

With a profit amounting to 315,163 liras, the balance of the 188 years of existence of the 'Monte' was, on paper, positive. However, after careful examination the situation seems less favourable. In fact, the assets column included a considerable amount of accounts receivable from employees, the nature of which were either 'mediocre' – that is to say, only recoverable up to a limit of 50 per cent – or totally irrecoverable owing to the insolvency of the debtors. It included another 31,442 liras in accounts for which there was no hope of being repaid since they concerned insolvent debtors. This meant that, out of the 461,868 liras contained in the last three items of the assets column, all the 'Monte Pio' could actually claim was the notably lower sum of 74,868 liras. As a result, the 'Monte's' assets did not total 894,829 liras, as indicated on the balance sheet, but only 507,000 liras. They were therefore down by 387,000 liras on liabilities. The consequences of this discrepancy were threefold. Firstly, the profits did not exist anywhere else but on paper. Secondly, charitable loans for which the 'Monte' had received 546,317 liras in the form of initial donations and deposits were limited to 363,907 liras, including outstanding interest. Lastly, the 'Monte' was not solvent, since, with assets reduced in practice to 507,000 liras, it was not able to meet the 579,666 liras debt that figured in the first three items of the liabilities column.

The situation of the 'Monte Pio' can therefore be summed up in two phrases: limited financial activity and total insolvency despite apparent profits. These two disadvantages shared the same origin: age-old corruption by which unscrupulous officials had defrauded the institution, appropriating not only the profits but also a part of its capital.

Partly or totally irrecoverable accounts were the result of the long series of frauds which had been rife in the 'Monte' since its beginnings: embezzlement and *scapiti di pegni* accounted for 69 per cent of the mediocre debtors and 89 per cent of the insolvents. The balance sheet of 1758 enumerated the guilty partners: the *camerlenghi* Aldieri Della Casa and Armanio Melari, who since 1589 and 1636 had been requested to repay 48,921 liras and 133,114 liras respectively; Girolamo Gori, who had appropriated 5,297 liras by means of counterfeited documents; Silvestro Sicuri, who, in his office of warehouseman, had managed to hoodwink 6,193 liras; the pawnbrokers Giuseppe Luri, Francesco Buoninsegni, Alessandro Baratti and Muzio Alberti, whom the 'Monte' held responsible for *scapiti di pegni* amounting to 42,523 liras, and so forth.[23] It was no exaggeration when the administrative governor of the 'Monti' in Tuscany, senator Neri-Maria Da Verrazzano, wrote that the 'Monte Pio' of Siena had been 'shamefully assassinated by its own employees.'[24]

*   *   *

The institutions mentioned so far all fulfilled a function and thereby contributed to the preservation of social organization. The 'Abbondanza', for example, had been allotted the function of guaranteeing adequate food supplies for the capital. The function of *provveditore* Gondi and the *auditore* Conti was that of counsellor to the sovereign. The 'Monti' aimed to provide the state, as well as individuals, with the means to resolve their financial difficulties. The cases of embezzlement, bribery and other illicit practices, which I have just outlined, represented as many obstacles to the fulfilment of these functions. From this point of view, they were more detrimental than favourable to social equilibrium. With the embezzlement from the 'Abbondanza', for example, the food supplies of Florence were at stake. The behaviour of men like Gondi or Conti did not necessarily lead the sovereign to make the best choice. The embezzlement from the 'Monte Pio' of Siena resulted in a reduction in the quantity of capital available for assisting the needy. What is more, these cases of illicit practices were not isolated. They occurred with remarkable frequency and subjected all parts of the state to constant pressure. They also had standardized features in as much as some simple principles were hidden under their different forms – appropriation of state funds, payment by individuals in order to influence the action of the state, unjustifiable appropriation of the income of private individuals under the cover of public authority. Lastly, the abuses, far from striking at society from outside, were produced by it and were a stable part of it. They constituted the 'dysfunctions', in the sense of the term indicated above, of organic processes which were detrimental to the preservation of the social system. The question to be asked now is whether or not that is all they were, or if behind the apparent 'dysfunction' lies, in fact, the reality of a function.

PART II

Dissolute Morals

Introduction

When tried for embezzlement, Maona, former secretary to the
governor of Milan, attempted to justify himself by explaining
that Charles V 'treated his servants very badly and for that
reason they were justified in trying to compensate by other
means.'[1] He thereby established a link between fraud and the
low salaries paid to public servants. He implied by this that
corruption served to compensate for the low wages the
monarch's servants received.

Maona's point has been taken up by several historians. W.
Paravicini, for example, pointed out that, 'since salaries were
low and paid on an irregular basis, officials compensated by
exploiting the office they paid for dearly.'[2] J. Hurstfield, for his
part, also associated corruption with poor wages,[3] and P. L. Rovito described Neapolitan abuses of officialdom as a 'system
which, by compensating for the low level of official salaries, had
ended up by considering extortion and embezzlement with
indulgence.'[4] Corruption could therefore have fulfilled a very
simple function: that of compensating the inadequacy of public
sector wages, of providing state office-holders the means to
survive and of making it possible for public service to work.

This first hypothesis can be enhanced with the notion of

social mobility. Seen in this light, it could be said that the function of corruption was not only to allow employees to survive but also to push them up the social ladder. This phenomenon can be observed, for example, in the new nations, where to enter the civil service is seen above all as a way of achieving self-advancement.[5] This is particularly true in Africa, where corruption is practised by 'unsatisfied' civil servants, in other words, lower-scale civil servants eager to reach the income level of former colonialists.[6]

Corruption, therefore, as a means of increasing a reputedly inadequate salary, would have provided underpaid employees with the means to survive. At the same time, it contributed to the renewal of the elite class. Suggestive as it may be, this first analysis gives rise to a number of questions.

To attribute corruption to low wages is to assume that wages were always low. This cannot, however, be verified empirically, especially in Milan where, as F. Chabod has clearly demonstrated, Charles V's agents could survive very well, even without the bribes.[7] To read into corruption a process of social mobility is tantamount to overlooking the fact that corrupt employees had often already reached the summit of society. We have only to take the 'Abbondanza' affair to see that the four men charged with embezzlement all came from the highest families of the Florentine patriciate. It must therefore be recognized that not all the observed forms of corruption served either to compensate for low salaries or as a means to achieve social mobility.

*   *   *

Another way of analysing the functions fulfilled by corruption is to examine the problem from a political point of view. Explanations can then be based on the idea that the existing political systems do not satisfy the needs of all social groups to the same extent. Although some no doubt are quite content with the situation, others must feel underprivileged, marginalized or excluded. Of course, there are legal methods to overcome the obstacles limiting political rights, freedom and economic activity. These include press campaigns, partisan action, parliamentary interventions and so on. However, the situation often seems so unfair and to be such a dead end that these citizens feel justified in turning to illegal means. They either resort to violence to overrun the regime they abhor, or else, more prudently, they are content to corrupt civil servants in order to obtain *de facto* changes in their status. Here, corruption can be said to have the function of counteracting the shortcomings that the existing political system comprises for certain social groups.

It is in this perspective that S. Huntington stated that corruption and violence fulfilled the same social function. 'Both', he says, 'are means by which individuals or groups relate themselves to the political system and effectively participate in it. . . . Corruption provides immediate, specific and concrete benefits to groups which might otherwise be thoroughly alienated from society.'[8] J. Scott went further by describing corruption as 'patterns of access and exclusion' belonging to 'the formal political apparatus' and stating that, with violence, it constitutes one of the two ways in which the socially excluded can retrieve status. 'Corruption by the wealthy is the functional equivalent of violence by the poor as a means of redress.'[9]

The analysis to which I have just referred leads to a clearer understanding of the part played by corruption in the relationship between the political system and the socially excluded. It enabled a new stability to replace a dead-end situation in which marginal groups are underprivileged. Thanks to corruption, the once-excluded minorities manage to recover a certain political status and redress the situation.

Of apparently less interest to researchers has been the effect, if any, that corruption had on the physiognomy and internal balance of political and administrative institutions. Let us take as an example a customs officer who, in exchange for a fee, agrees to facilitate the commercial activity of an ethnic minority normally banned from foreign trade relations. This officer doubtless helps to render more tolerable the inferior status imposed on this minority by the political system. In doing so, however, he is also assuming the right to a power which, in other cases, would be within the sole competency of the department responsible for granting, or refusing, exceptional export licences. In other words, he is replacing, without any authority to do so, the powers controlling foreign trade. Corruption, therefore, can be said to redistribute power within institutions in the same way that it redresses the balance of power between the political system and citizens.

*　　*　　*

The analysis of corruption gave rise to two hypotheses. The first one, based on the economic aspects of the phenomenon, sees the function of violations as being compensation for low incomes of employees, thereby enabling the smooth-running of the state and the renewal of the elite class. The second hypothesis looks at corruption in a political light, in relation to the needs of the socially excluded. It assigns to corruption the function of redressing the situation of these minorities without having to resort to more violent solutions.[10]

Neither of these hypotheses is completely satisfactory. The first cannot be applied to all the situations empirically observed and the second does not take enough into consideration the effects of corruption on the distribution of power within institutions.

The aim of my examination of the Florentine situation is to resolve these difficulties. I will try to show how the additional income gained from corruption could in fact fulfil functions other than those of making up for insufficient salaries or guaranteeing social mobility. Then, from a political point of view, I will indicate how the redistribution of power within institutions could be said to constitute an important function for corruption.

By this stage in the analysis, I will have outlined several functions fulfilled by corruption. The question will then be raised as to whether or not these functions were recognized – in other words, if functionaries engaged in corrupt practices in full awareness of the effects their behaviour could produce. To answer this second question, I will examine the way corruption was lived, the way it was interpreted, perceived and understood by those concerned and by the government. This will reveal that, for the men of the time, corruption was not so much an economic or political issue as a moral problem: only the dysfunction was manifest; the function was latent and, as such, was neither intentional nor recognized.

3

APPROPRIATING THE STATE

To talk about corruption is first and foremost to talk about money. It is to talk about the small gifts, the juicy bribes and the grand embezzlements which were the bane of the state and the joy of unscrupulous officials. It means drawing up lists of figures with strings of zeros and entering into the dizzy financial round in which money changed hands all the more easily in that it did not belong to those who handed it out. A question arises: what happened to all this money – for example, to the 16,000 *scudi* appropriated by the Teri brothers, or the 25,000 *scudi* purloined by Vittorio Nelli, the 42,000 *scudi* misappropriated by the Malegonelle brothers and the 50,000 *scudi* embezzled from the 'Abbondanza'? Where did all that money end up and, above all, what does it all mean? What is the significance of these endlessly repeated crimes? Could they not be said to conceal a common function or meaning?

The aim of this chapter is to explore that meaning. I will firstly analyse the consequences of corruption in order to compare them with the social situation observed in the Grand Duchy. I will then attempt to indicate the functions fulfilled by corruption in this political formation.

*   *   *

There is no doubt that the figures are misleading. The colossal capital misappropriated by Florentine accountants did not disappear in one day. The highest sums embezzled were generally appropriated by office-holders who had been in service a long time and whose crime, in reality, consisted of a series of meticulous and repeated pilferages carried out over the years. The 'Abbondanza' was despoiled over a period of twenty-five years. Francesco Maria Malegonelle, treasurer of the military bank, had been in office for thirty years when he died. Giovanni Ubaldini, cash clerk employed at the 'Possessioni', had been serving for sixteen years when his problems with the law began. Thus, if we examine average yearly figures, the cases of embezzlement take on more reasonable proportions. Francesco Maria Malegonelle doubtless owed more than 24,000 *scudi* to the Treasury, but all things considered that amount represented a yearly embezzlement of approximately only 700 *scudi*. Ippolito Niccolini very modestly appropriated only 120 *scudi* per year, Franceso Bindi, 247, and Giovanni Ubaldini, 250. Giovanni Bati and Alessandro Degli Alessandri were a little more greedy: they misappropriated 515 *scudi* and 560 *scudi* respectively. The *camerlenghi* of the 'Monte Pio' in Leghorn broke the record set by the treasurer of the military bank. One of them, Cremoni, obtained no less than 876 *scudi*, and the other, Chiti, a soaring 1,222 *scudi* per year. These were nevertheless exceptional cases.[1]

An 'average' accountant could therefore appropriate a few hundred *scudi* per year. The most skilled no doubt made more, but they were few and far between. As for employees who accepted bribes, it is unlikely that they gained much more from their misconduct. Here again, it is important not to be misled by the figures. 40,500 or 1,000 *scudi* in terms of wealth were, of course, not huge sums. However, in terms of income, they were far from negligible. Francesco Maria Gondi, as *provveditore* of the 'Gabella dei Contratti', earned an annual salary of 400 *scudi* and spoke of this sum as a 'considerable wage'.[2] In fact, a survey carried out in 1768 reveals that the *camerlengo generale* at the 'Tassa del Macinato', the office handling taxes on corn milling, earned only 250 *scudi* per year, while the cash clerk of the 'Magona', the iron production monopoly, earned less than 200. The salt tax *camerlengo*, who earned more than the others, managed to scrape up 320 *scudi* per year.[3] What is more, *camerlenghi* were far from being the most badly paid of Tuscan civil servants.

A last illusion to be avoided: the salaries I have just mentioned were by no means low. In fact, two or three hundred *scudi* was, all the same, much more than the forty or forty-five *scudi* that in the mid-eighteenth century a Florentine worker could hope to earn in a whole year. Even a fully booked-up stonemason earned only ninety *scudi* or so.[4] The salaries of civil servants in the Grand Duchy of Tuscany, at least those of medium and superior levels among whom affairs of corruption were the most frequent, were therefore far from inadequate.

The financial consequence of corruption on individual budgets seems therefore clear. Although they did not bring about an extraordinary social ascension, corrupt practices substantially boosted official incomes which were, in themselves, not insignificant. The question to be answered now is what did the employees do with this extra cash?

*   *   *

At the end of Autumn 1719, Antonio Maria Gherardini had just turned twenty-six. He was hopelessly in love with the wife of *cavaliere* Isidoro De'Rossi, a beautiful Sienese woman called Aretafila, or lover of virtue. Given his patriciate origins and the fact that he was the son of a Portinari and the brother of a knight of Santo Stefano, he knew no other way of expressing his feelings than by spending outrageous sums meant to touch the heart that resisted him. Thus, not only was his passion tragic, it also created a bottomless pit. Since his own resources were insufficient, he had to resign himself to defrauding the salt tax funds which had been entrusted to him three years earlier, and from which, in his blindness, he stole several thousand *scudi*. The fact came to the law's attention and he was prosecuted. He confessed but did not repay the money and consoled himself some time later by marrying a young Florentine woman.[5]

Women, then, provided one way of spending money. But

there were others. A lot of money was lost in gambling. Benini, for example, the man presumed guilty of the 'Monte redimibile' embezzlement, had the reputation of being as unlucky as he was persistent. Another gambler, Lodovico Teri, may well have won money in public games, but lost much more in private circles. He was ruined, apparently, in the salons of senator Spinelli, where he came to play in the evening with the mistress of the house and other women of high society. It was 'gambling and conversations' that, according to the chronicler Squarcialupi, caused the downfall of Antonio Francesco Durazzi, who fled in 1748 after many years of pilfering from the 'Monte di Pietà' in Florence[6].

Other more down-to-earth officials used their illicitly earned state funds to provide themselves with the material accompaniments of an aristrocratic existence. Vincenzo Gaspero Borgherini, one of the men charged with the embezzlement from the 'Abbondanza', used the money to buy himself a villa in Fiesole. He helped himself to three hundred *scudi* to restore his apartments when he married, and paid his coachmen and his chaplain with public money. As for Gaetani, he had his domestics served by the 'Abbondanza' and Roncalli, the salt magistracy chancellor arrested in 1677, was accused of having a bed decorated with four figures which he had made at great expense, but not his own.[7]

Corruption sometimes had more altruistic ends. Some officials did not keep the money for themselves, but distributed it to third parties in order to display their power. The case of the 'Abbondanza' is typical. In fact, when pressed by his judges for an explanation just before his second departure, Lorenzo Rossi provided another list of debtors. The names on this list were not all those of civil servants. They included individuals of all extractions to whom either Borgherini or Rossi had been generous. Among the beneficiaries of these little gifts were the *provveditore*'s own father-in-law, two other relatives, his gardener, his stonemason and the peasant worker of Rossi's sister-in-law, as well as a functionary from the 'Grascia', a colleague of *sotto-provveditore* Libri. Also on the list were some of the town's nobility, such as the prior Melati or the senator Dragomanni,

and above all there appeared a large number of peasants for
whom powerful masters had procured grain from the supplies
of the 'Abbondanza'. These included Sollazzino, Burzichelli,
Pierino and Paoletti, some of whom cultivated the land of
Alessandri, others that of Capponi or of Count Della Gherardesca, or even that of the Benedictine monks of the Badia.
Nobody had been excluded.[8]

Love of women, the pleasure of gambling, the taste for
comfort, the eagerness to keep up appearances, this is how the
money gained from corruption was spent. Some officials, such
as Gherardini, indulged in only one of these activities while
others took a more eclectic approach and tried their hand at all
of them. A cash clerk of the 'Decime' in Florence, for instance,
was reported to have got through 18,400 *scudi* 'by paying his
debts and those for which he was guarantor, by lending to
numerous individuals, by buying furniture, by repairing buildings, by providing his family and himself with food and clothes,
by placing bets on the election of papal sovereigns and on the
creation of cardinals, and by other means.'[9]

All these uses had a common factor. Whether it was a
question of parading in front of loved ones, of losing at cards
with noble indifference, of displaying one's luxury or power
through generosity, the resulting effect was always the same:
ostentation made possible by misappropriated or embezzled
money.

It is not a given fact, however, that money was appropriated
with the aim simply of making the dreams of a sumptuous
lifestyle come true. It was rumoured, in Florence, that *camerlenghi* used the funds from the coffers of the state for more
productive ends: in other words, that they engaged in traffic
with state money. This practice was apparently so common-
place that exceptions rather than the rule were remarked upon.
When recommending to the emperor a candidate to succeed
Borgherini, Count Richecourt stressed the fact that the candidate's brother who was employed as cash clerk at the 'Monte'
had 'never traded with money from the till', and he added
sententiously that it was 'no meagre praise for a cash clerk of
this country.'[10]

In certain affairs, the torch of commerce seems to have lighted the misdeeds of the Grand Duchy's employees. Vittorio Nelli, the treasurer from Siena who was sent down in 1666, had been food commissioner and supply officer for the 4,000 infantrymen sent to Milan in 1635 to aid the king of Spain. His interest lay mainly in the trading house opened in Bari by his brothers Francesco and Lorenzo. Giuseppe Verdi, cash clerk of the 'Magona' in Florence, lent the money left in his custody to individuals; Florentine patricians such as Amerigo Antinori, Francesco Tempi and Ippolito Niccolini were among his debtors. It came to light in the end that Vincenzo Borghigiani, agent of iron monopoly in Leghorn, also traded there. His bad, purely private business led to his voluntary exile and to the missing funds amounting to more than 11,000 *scudi* from his administration.[11]

The money obtained through corruption therefore had two effects: the less obvious and more difficult to verify concerned trading and made use of public funds for private business. The more manifest and better documented used state funds as the instrument of ostentation and social prestige. Corruption, however, was not only an issue concerning money: it also had political implications.

* * *

The institutions in which corrupt affairs occurred were organized around a very simple model governed by a statute and other legal texts. They fell first under the authority of the sovereign, the eminent and absolute ruler of the whole administrative machine of the Grand Duchy. Each magistracy had a special function to accomplish: the payment to troops, the upkeep of roads, the provisioning of Florence, the maintenance of public order in the countryside, and so on. The operation of these magistracies depended on three elements: regulations, which endowed the administration with rights and imposed obligations on subjects; cash, needed to carry out the regulations; and men, or staff, who applied the regulations using the cash. The functionary was not meant to be the master of the game. His role was to fulfil a function – not in his own interests, but in those of the sovereign. He was under the control of the master's will. Even at the highest level in the hierarchy, he was merely a cog in the state machine, not the owner of it.

The main characteristic of corruption was that it profoundly modified the terms of this organization by operating a massive redistribution of power. This is illustrated clearly by the example of Zanobi Paoli, director of the mint in Florence.

In Florence, as in all major European centres, there was a mint which struck gold and silver coins. The mechanisms of this establishment were, at the beginning of the eighteenth century, most elementary. Merchants who wished to have metal coined simply handed it to the employees who struck the corresponding money. The product of the conversion into cash was then divided into two parts: most of it went to the trader, while the mint kept a small share, as royal duties and mintage duty. This duty was in fact a tax paid to the sovereign when coins were minted. For gold, it amounted to four liras per pound of metal. Two changes were made to this system during the first half of the eighteenth century. Firstly, from 1714 onwards, traders wishing to have coins struck had to obtain prior permission from the Grand Duke, specifying the amount of metal to convert. At the same time, the mintage duty was raised to five liras. After the extinction of the Medici dynasty, however, it was reduced to four, and then to three liras for gold.[12]

When the Lorraines arrived in Florence, the mint was directed by Zanobi Paoli, who had held the position since 1735. Paoli had succeeded his father, Giovanni Pietro, who had governed the same administration from 1721 onwards. His sister, Francesca Maria, was married to Carlo Del Feo, the *camerlengo* of Portoferraio who, in 1738, fled to Rome with the cash from his administration. Zanobi Paoli was not only master of the mint, he was also the business partner of his subordinates Coletti, Cianfi and Traversagnoli in one, if not two, commercial companies specializing in operations on precious metals. He was, therefore, in the ambiguous situation of being director and at the same time client of the mint.

The Paoli affair broke out just after the government had ceded the mint to a new farm-general. It reached its full development in 1742, when the ex-director set fire to part of the records and took refuge in the church of Santa Croce in Florence. The affair then became one of the battlegrounds between the Lorraines and the Spanish parties in the dispute for power in Florence. As a result, the affair, which was already full of unsolved mysteries, became deliberately clouded by lawyers who did not necessarily have the good of the law in mind. The trial dragged on, being reopened then postponed, reopened and postponed again. The most rigorous severity alternated on the part of the same ministers with demonstrations of a clemency which was perhaps only calculation. The truth, subjected to numerous contortions, became more and more difficult to ascertain. However, with all due reservations, we can render a more a less correct version of what happened.

Paoli was accused of not having declared all the money struck in the mint and of having appropriated the profits. Paying little attention to the regulations concerning permissions he apparently accepted metals that merchants brought directly to him. He struck the coins without informing the grand ducal authorities and pocketed the mintage duty. Moreover, it appears that he continued charging merchants the higher duty of five liras. The difference between the old and new rate was never received by the treasury and could therefore only have been kept by Paoli. He was also accused of having run the mint in the interests of the companies in which he had shares. On the one hand, he was alleged to have agreed to his partners bringing metal to his bureau, and to convert it without completing any of the required formalities concerning licences and duties. On the other, he apparently used funds from the mint to acquire precious metals which were then to be struck for his personal benefit and that of his colleagues. The mint thus became the private bank of Paoli's partners. The judges had no difficulty in making figures expressing profits made by the

companies in which Paoli had shares, and which amounted to
more than 32,000 *scudi* since 1734, tally with those of the mint
which had a deficit balance.[13]

The political effects incurred by corruption are, in the case of
Paoli, perfectly clear. The rules decreed by the prince were
scoffed at and replaced by another tacit system of standards, of
which the director of the mint was both author and guarantor.
The cash kept in the till was never placed in the treasury or
used by the mint department; it was used for the private
activities of the director. The benefits of the institution were
partly diverted to individuals. In this way, the mint, which was a
public institution under the authority of the Grand Duke,
tended imperceptibly to become a private enterprise run by a
director-owner. Indeed, in the archipelago of the state, a small
island was gradually dividing itself off.

*   *   *

The balance of power produced by corruption therefore differed to the one designated by law. Firstly, corruption operated
a vertical transfer of authority. It created a situation in which
the sovereign power became a mere formality and tended to
fade away before that of office-holders who were recognized by
the citizens as having complete authority. The mint, therefore,
was no longer the affair of the Grand Duke but that of Paoli
himself. The 'Gabella dei Contratti' had become Gondi's private office, the silk guild that of Uguccioni. This evolution was
reflected in the comments of the officials. When he was
dismissed in 1743, Francesco Gondi declared that, for twenty-
two years, his position as *provveditore* had been characterized by
'complete authority without interference' in his department.
He mentioned only parenthetically the 'normal and advantageous dependence by which, in conformance to the law and
customs in force, it was always an honour to find oneself
vis-à-vis His Royal Highness and his most important
ministers.'[14] As for the governor of the 'Parte', Filippo Guadagni, he replied to the accusations made against him by protesting
that, 'by a clear will of the sovereign, the upkeep of the roads

[in Florence] has always been left privately to the vigilance, the care and the administration of the *provveditori*', who, 'have always settled road matters freely and independently of all rescript, decree or order in the way which, given the circumstances, seemed to them the most advantageous to proceed.'[15]

Corrupt officials completely usurped regulations. They no longer applied the rules, indeed they rewrote them. Thus, Bronzuoli, the pawnbroker employed at the 'Monte di Pietà' in Florence, did not estimate the value of the objects by applying the rules of the institution, but in proportion to the bribes paid to him. He thereby substituted a rule under which he was to give an evaluation that corresponded to the intrinsic value of the pledged objects for one in which the value of the objects had no relation to their nature, but rather to the bribes that accompanied them. Likewise, the door-keepers of the secretarial offices discarded the procedures governing the delivery of passports and thereby founded a system by which the granting of these documents was based on standards that were as empirical as they were personal. *Auditore* Conti and *provveditore* Gondi procured unwarranted tax relief for certain tax payers by introducing a new way of calculating death taxes that was based on influence more than on arithmetic.[16] Everyone therefore created a law to suit himself.

Lastly, with corruption, cash changed hands. Public reserves, which should have been under the sole control of the sovereign, fell under the surveillance of those who, by statute law, were no more than trustees. Corruption therefore dealt the cards out differently between the sovereign and officials. It created a new economic circuit in which money no longer flowed from tax payers to the Grand Duke but from tax payers to officials. More than any other crime, it symbolized the disintegration of the state.

Corruption thus profoundly affected the organization of institutions. The organizational model by which three elements – regulations, cash and staff – were placed under the authority of a leader– the Grand Duke – was empirically substituted by another in which the staff usurped the authority of the leader and took over the other elements to exploit them for their own interests. Officials and simple subordinates thereby became masters of the institutions. They dictated laws and became the owners of public money. Bribes, the new form of fee paid to these new masters, were proof of recognition of their new authority. They represented the personal power acquired, to the detriment of the state, by men who should have been mere docile servants of the prince and who, in reality, had become powers to be cajoled. They illustrated a new order which, in turn, satisfied the needs of a society that we will now examine.

*   *   *

From the end of the fourteenth century onwards, the upper strata of Florentine society was characterized by an irreversible tendency towards aristocratization. When an oligarchic regime was definitively established, the elite classes had gradually left behind the relatively frugal and parsimonious lifestyle typical of masters of guilds. They had begun to enjoy a new, more lavish way of living in which they tended to distinguish them- selves and their new social status through ostentation.[17] This evolution continued despite the advent of the monarchy in the 1530s. In fact, the constraints of court life, the creation of the order of the knights of *Santo Stefano* and the fascination for foreign models all contributed to reinforcing the tendency that had marked Tuscan society for one and a half centuries. Throughout the seventeenth and eighteenth centuries, there- fore, the lifestyle of the Grand Duchy's elites remained pro- foundly aristocratic, with all its implications in terms of luxury, liberality and ostentation.

Family patrimonies were not necessarily in keeping with the requirements of this way of life. I would even go so far as to say that it was impossible for them to suffice, since social conven- tions fixed no limits to expenditure. No income, no matter how high, could cover expenses which by their very nature had no limits. Budget problems, debts and other financial straits were therefore common in many families. Even the richest were not spared. The Riccardi family, who had one of the greatest fortunes of the capital, caused its own downfall by indulging in too exalted a lifestyle.[18] This case was not unique. Tommaso Buonaventuri, the famous senator involved in the 'Monte redimibile' affair, died not only at an assassin's hand, but also completely ruined by his debts or those of his brother. The Malegonelle brothers, authors of two cases of embezzlement that caused a great outcry, had a series of outstanding 'old debts' that had caused them to be caught up in a web of loans and repayments.[19] As for the men accused of the 'Abbondanza' embezzlement, their private finances were hardly more healthy.

One of these men, Braccio Degli Alberti, disposed of personal wealth amounting to 17,425 *scudi*. His debt, however, totalled 19,587 *scudi*. 'His income', added Lorenzo Rossi in a statement, 'was modest and he spent a lot, especially on his mother, to whom he paid fifty *scudi* a month. He paid another ten to his wife, and his children also had their monthly allowance of two or three *scudi* each. Then there were the servants and the upkeep of the house. Every year he had to pay interest on a number of debts.' The statements of the former custodian of the 'Uccello' are confirmed by evidence used in the trial. It included this eloquent letter addressed to Rossi in 1732: 'My mother is on her deathbed and I have many expenses. Hence I ask you the favour of a mandate for six hundred *staia* for which I should be infinitely obliged.' Ten years later, in 1742, Alberti wrote again: 'Signor Lorenzo, I am in need, great need of some money today, and which I must pay without fail before midday; please do what you can and don't let me down.'[20]

One of the other culprits of the 'Abbondanza' embezzlement, senator Gaetani, was also in dire straits. His fortune, amounting to nearly 31,500 *scudi*, was certainly not negligible. But his debts soaked up more than two-thirds of this and, in the end, all the senator was left with was about 9,500 *scudi* of which, say the experts, only 6,000 were recoverable. Thus *provveditore* Gaetani, who kept seven servants, found himself with budget problems. To overcome them he had to borrow, which he did, for example, when his daughter married. In order to face the unexpected expense for that occasion, he opened up a credit account with a baker. This type of borrowing was not, however, sufficient to balance his domestic finances, and in order to pay his servants he was forced to help himself to some grain from the 'Abbondanza'.[21]

Two features, therefore, characterized, to a greater or lesser extent, the private economy of a number of aristocratic families: on the one hand, the requirements of a sophisticated lifestyle and, on the other, the financial constraints imposed by an insufficient income aggravated by inevitable debts. These problems, however, were not necessarily reserved only for members of the nobility. A member of the middle class such as Benini, the second protagonist of the 'Monte redimibile' affair, was, as we have already seen, a consummate gambler, as was Durazzi, a functionary at the 'Monte di Pietà'. As for Roncalli, *cancelliere* at the salt tax office, he was a prodigal spender. It is thus quite possible that certain patterns and therefore certain difficulties, had reached beyond the strictly closed circle of aristrocratic families and into the 'bourgeoisie' or 'legal professions'. These middle and upper classes, which held salaried posts in government office and whose members had a taste for expensive living, were prone to crucial financial difficulties. Of course, not all members of the nobility and the middle classes shared these tastes and many did not have such problems. But it is nevertheless clear that a certain section of the leading class – in the widest sense of the term – was prey to a constant need for cash.

Politically, since 1532 Tuscany had been a monarchy under the authority of a Duke and then a Grand Duke. This new constitutional regime had replaced the oligarchic government that had held power in Florence, one of the main republics of the peninsula, for a long time. The change did not, however, bring an end to the political influence of the great aristocratic families of the town. After a difficult beginning, in fact, the cohabitation between the traditional elites and the new sovereign had gradually turned into an even tighter collaboration, so that the reign of Cosimo III at the end of the seventeenth century marked a 'symbiosis between the personal work of the prince and a council of upper courtiers, themselves representatives of a nobility firmly consolidated in the absolute state.'[22] The organizational order of institutions bore the traces of this entente: the highest posts in Florentine administration were more open to nobles at the beginning of the eighteenth century than ever before.[23]

However advantageous it was for the nobility, this political situation did not manage to eradicate the republican sentiment that continued to penetrate the hearts of many Florentines, who were stubbornly hostile towards the monarchic regime. In 1673, more than 140 years after Alexander de'Medici came to power, a French observer noted that the 'Grand Dukes are disliked in their States, if not hated. All their subjects are still nostalgic for the republic. They tolerate their domination because they are forced to. They do not dare to express their feelings, but it shows on their faces. An inviolable secret is kept on this subject in all their States.'[24] This evidence, offered by Monsieur de Lamayène, a gentleman from Avignon, may appear to be no more than rhetorical exaggeration. It was nevertheless confirmed fifty years later by another observer of the Florentine situation, *cavaliere* Bartolini. Bartolini, a courtier of Cosimo III, was also one of the Emperor's agents. As such, he informed the emperor's ministers about the situation in Florence, which meant that he corresponded, among others, with the Marquis Corpa. In 1715 he sent the latter a note, which is unpublished to date, concerning the political opinions of Florentine nobility. It classed aristocrats in three categories: friends of France, partisans of Austria and Republicans. Of these three parties, the smallest was the Austrian one, which numbered only sixty-two families. The French side was slightly better supported with 182 families, but the highest score went to the Republicans with 232 families, more than half of the list drawn up by Bartolini.[25]

A part of the aristocracy, therefore, preserved its political hostility, despite a balance of power weighed in its favour by the Medici family. In fact, even up to the eighteenth century a good number of noblemen continued to resent the frustration suffered in the sixteenth century when Alexander, and then Cosimo de Medici, took over the government. Hence they were constant applicants for power.

Lastly, from an economic point of view, Tuscany, although profoundly agricultural, possessed a capital city, Florence, where the industrial activities inherited from the Middle Ages still thrived. Silk, and also trade, had long provided the main occupations in the principal town of the Grand Duchy. Until the 1740s at least, the nobility played a major role in the funding of these activities. However, the capital from the nobility was not always sufficient to meet the needs of business and additional funding was often required, especially in times of crisis.

This very brief summary of the situation in Tuscany demonstrates several requirements of the social body: need for cash, on the one hand, brought about as much by an outrageously expensive lifestyle as by business interests; the desire for power, on the other hand, formulated by the social elite who were unable to recover from their prior frustration. These needs were generally those of the leading classes. The fact that it was these very same classes who held public offices is of fundamental importance. A survey carried out over the years 1708–37 shows, in fact, that more than four-fifths of *provveditori* and more than half the *camerlenghi* posted in Florence were members of the aristocracy from the Grand Duchy and, for the most part, from the capital.[26] Thus the prominent families, assisted by 'middle-class' technicians, controlled or, to put it better, occupied the institutions of the Tuscan state.

The Grand Duchy's officials, therefore, came from the leading classes and were also the beneficiaries of the profits made through the abuses of officialdom. They desired ostentation, they coveted cash and they longed for power. Corruption gave them all that. It offered them authority and provided them at the same time with the financial means to obtain their desired lifestyle and business. It constituted a process by which the elites defrauded institutions and exploited them for their personal needs. This confiscation of the state, which constituted the real function of corruption, may be illustrated by a last example, that of *provveditore* Guadagni.

*   *   *

Cavaliere Guadagni was posted in 1735 at the head of the public works magistracy in Florence. He retained his position after the end of the Medici dynasty up until the first years of the reign of the Grand Duke Peter-Leopold, the second sovereign of the Habsburg-Lorraine house. He was made a senator in 1736, and between 1750 and 1768 was farmer-general and the emperor's chamberlain. He was thus one of the most important men in the Florentine administration at the beginning of the 1760s and among those whose career had suffered the least from the political changes that occurred after the arrival of the Lorraine dynasty.

He and his department, however, had long since aroused suspicion. As early as 1743, the *cavaliere* had been the target of a very critical report drawn up by Count Richecourt, the regent for the Grand Duke in Florence. He accused the 'Parte' – as the public works department was called – of spending considerable sums for the benefit of a few individuals.[27] Some years later, in 1753, a new affair broke out while Count Richecourt was in Vienna. It appears that funds had been misappropriated by the accountant of the 'Parte', or at least by his assistant, who had demanded payment of 'interest on capital which did not exist in the accounts books.' In the absence of the regent, Florentine ministers did not dare take them to court and the scandal blew over.[28] But suspicion did not die down. In 1758, Baron Toussaint, financial adviser to Francis-Stephen, warned the Marquis Botta-Adorno, head of the Tuscan government, against the public works official. He even spoke of a 'trial' that was said to have been initiated against senator Guadagni, *provveditore* of the 'Parte', who owed 70,000 *scudi* to his magistracy, a trial which had been closed when he became farmer-general.'[29]

Finally, on 13 October 1766, with twenty-five years of suspicion weighing heavily on the 'Parte', the Grand Duke Peter-Leopold delegated a commission to carry out a 'universal review of the system and regulations, of the accounts, incomes, expenditure and cash' of the magistracy. The four judges who comprised this new authority remained in office for three years during which they had to overcome many human and technical obstacles. Firstly, the attorney of the 'Parte', who had been named by Guadagni, refused to proceed against his master. Then the chartered accountant designated by the commission came up against complete disorder in the entries in the books. In most offices of the department the accounts books had not been drawn up systematically, which made the task of inspection extremely arduous. None of these difficulties, however, discouraged the judges, who, with the strong support of a sovereign intent on concluding the affair, succeeded in uncovering a number of errors and examples of professional misconduct.

The office directed by Guadagni had attempted to become independent from its two governing bodies, the Grand Duke and the 'Capitani di Parte'. Indeed, without having the authority to do so, the *provveditore* had imposed a new tax on street paving in Florence, leased wooded land belonging to the magistracy, created posts, appointed officials, raised salaries, accorded favours and ordered works without consulting anyone else. More seriously, he had misappropriated 17,744 *scudi* reserved for office expenses and used the money to pay for works the cost of which should have been borne by the residents, namely the canalization of the Bagnolo river downstream from Prato, and the repaving of Florence. Lastly, lower-ranking officials emulated Guadagni and, without any official authority to do so, would sometimes abandon legal proceedings against debtors, sometimes open them up against others.

Guadagni used from time to time the power he had attributed to himself for his personal gain. From 1742 to 1764 he had the department deliver to him 103 cart-loads of firewood, which went up in flames in the chimneys of his Forbici villa overlooking Florence. Another incident concerned the disappearance of a considerable quantity of standing and felled timber, for which he was unable to account.

The 'Parte', in fact, through work carried out on waterways, sometimes gained land from river-beds and in particular from that of the Arno. This land was immediately cultivated, and after a few years the wood that had grown there was sold standing or in planks. From 1736 to 1767, 23,098 trees had been planted by the department, 8,385 of which had been sold or were still standing when the commission began its investigations. The others, however, had disappeared without trace. Besides this, several thousand square yards of sawn wood was missing. From this episode alone, Guadagni was declared to owe the state 14,000 liras.

The *provveditore* also made full use of his authority to demonstrate his generosity towards his friends or dependents. He distributed to his employees eighty-seven cart-loads of firewood. He leased land to his colleague the farmer-general Serristori for a peppercorn rent. Every year, during the public fesitivities, he had a platform erected in the Santa Maria Novella square at the expense of the department and he distributed places generously to the members of nobility. He arranged for the pay clerk, Uguccioni, to be unduly remunerated with sums which, having accumulated over fifteen years, totalled 5,137 liras. He awarded a salary rise to the accountant and the paving commissioner and raised the wages of the agent responsible for the roads – whom, moreover, he had nominated personally.

Last but not least, the *provveditore* covered up for, indeed facilitated, the abuses committed by his inferiors. An example of this is the case of the paving commissioner, a certain Agostino Fortini. Guadagni turned a blind eye to Fortini's dealings concerning three tribunes he had had erected by the department for public ceremonies and for which he pocketed the profits. When Fortini was accused, and rightly so it seems, of having added an extra four hundred *soldi* to the cost of the paving of Via Degli Alfani, behind the cathedral, Guadagni came to his defence. Lastly, he was involved in a case known as the Ponte Vecchio affair.

The Ponte Vecchio, as we all know, crosses the Arno a little downstream from the Uffizi and links the heart of the city to the street that, on the other side of the river, leads to Palazzo Pitti, the former court residence. In the eighteenth century, as today, the bridge was lined with jewellery shops. At the beginning of the reign of Peter-Leopold, Guadagni made out an order for the restoration of seven of these shops considered dangerous. This order was based on a decree from the Grand Duke himself referring to other matters. The file was immediately entrusted to Fortini, who, without consulting the interested parties, went ahead with drawing up plans and agreements with the building companies and had the work carried out for a price that was apparently excessive. When the bill arrived the jewellers protested, and the paving commissioner was suspected of having come to an agreement with the builders to raise the price, promising them a share of the benefits. Fortini was thrown into prison and interrogated. He defended himself by laying the blame on the *provveditore*, against whom the judges did not dare to proceed considering he was a knight of *Santo Stefano* and the emperor's chamberlain. The affair was therefore brought before the Grand Duke, and in the end Guadagni was held sufficiently responsible to be obliged, together with Fortini, to have the shops restored to their original state at his own expense.[30]

The public works department, an institution charged by the prince to administer, under his authority, the roads, bridges and waterways, had therefore become the instrument by which the *provveditore* turned these things into his private kingdom. He not only imposed the law, but also reorganized it, conferring upon himself a new function: to serve the interests, the power and the glory of a Florentine knight rather than the needs of hundreds of thousands of subjects who used the roads, crossed the bridges and had to protect themselves from the rivers. Little by little, Guadagni made himself the master of a small part of the state, which at the same time he distorted.

*　　　*　　　*

Let us now re-examine the questions that were raised at the beginning of part II. In the cases we examined, did corruption have the function of compensating for low salaries? The answer is no, because, more often than not, the salaries of the officials in question were far from negligible. Was corruption a factor in social mobility? Again the answer is negative, since in many cases the personalities cited were members of nobility from Florence or other cities in the Grand Duchy. Lastly, was corruption the answer to the political needs formulated within institutions by those excluded from the regime? Nothing in the current state of documentation enables that hypothesis to be confirmed. Corruption was therefore associated with other constraints and needs. From an economic point of view, it originated not so much through the level of incomes as from the extent of expenditure, or more precisely the impossibility of fixing a limit to this expenditure. From a political point of view, the incentive came not so much through the pressure exerted by those who were excluded as from the demand for power formulated within the institutions on the part of officials.

Corruption therefore fulfilled two functions in Tuscany. It helped to redistribute power within the state mechanism by attributing greater authority to office-holders, many of whom belonged to a politically frustrated class. It facilitated appropriation and venality, the product of which afforded aristocrats – or those wishing to imitate them – the lifestyle fit for their social status and enabled them to face the subsequent financial difficulties. Corruption thus completed the family strategies by which the leading citizens took control of posts. Lastly, it made possible the transition from simple office-holding to appropriation of the state.

Corruption was therefore doubly subversive. On the one hand, it constituted the dysfunctions that jeopardized the correct functioning of institutions and prevented the ruler's will from being accomplished. On the other, it established counter-powers within the state which functionaries exploited for personal interests. It made it possible for a lot of independent elements, which were more or less connected to central power, to prosper within the monarchical regime.

This interpretation immediately raises two questions. First of all, if corruption met the monetary and political needs of the leading classes, why is it that not *all* the officials from these social groups were corrupt? Why did some of them remain incorruptible, when everthing incited them to illicit practices?

Then, if corruption was subversive and sapped the authority of the prince and the cohesion of the monarchic state, why did the Grand Dukes not react more vigorously to the danger threatening them? To answer these questions, it is necessary to change perspective and to explore the matter beyond an analysis limited to the relation of the effects which have been observed with collective needs. The analytic procedure to be adopted now must centre more on the individual so as to examine corruption as it was seen, in reality, by contemporaries.

4

THE MISFORTUNES OF VIRTUE

Corruption produced ostentation, accumulated ready cash and conferred power. By appropriating the state, it satisfied the social needs of dominant groups who were firmly installed in public offices. Two centuries later, and thanks to the conceptual tools of modern research, this interpretation of corruption seems obvious, so obvious in fact that it is hard to believe that it was not always accepted by everyone. Yet it is far from a given fact that in the seventeenth and eighteenth centuries corruption was seen in the same light as we see it today. Indeed, it is quite possible that it was seen from quite a different point of view. It is the latter we must particularly bring to light, since it is this view of corruption and not contemporary analysis that determined attitudes towards misbehaviour. Without re-establishing it, we will be able to explain neither the state of mind of the culprits nor the resistance of the innocent, nor account for the decisions taken by the state.

*   *   *

'Justice ... is virtue entire' wrote the lawyer Savelli 'and not a part of virtue. ... As the incarnation of justice, a judge must therefore possess all virtues.'[1] A good judge, then, was a wise man, a lover of truth and a man impervious to passions. As such, he shunned excess and sought the golden mean. His ideal could be no less than to appear, in the words of another commentator Berart y Gassol, to be 'equal and equitable, holding the scales in balance between the parties, without leaning to the right nor to the left.'[2]

If the good judge was a paragon of virtue, the bad judge was the assassin of justice.[3] In other words, he was a slave to passions and above all to four of them which particularly threatened the law courts: love, hate, fear and avarice.[4] The corruption that was typical of bad judges had no other origins than these.

Corruption: the effect of human passions. This interpretation of corruption was to have a long success story. Just before the outbreak of the French Revolution, it was adopted by the Frenchman Dareau in Guyot's legal encyclopedia: the corrupt judge, he wrote, is a 'monster of horrifying appearance whose breath poisons the air he breathes. . . . He exploits the most sacred of laws to satisfy his passions and his greed.' He sacrifices his integrity to 'an excessive love of wealth' or to 'the appetite of his senses.'[5]

If this analysis has lasted so long it is because it is founded on a philosophy which has had an enduring influence on European thought: the philosophy of Aristotle as expressed, for example, in *The Nicomachian Ethics*.

Indeed, for Aristotle, justice is 'perfect virtue'. As for virtue itself, it is a disposition which allows us to control excesses of passions and therefore to follow the middle way between extremes. From the point of view of ethics, it is 'a mean between two vices, one of excess and the other of defect; and that is such a mean because it aims at hitting the middle point in feelings and in actions.' It follows logically that what is just is 'a mean' and that justice is the 'golden mean'.[6]

Virtue is inseparable from reason. It is perverted, however, by the effects of passion. It is often the case for judges. 'In their opinion, love, hate or personal interest are often involved, so that they are no longer capable of discerning the truth adequately, their judgement being obscured by their own pleasure or pain.'[7] Here again, passion leads to misconduct.

This gave rise to a moralistic interpretation of corruption, centred on simple oppositions between vice and virtue, passion and reason, excesses and the middle way. Steeped in Aristotelian theory, this interpretation saw corruption as the triumph of vice, passion and excess over virtue, reason and the golden mean.

Another quality expected of a judge was that he be filled with grace and God fearing.[8] As a Christian magistrate, he had to respect Divine Law and therefore to heed the admonitions proffered by the Holy Scripture against corrupt judges. Deuteronomy says: 'Thou shalt not wrest judgement; thou shalt not respect persons, neither take a gift: for a gift doth blind the eyes of the wise, and pervert the words of the righteous.' 'And thou shalt take no gift', says Exodus: 'for the gift blindeth the wise, and perverteth the words of the righteous.' Ecclesiasticus takes up the theme: 'Presents and gifts blind the eyes of the wise and stop up his mouth that he cannot reprove.' Isaiah, after having promised woe to those 'which justify the wicked for reward, and take away the righteousness of the righteous from him', sings the praises of 'he that walketh righteously, and speaketh uprightly; he that despiseth the gain of oppressions, that shaketh his hands from holding of bribes', for such a man 'shall dwell on high: his place of defence shall be the munitions of rocks: bread shall be given him; his waters shall be sure.' We find this eulogy again in one of the Psalms of David: 'Lord, who shall abide in thy tabernacle? who shall dwell in thy holy hill? . . . He that putteth not out his money to usury, nor taketh reward against the innocent.' Finally, Job sums up the issue in one sentence: 'Fire shall consume the tabernacles of bribery.'[9]

Corruption, therefore, was not merely a vice: it was also an offence against Divine Law, in other words, a sin. The Christian message fostered the Aristotelian approach by giving it roots in the theory of sin. What the two approaches had in common was that they considered corruption not as a social phenomenon, but as a personal defect, regarding it not as a political danger but as a moral problem. Thus there was a tendency, in the societies that concern us here, to see corruption as a matter of individual morality.

*   *   *

Nowadays the term corruption tends to be used in a more technical sense, mainly to designate the misconduct of state officials. Its usage and meaning in the early modern period were far wider.

Indeed, for our ancestors corruption was above all moral corruption and a depravity concerning not only the relations between individuals and the state but the entire moral life of mankind. In effect, the *Dictionnaire de l'Académie* defined corruption as 'any moral depravity, and principally that concerning justice, loyalty and modesty'. As examples, it offered the following expressions: 'corruption of morals; corruption of the century; corruption of youth; corruption of a man's heart; sin has left a trace of corruption in the whole of human nature. The world is only corruption. A judge suspected of corruption.'[10]

During the same period, the Italian language dictionary published by the Crusca Academy in Florence attributed to the term corruption (in Italian: *corruzione*) a similar meaning. On the one hand it refers to the 'spiritual and corporal corruption of the masses', and on the other hand to the 'darkness of our corruption', opposing it to 'superior spirits'.[11]

A multitude of similar quotations could be found. Towards 1560, Boaistuau, in his *Théâtre du Monde*, spoke of 'a century such as ours, so corrupt, so depraved and full of all sorts of vices and abominations'. In the words of Sainte-Marthe, 'natural corruption steeps our hearts in vices which misguide us and makes us abhor all virtue'. Bourdaloue evoked 'all that is perverted and corrupt in our hearts.' Last but not least, the *Prêtres de la Mission* when hearing sacrilegious confessions exclaimed, 'what strange corruption, what terrible blindness!'

As is made clear in the *Dictionnaire de l'Academie*, this wider conception of corruption was closely linked to that of sin. Saint Thomas Aquinas observed that 'nature has been deprived of grace through the corruption of original sin'. According to Bellarmine, the key to the debate between catholics and protestants was to determine whether or not 'corruption of human nature between catholics and protestants was to determine whether or not 'corruption of human nature and moreover concupiscence itself, found in the baptised and the righteous, can be defined as original sin'. Lutherans for their part, considered that 'all men . . . are conceived and born in sin' and that 'this innate corruption, this original sin, is well and truly a sin'.[12]

For men of the early modern period, therefore, the term 'corruption' covered much more than it does today. For them, it was not only the misconducts of judges or the fraud committed by officials. It was, in a wider sense, the depravity of morals, or even that of human nature, governed by and closely related to sin. It followed that the technical acceptation of corruption, that is, lack of integrity, was merely a part, one just of the many possible forms, of a much larger phenomenon which was perhaps inherent in human nature and in the human soul.

In the twentieth century, the term corruption has become specialized and interpreted as the response to social needs. It is probable that our ancestors saw the matter in a completely different light. For them, corruption was the weakness of human nature, the depravity of mankind, the failure of virtue, the triumph of passions, the outbreak of sin. This corruption of morals, for which both Aristotelian philosophy and Christian law could account, was closely associated with sin from the very start. Indeed, if corruption was considered to have firm roots in human nature, it could even be regarded as the origin of all faults. Its bounds knew no limits and stretched far beyond the moral standards of public officials.

In this context, failure of integrity, which constitutes corruption today, was first and foremost conceived as a moral problem where conscience and personal culpability of individuals were involved. Its meaning was then extended to cover the wider notion of a corruption having almost metaphysical qualities. That is the reason why corruption – in its modern and technical meaning – had no chance of being the subject of a specific study. Nothing induced people of the time to follow the track that today we are so easily inclined to take: that of a social and political survey.

* * *

The term corruption had yet another sense. It designated, in the words of Diderot and d'Alembert in their *Encyclopédie,*

> the state in which a thing ceases to be what it was.... An egg is corrupt when it ceases to be an egg and a chicken has taken its place; for here corruption is not used in the vulgar sense. Whence the philosophical axiom that the corruption of one thing is the generation of another. Corruption differs from generation as two opposites differ from each other. It differs from alteration as the most from the least, or the whole from a part. An object is said to be altered when it has not changed so much as to be unrecognizable and conserves its former name. However, after corruption, neither one nor the other subsists any longer.[13]

None of these ideas were new. They originated, like others already mentioned, from classical philosophy. Aristotle stated that 'the passing away of this is a coming-to-be of something else, and the coming-to-be of this is a passing away of something else.' He then demonstrated how alteration differed from corruption.[14] Although ancient, these ideas had not lost their universal value and were useful in explaining the political implications of corruption.

What happened, in fact, when corruption of morals became so widespread among a large number of citizens that it became the behavioural norm among the population? Was it not to be feared that in the end the state itself would become contaminated, altered and finally corrupted, and that from its corruption another political regime could arise? Finally, was not corruption of morals the origin of the corruption of institutions? This question was duly raised and often answered in the affirmative.

Machiavelli, for example, associated corruption of the state with a lack of civic sentiment. It occurred when citizens lacked the sense of general interest and the taste for freedom. It did not affect Germanic states which, being more primitive, were also less corrupt. But where it was most rife, in particular in Italian states, it was exacerbated by wealth, catalysed by an unequal distribution of power and stimulated by the absence of a suitable religious feeling. In a context such as this, corruption was bound to become an irreversible process. As the consequence of individual depravity, it meant the end of freedom and the triumph of tyranny. State corruption could thus be explained by that of individuals.[15]

'The corruption of every type of government', explained Montesquieu, 'almost always begins with the corruption of its principles.' Democracy founded on virtue, had therefore two excesses to avoid: 'the spirit of inequality, which leads to aristocracy, or to the rule of a single person; and the spirit of extreme equality which leads to despotism under one ruler.' Both extremes originated in the depravity of individuals. They were moral phenomena in the same way that, in previous times, a moral principle, that is to say virtue, had ensured social stability in the state. Thus for Montesquieu, as for Machiavelli, corruption of the state resulted from that of men. They were not tyrants who swept away strong republican virtues, but the citizens themselves who, through the corruption of their morals, hindered the survival of the republic and prepared the way for despots.[16]

Several characteristics appear to summarize the early modern world's view of corruption. Seen in its relationship with public offices, it was a vice, a fault, a sin. It was thus denounced unequivocally, and anyone found guilty of corrupt practices had committed a grave offence against divine law. Then, corruption among public office-holders was just one of many forms of corruption of morals, that is to say, of a much wider phenomenon within which it did not appear to have a specific place. Like all forms of depravity, however, it was seen far more as a moral and individual defect than a social or political problem. Lastly, public corruption was not the subject of an autonomous political thought, but naturally contributed to the catastrophic consequences that moral depravity implied for the states. It did not, however, constitute more of a danger than other perils. In a democratic system, the venality of judges was, all things considered, less dangerous than the spirit of extreme quality.

*   *   *

As corruption of public officials was a particular expression of universal depravity, the authorities had to deal with it in the same way as with other forms of corruption of morals. Venal judges, accountants guilty of embezzlement and officials convicted of extortion had to be punished in the same way that thieves had to be hung, murderers beheaded and regicides burnt alive. The state response to corruption was, with a few exceptions, less of an immediate political confrontation than of a criminal penalty sentenced by a judge. It was not directed against a dangerous class, but against individuals deficient in integrity. It was not directed to a collective threat to the throne, but to a multitude of scattered crimes of which the only common factor was the corrupt nature of man. The prince, in his repressive action, had only one enemy: the individual guilty of having violated God's will and who deserved, for this reason, to be crushed by the arm of Justice.

Let us take here again the example of Tuscany. Of course, the political effects of corruption were perceived by a few isolated observers who, being particularly perspicacious, put their finger on the independence of officials and the resulting desegregation of the state. In 1738, a few months after the arrival of the Lorraine dynasty, the author of a note which remains anonymous observed that the customs officers of the Grand Duchy 'often act as if they owned the customs stations and hardly obey orders from superiors.'[17] Even more of a clairvoyant was Count Richecourt, who was by no means taken in by the tricks used by higher ranking functionaries to escape the control of central authority. Thus, in 1753, in his comments on the new rules of the farm-general, he noted that each farmer wanted to have 'his own management and monopoly.' They all, he added, wished to carve themselves an 'individual sovereignty' or 'private kingdom.'[18]

It was no doubt Richecourt who took this type of analysis the furthest. As a foreigner in a hostile country, he was more far-sighted than the natives, and for this reason he was one of the rare observers to realize the political implications of misconduct: 'Once fear', he said, 'which is the only means of ruling Florentines had passed, they went back to being republicans.'[19] What must be underlined, however, is that Richecourt's thought is late in coming. What is more, it is somewhat of an isolated case. It does not really represent the situation in which the problem of corruption of officials was, in fact, a legal issue, expressed in terms of individual punishment. It did not, therefore, reflect the attitude nor the dominant idea on corruption.

In Tuscany corruption was seen from the point of view of penal consequences set out by appropriate legislation. Bribery was firstly dealt with by two legal texts given by the Grand Dukes Cosimo I and Francis I, published in 1550 and 1576 respectively. Under these laws, it was strictly forbidden for judges and other public office-holders to accept 'gifts' either before, during or after the trial or the handling of the case in question. This interdiction also covered those who, although they did not pass sentences or take decisions themselves, could be tempted to use or abuse their influence on magistrates or officials. Heavy penalties – fines, administrative sanctions and so on – were imposed on offenders.[20]

As far as embezzlement was concerned, the Grand Dukes had taken certain measures which were both preventive and punitive. These measures were added to texts dating from the republican period. A law dated 1622 had defined rather strict procedures by which *camerlenghi* had to submit their accounts for inspection. They were obliged to present on a monthly basis the balance of their tills to the *auditore fiscale* and to the *depositario generale*, that is to say to the state's highest judicial and financial authorities. As far as punishment was concerned, the oldest text was the statute of Florence, dated 1415, which imposed very heavy penalties on dishonest accountants. The culprit was to be attached to the tail of a donkey and dragged around the town. He was then to be buried up to the waist and the part of the body that was above ground was to be burned. All the wordly goods of the punished man were, of course, confiscated. New measures were added to this already awe-inspiring programme. For the State of Siena, which did not come under the jurisdiction of the statute of 1415, a measure dated 1562 decreed very heavy fines for minor acts of embezzlement (less than one hundred liras) and, for the others, death by decapitation or hanging. Lastly, in 1681, the Grand Duke Cosimo III included the crime of embezzlement in the new law on theft that he decreed. For up to fifty *scudi*, a public accountant convicted of having stolen money had to restore four times the sum and ran the risk of having to suffer corporal punishment which could be as severe as being sent to the galleys for life. For crimes involving from fifty to a hundred *scudi*, the judge still demanded the restitution of the sum stolen multiplied by four, but could also hand down a death sentence by hanging. Beyond this sum, the law stated that the culprit be hung and that his worldly goods be confiscated.[21]

In Tuscany, therefore, the official position on corruption was above all expressed in terms of punishment. It concentrated on individuals rather than groups and its explicit goal was that of creating an obstacle to corruption of the soul.[22]

*   *   *

In the first three chapters of this book, I considered corruption as a social phenomenon and attempted to provide a definition of its function. This led me to confirm that, through corruption, the state was appropriated and the needs of certain social groups were thereby satisfied. I am now able to complete those first indications by underlining the fact that contemporaries probably had no overall vision of a function which was basically latent. The way they interpreted infringements was not from a social point of view but from a moral one. They saw corruption as an individual sin requiring individual punishment, and not as a collective phenomenon manifested by a redistribution of political power. This interpretation, faithfully reflected in legal texts, had two advantages. On the one hand, it culpabilized corruption. On the other, it de-dramatized the situation.

By censuring corruption, the moral interpretation of the phenomenon naturally prevented the spread of abuses. As soon as guilt comes into play and consciences are pricked, people hesitate before acting. To classify corruption as a sin was, of course, of no importance to those who were dominated by overwhelming needs and incapable of resisting temptation. But, it did, on the other hand, awaken scruples in more honest people who were then stopped from engaging in corrupt practices. The moralization of corruption thereby put a brake on its generalization, which explains why not all employees were corrupt.

This moralization was at the same time a way of de-dramatizing the situation. It substituted collective danger with individual errors.[23] It enabled the sovereign to regard corruption as just another form of crime, rather than subversion. It made tolerable what would otherwise have been an attack on his majesty and saved the sovereign from a large-scale political struggle the outcome of which would have been far from certain.

The contemporary interpretation of corruption can therefore be summarized in three terms. Firstly it was linked to morality and guilt. Secondly, its expansion was checked by the very fact that it was associated with morality. Lastly, the moral interpretation rendered infringements more tolerable by eliminating the subversive aspect. The consequence of this interpretation was twofold: it limited havoc and made the problem more tolerable. In short, it held corruption under control while ensuring its survival.

In this system, the role of the law was clear. It had the explicit function of authorizing the punishment of the culprits. Its declared goal was therefore the extirpation of corruption. More profoundly, it made it possible to see as isolated criminals those who otherwise would have been seen as a group of opponents. It brought what in fact was a permanent *coup d'état* down to the level of minor morality issues of no consequence. It concealed a situation which, had it been conceptualized, would have been intolerable. It rendered tolerable and by doing so made possible the very phenomenon it aimed to stamp out: corruption.

Is there a universal model?

The object of parts I and II of this work was to weigh up the various functional effects of corruption. Firstly, I established that misconduct among officials had become standard behaviour which, founded on a few simple principles, was repetitive in nature. At the same time, I observed that this misbehaviour was detrimental to the adjustment of the social ogranization in question because, as a dysfunction, it went against the accomplishment of the functions to be fulfilled by institutions. These negative aspects nevertheless appeared to me to be balanced out by positive consequences with regard, if not to society as a whole, at least to certain groups. In a monarchy such as Tuscany, for example, corruption satisfied the needs of the leading classes through the intermediary of officials who were themselves members of the social elite, thereby producing the desired effects, both monetary and political. To do this, they appropriated government institutions. For this reason, corruption was eminently subversive. The moral interpretation of this phenomenon was inclined to thwart its spread while at the same time it de-dramatized the situation. This interpretation found its concrete expression in a law which, while proposing overtly to punish the culprits, also had the advantage of transferring the problem of corruption from the field of political struggle to that of individual criminality. The law thus created the ideal conditions for corruption to be de-dramatized, in other words, to be stabilized.

No matter what the time or place of origin, quotations on corruption echo each other in many ways. Count Richecourt's invectives against corruption in Tuscany, for example – 'this evil is so widespread and sanctioned so strongly that, far from being condemned, it is commonly said of such a man that he is well-versed in business matters'[1] – is very similar to the pessimistic lines written: on corruption in Azerbaidjan by a soviet sociologist in 1976:'if a man steals, he is said to be smart; if he is cunning or dishonest, he is a real businessman.'[2]

The same author, Zemtsov, continues further on: 'the [Soviet] man must have a split personality in order to survive: at work, he accepts the hypocrisy of others and he in turn is hypocritical.' But 'in a small circle of friends', 'he is obliging and as honest as possible, for here the moral standards discarded at work become even more demanding.'[3] This calls to mind another judgement. It is a quotation relating to Nigeria mentioned at the beginning of this work: 'to put your fingers in the till of the local administration', stated Wraight and Simpkins on the subject of Nigerian officials, 'will not unduly burden your conscience. . . . To steal the funds of the unions would offend public conscience and ostracize you from society.'[4] This double-sided morality, with a public and a private face, is therefore not reserved for one particular society.

Can these similarities, which are actually rather striking, inspire the hypothesis that, despite the various forms it takes, corruption can be explained by a universally valid model? In fact, nothing permits such a naive conclusion to be drawn. Just one example, chosen deliberately from a radically different context in time, politics and place from that of the Grand Duchy of Tuscany, makes it clear to what extent comparison is limited.

The example chosen is that of the Soviet Union in the 1960s and 1970s. It appears that corruption was so widespread that the writings of Zemtsov on the hierarchy of the racket in Azerbaidjan[5] differ very little from those produced more recently by P. Veyne on the same practices during the late Roman Empire.[6] This corruption, we are told, fulfilled certain functions. It apparently enabled dignitaries to build up vast fortunes which themselves guaranteed the necessary protection against the possibility of economic instability. In a regime where political careers were very often uncertain, it answered an intense need for security.[7] For a historian such as A. Besançon, however, corruption had a more essential function. It quite simply enabled the regime to run, for without it the economic machine would have come to a halt. At the same time, the political consequences were considerable. Corruption was the counterpart of dissidence, which attacked official truths in the aim of eliminating them, in that it liberated men through lies and trickery. It therefore threatened the communist regime which, for this reason, systematically stamped it out.[8]

The official interpretation of corruption, however, did not always tend to see it as a political problem. The lessons of the *Great Soviet Encyclopedia* are, in this respect, very revealing. Two articles can be found on the issue. The first, entitled 'Corruption', considers it as a political phenomenon and indicates that it is 'known in all forms in the exploitative state'. The author underlines, however, that 'a particularly widespread corruption is inherent in the imperialist state'. He concludes by observing that 'it is widespread in the USA.'[9] Not a word about the Soviet Union. The second article, on the other hand, is entitled 'Bribery' in the American edition. This article is purely juridical and examines the crime of corruption. It describes corruption as 'a disgraceful vestige of the past; it was widespread in the pre-revolutionary Russian state apparatus.' It then analyses Soviet legislation on the matter before concluding that the government of the USSR considers 'the struggle against bribery one of the most important tasks of Soviet agencies fighting against crime.'[10]

The *Great Soviet Encyclopedia* therefore reflects a situation in the USSR in which corruption could be spoken of as a form of criminality – inherited from the past – but not as a structural characteristic of the regime. For writers such as Ilja Zemtsov and Constantin Simis, who refused this elementary truth, life was made difficult. They usually ended up either in Israel, or in the United States – the price they paid for their refusal to moralize about corruption, that is to say, to associate it with guilt and crime and to depoliticize it.

The Soviet situation in the 1960s and 1970s differs from the situation observed in certain pre-industrial monarchies, in that the moralization of corruption remained somewhat superficial. It did not seem to have a hold on a population for whom morality had nothing to do with public affairs.[11] It did not, therefore, stop corruption from taking on considerable proportions and from becoming, whether the government liked it or not, a problem of authority and politics. That, it seems, was the case in Azerbaidjan where, according to Zemtsov, 'a situation that threatened the existence of the regime had been established. Corruption was the product of the Soviet system.... But, in Azerbaidjan, this corruption was now in conflict with the system.' And when Leonid Brezhnev disgraced the first secretary of the local Communist Party's central committee, it was not so much in order to punish him for his crimes as to re-establish a situation which had become politically unbearable.[12] In actuality, the authorities had therefore to revert to a political interpretation of corruption that they had officially rejected. The moral and juridical interpretation was not adopted.

The moralization of corruption had therefore more chance of success in a small agricultural monarchy of the *ancien régime* with its elites steeped in Aristotelism and Christian morality than in a great dictatorship where virtue is not based on classical philosophy but on socialism. However, even when it managed to take root it was not without problems, as much for employees whose consciences it pricked as for princes whose sense of justice was called into play. I shall now explore the solutions applied to these problems.

Part III

CONSCIENCES AT PEACE

Introduction

Whenever the holder of a public office, dignity or function commits a serious professional fault, he must be dismissed. . . . It is absolutely essential for the Republic that the men assigned to public offices be capable and full of integrity, and have a good reputation, judgement and moral standards. . . . The wrong choice of officials, on the other hand, subverts everything and destroys the world. . . . If the prince . . . designated subjects that he esteems fit, and if afterwards he realizes that they are incapable and that they do not have an appropriate character, he is obliged to dismiss them and substitute them with persons suitable for the task.[1]

The author of these harsh words was Giacomo Conti, a nobleman from Ascoli, doctor of law and theology, consultant to the Holy Inquisition and *primo auditore di Consulta* of the Grand Duke of Tuscany. They appear in a collection of his decisions as published for the edification of jurists.

This grave magistrate is not unknown to us. We have already seen him at work with regard to Prince Strozzi's inheritance. And we know under what terms this affair was settled: the prince was the beneficiary of a considerable tax exemption in exchange for which doctor Conti received a lavish gift.[2]

The eminent *auditore* therefore accepted the moralization and the penalization of corruption, but at the same time infringed the grand ducal laws of 1550 and 1576 which forbad judges to accept any gifts, even once the lawsuit had been closed.[3] He thereby incarnated the contradiction in which were involved those who, on the one hand, were aware of, indeed commentated on, the principles and the laws, and, on the other hand, flouted them.

There were only two ways of resolving that contradiction: by complying with the laws or by neutralizing them. The first solution required an unattainable moral heroism from men who were already steeped in error. It was therefore necessary for the majority of dishonest functionaries to adopt the second course, by trying to distance themselves from the temporal and spiritual threats proffered by divine and human law.

The corrupt man thus faced two problems. Being fully conscious of exposing himself to more or less ignominious punishment, he tried firstly to limit the risks, in other words, not to be seen or caught. Hiding his crime, however, did not calm his troubled conscience. Thus, in order to be completely at peace with himself, the culprit had still to reclaim his virtue by finding a moral justification for each action in order to override or at least to shake off the fetters of religious interdictions. He therefore had two objectives. Firstly, to be seen in the eyes of others as somebody he was not, and secondly, not to be seen, in his own eyes, as somebody he was.

The aim of the third part of this work is to demonstrate how lies and casuistry enabled these goals to be obtained. I will thus show how these two arms made it possible for even the most venal of judges to become, in the eyes of the world as well as in his own eyes, a model of justice. I will also show how the moralization of corruption, the exaltation of justice and the oppression of defenceless beings could co-exist, fairly easily and at the cost of a few compromises with truth and righteousness.

In a monarchic regime, this reconstructed honesty needed to be sanctioned, however, by the sovereign. The question was therefore to ascertain whether or not the prince would play along – in other words, if he would pretend not to see, affect not to understand, in short, if he would accept a situation which considerably limited the extent to which human law and divine dictate could be applied. I will therefore explore, in part IV of this book, two possible forms of answer. The first was based on the recourse to clemency so that infringements were tolerated without actually being disculpabilized. The second used the exaltation of punishment to discourage employees and obliged them, with threats of the most dreadful penalties, to adhere to the concepts which had been instilled in them.

On the Strength of Lies

Corruption was therefore a vice. Vice, being the opposite of virtue, threatened honour. It was, besides this, punishable by law. Dishonour and punishment awaited those who gave in to their passions, deceived their masters and engaged in illicit practices. These traitors had to be caught, prosecuted, and marked forever by the indelible stain of infamy.

It is wise, however, not to insist too much on the perils attached to corruption. Many tribunals were very lax in executing the laws entrusted to them. In Naples, for example, where corruption prevailed on a large scale, a jurist of the second half of the eighteenth century, Carlo Petra, found in the entire body of previous court literature only eight sentences of criminal punishment passed for charges of lack of integrity.[1] This was indeed a small number, and for anyone considering indulging in the crime it was all the more encouraging, as they felt they could count on the clemency of public opinion: 'They are the douceurs that everyone takes', declared Francesco Grassi, Grand Chancellor of the State of Milan, on the subject of the bribes he was accused of accepting. Charles V himself recognized that the crimes of which Ferrante Gonzaga, governor of Lombardy, was accused did not stain the reputation of this great personage.[2]

It would be wrong, however, to exaggerate the situation in the opposite direction and to state that laws were never applied or principles were always taken lightly. In fact, not all tribunals were as easy going as the Neapolitan ones, as I will have a chance to show further on.[3] In certain political formations, those who had violated the code of ethics were firmly marked as infamous. For instance, in Venice, 'the list of people guilty of embezzlement was re-read every year before the grand council so that their infamy should neither be diminished nor forgotten.'[4] Tuscan society was not much more lenient. Lorenzo Libri, who had returned to Florence after years of exile for embezzlement, apparently found himself 'shunned by most people'.[5] Another example is that of Lodovico Teri, the *camerlengo* of the capital's 'Abbondanza', who was the protagonist in a major case of embezzlement at the beginning of the eighteenth century. His compatriots did little to defend him. On the contrary, they completely ran him down, rebaptizing him Luther (one could be forgiven for thinking, then, that officials convicted of embezzlement were automatically classed as heretics). Teri-Luther, therefore, was the object of a satire which spread across the capital entitled: 'Luther, dreaming that he is being led to the gallows, makes his last confession.' He began by confessing, 'I was a Cain for my brother', before stating that he had never shown any filial love or attended mass or sermons, that he swore, gambled, terrorized his peasants, did not pay his debts and left the 'Abbondanza' administration with 'a missing sum, I know not how big; not much, 8,000 *scudi*, not as much as everyone is talking about.'[6]

These rebuffs made less imprudent people think twice about engaging in corruption. The Marquis Niccolò Francesco Antinori, the special Tuscan delegate sent to Vienna, observed in 1708 that at the emperor's court nobody wished to expose himself to the suspicion of corruption. Ministers, of course, did not refuse money in 'issues for which they had a special competence' and that they could settle personally. But they became incorruptible when it came to matters that were liable to be discussed in a conference, that is to say in ministerial meetings, where their venality may have transpired.[7]

Tuscan employees felt an equal concern for their reputation. When Giovanni Ubaldini, for example, was accused of embezzling more than 2,000 *scudi* from the 'Possessioni' administration, he immediately contacted a member of the reigning family, the prince Giovanni Carlo, asking him to support a project for a financial transaction that would have spared him court proceedings and a subsequent scandal. He admitted that his motive for this was to 'save his reputation'. The same concern was shown a century later by the treasurer of the military bank, Francesco Maria Malegonelle. When his balance sheets were inspected by revisors, Malegonelle begged his subordinates not to speak 'so that his reputation would not be shattered'.[8]

Avoiding proceedings and the infamy that followed the confession or discovery of corruption, due to its official moralization, must have been the primary preoccupation of many officials. The well-established means for doing this consisted in lying, for lies, while giving the appearance of virtue, offered the way to escape all censure.

*   *   *

'A man of honour is not to be crudely bought by social inferiors if he does not wish to lose prestige in the community.' Bribes should thus be paid 'with *finesse*'. These remarks were made by the British anthropologist John Campbell,[9] referring to contemporary Greek communities. They doubtless have a far more universal value, and could easily have been applied to eighteenth-century Florence. In both contexts, a gentleman refused to be openly corrupted. He preferred to receive discreet marks of affection or gratitude. The *auditore* Giacomo Conti did not actually receive money from prince Strozzi, but a gift which was 'proportional to his magnanimity and to the esteem and merit of the *auditore* himself'. The *provveditore* Gondi accepted cash on only one occasion and that was from the De'Nobili household, a family on a social par with his own. But from his subordinates he received only gifts. True, he had them meticulously evaluated and, if need be, took them to the nearest jewellers to resell. But they were gifts all the same and certainly not bribes.[10]

Thus, to all appearances, Gondi was not a venal leader, but a caring employer whose servants were full of gratitude. Conti did not look like a corrupt magistrate. He made himself out to be more of an obliging adviser whose discretion did not permit him to refuse a gift offered by a man of the world for whom he had done a favour and who would certainly be offended by a refusal.

Lies, therefore, were part of custom. Not even the slightest mention was made of corruption. On the contrary, efforts were made to deny obvious facts and to show an honest face, the ingenuity of which discouraged critics. Vincenzo Gaspero Borgherini, the *provveditore* of the 'Palco dell'Uccello', excelled in this art. True, the storehouse had been completely depleted during his long administration. That fact he did not deny, but he also pointed out that most of his functions had been carried out by his deputy. This was only fair, he continued, for his work comprised a number of tasks which were 'quite unsuitable for a knight of his quality, for example that of having to remain for ever in that heap of dust.' It was impossible under those conditions to attend the office on a regular basis. It was absolutely impossible for a gentleman like Borgherini to deal with the petty administrative details of his magistracy. His aristocratic ethos forbad it. At the same time, it disincriminated him since it constituted the cause of and the excuse for his being unaware, as the good *provveditore* claimed to be, of the real situation. The culprit, therefore, could be no other than Lorenzo Rossi, that scoundrel and cad whom he had trusted and who had shamefully deceived him.[11]

Thus, nobody in the capital of the Grand Duchy admitted to being corrupt. Office-holders would say instead that there were, unfortunately, among the crowd of Florentine administrators who were highly respected by their subordinates, some absent-minded gentlemen who were often swindled by less scrupulous collaborators. Social rites thus supported a comedy of innocence – an innocence made all the more convincing by the protestations of those involved. This comedy, however, was valid only to the extent that there were no facts to contradict it.

*   *   *

The first precaution to be taken was to arrange for the institutions to be totally sealed off to outsiders. Some officials were very successful in doing this. It was a recognized fact that Tommaso Buonaventuri, *provveditore* of the 'Monte redimibile' in Florence, was the only person able to 'see the real state of the Monte, of which he was extremely possessive'.[12] The situation was similar at the 'Abbondanza', on which, according to the imperial Council of Vienna, Count Richecourt had not managed to gather satisfactory information on account of the 'secrecy with which the members of the same magistracy covered up their operations.'[13]

It was no easy task to keep so many secrets. Indeed, secrecy, so as to discourage curiosity and avoid indiscrete remarks, was secured only at the expense of constant pressure on citizens, colleagues and subordinates.

A certain Pier Antonio Betti, grain measurer at the 'Abbondanza', thus paid dearly for having discovered illicit practices. He declared to the judges that, in 1733 or 1734, he had caught one of the storehouse porters stealing a sack of grain in order to give it to a peasant. His conscience obliged him to go straight to *cavaliere* Borgherini and denounce this misconduct. The porter was immediately dismissed, but hired again a short time later. The scandal then turned against the person who had brought it into the open. Lorenzo Rossi, explained Betti, 'had me reprimanded by *cavaliere* Borgherini, who told me that I should concentrate only on my job, and not pay any attention to other people's business. He said I should keep away from the silos, otherwise he would dismiss me as well.'[14] It was obvious that inquisitive people were not well-liked at the 'Abbondanza'.

The treasurer of the military bank also urged his employees to be discreet.[15] In fact, and luckily for him, his embezzlement was not discovered until after his death. But not everyone was as fortunate as he. Antonio Francesco Durazzi, employed at the 'Monte di Pietà' in Florence, attempted in vain to silence his assistant, a certain Tommaso Mori-Ubaldini, who had stumbled upon proof of his master's corrupt practices. He did not succeed and was forced to flee to Venice.[16]

The law of silence, however, was the rule in several states. In

Milan, for example, at the time of Charles V, investigators admitted that they had a lot of trouble in persuading people to talk. Witnesses were, in fact, convinced that any declaration would have rendered them 'abject and unworthy'. This sentiment was all the more acute owing to the fact that, in the capital city of Lombardy, political power was weak, the Spanish monarchy far away and the risk of exposing oneself to revenge considerable. A certain Urbano da Landriano, for example, who had thought fit to denounce abuses, was far from thanked for his trouble. He was chained up in the Merchants Square 'with his tongue *ingiovada*, that is to say, half pulled out and wedged between two pieces of wood. He was also made to wear a painted mitre on his head.' It was far wiser to follow the example of a senator who, when questioned by the investigators, declared that 'man's memory is fragile and that to remember everything is more an attribute of the holy spirit than of the human mind.'[17]

In Tuscany, the proximity of the prince, which was both protective and threatening, no doubt encouraged tongues to wag. One of the best jurists of the Grand Duchy pointed out, however, that, when it came to corruption, there was always 'a lot of reticence, and few people who wished to testify in favour of the state.'[18] Sixty years later, Richecourt echoed this theme. According to him, there was no doubt that many officials nominated by the Grand Duke Gian Gastone, the last of the Medici, were corrupt, but it was difficult to catch them 'owing to the general prejudgement that to save a criminal is a good deed as well as to the fear people have of exposing themselves to his or his family's vengeance. In fact, in this country, we cannot get witnesses to testify against the worst criminals and the dregs of society except by putting them in jail. As for testifying against people of a higher social rank, and chiefly well-protected people with influence, it is impossible.'[19] The investigation of the 'Abbondanza' embezzlement fully confirmed these pessimistic words.

One of the main witnesses, Ciacchi, was formerly butler to senator Alberti. When interrogated on 28 August 1747 on the subject of the false money orders that Lorenzo Rossi accused him of having drawn up for his master, he denied the accusation outright and was immediately put into jail. A few days later, having realized that by then the former guard of the 'Palco' would have revealed all, he confessed, but only partially, and was sent back to prison. When interrogated again on 2 September, he still did not satisfy the examining magistrate and was sent back again. It is more than likely that Ciacchi had not told the judge everything he knew.[20]

The court, of course, tried to make other witnesses talk. Among them was Giuseppe Vergili, one of Borgherini's former servants. He was imprisoned and questioned about a certain money order that his master had asked him to cash at the 'Abbondanza'. His reply: 'I did not know what it contained, for servants are not supposed to know the affairs of their masters, and must only obey orders.'[21]

The trial also brought to light the fact that several people had been aware of what was happening at the 'Abbondanza' for a very long time but had said nothing. A certain Abbott Pecorini, attorney to the convent of Santa Marta in Florence, having cashed, on behalf of Ciacchi, a false money order for the amount of 750 *staia*, went to Rossi and said that 'he had received the money order from [him],' and he added that 'for [him, Lorenzo Rossi] it was a disgraceful thing to have superiors in need of cash.'[22] Nevertheless, Abbott Pecorini did not let the law know of this problem. As for Vincenzo Gaspero Borgherini, he confessed that he had been informed as early as 1733, that is, fourteen years before the scandal broke out, about the illicit practices of his colleague Alberti. He said nothing of it 'so as not to render the affair public through respect for Alberti's family and for his father-in-law, Marquis Torrigiani.'[23] As for the grain merchants who, shortly before Rossi's departure, had profited from the illicit bonus distributed by the latter, the news had certainly spread among themselves but not a word was said in public.[24]

Many reasons could no doubt explain this reluctance to testify. It is worth mentioning at least one of them: the heavily dependent relationship between subordinates and their masters. This observation, of course, will surprise anyone who knows that several public offices were allocated by the Grand Duke in person.[25] It is, however, important to be aware of the fact that office-holders were not owners of their posts, that they often obtained them through recommendation from their masters and that, besides this, they enjoyed in their daily work no special protection from the authority of their superiors. Finally, some posts, were not designated by the sovereign but by administrative officials themselves. For all these reasons, the relationship between Vincenzo Gaspero Borgherini and his subordinates at the 'Abbondanza' may, in respects, be considered to be symbolic of a more general situation.

The administration of the *cavaliere*'s private affairs often overlapped with that of the storehouse. Lorenzo Rossi, before joining the 'Abbondanza', had been working for the Borgherini household from 1718 onwards. It was not until two years later, in 1720, that he entered the 'Palco', as deputy to the *custode* of the time, a certain Becalli. But he continued to handle his master's household. Indeed, in 1747, he was generally considered to be Borgherini's secretary or butler. 'He dealt with all the affairs of the house'[26] explained Richecourt. Another of the *provveditore*'s collaborators, his personal secretary, Cappuccini, was also employed from 1731 to 1734 as deputy to the *custode* at the 'Palco' of the 'Abbondanza'. He was still responsible in 1747 for retail sales of grain on the public square.[27] As for the other subordinates of the 'Uccello', unaware of all the higher authorities of the 'Abbondanza', they considered themselves to be totally dependent on Lorenzo Rossi and on the *provveditore*. Giovanni Battista Bianchi, Rossi's deputy, declared that he had been given his post by his superior. The porter Chiavistelli said he owed his job to Borgherini alone. Nobody imagined that the supreme authorities of the 'Abbondanza' had any say in the matter and everyone recognised that the *provveditore* of the storehouse had the absolute right to nominate and dismiss his subordinates as he saw fit.[28]

Strong personal links and at the same time relationships of dependency meant that subordinates were not eager to reveal the fraud practised by their superiors. In this context, the trials and tribulations of Antonio Francesco Durazzi, who did not succeed in silencing his deputy, seem to be somewhat of an exception to the rule. In most cases, nobody was ready to go gossiping outside or take the matter to law. And what happened inside the offices was carefully sheltered from inquisitive ears.

*   *   *

As ill luck would have it, there existed in Tuscany official boards which had the task of inspecting the management of officials in the Grand Duchy. Two of these divisions in particular were in charge of auditing accounts. One of them, the so-called 'Soprassindaci', had been founded as early as 1549 and gradually became organized under the reign of the Grand Duke Cosimo I. At the end of the Medici period, it comprised four accountants assisted by twelve deputies and directed by four *soprassindaci*. The other board, that of the 'Sindaci del Monte', was even more ancient. It numbered, in 1737, two *sindaci* assisted by several deputies.

Sindaci and *soprassindaci* carried out regular audits of state accounts, the task of which they shared between them. The 'Soprassindaci' also made special unexpected inspections of the books kept by individual accountants. If carried out scrupulously, these operations involved extensive checks. All entries had to be carefully examined to verify their authenticity and to check their accuracy.

Like all Florentine administrations, these boards were comprised mainly of members of the aristocracy. A survey carried out over the first half of the eighteenth century shows that, in fact, all the *soprassindaci* having served during the time were of patriciate origin and that, more generally speaking, three- if not four-fifths of functionaries were of the same social extraction. This meant that the agents of the 'Sindaci' and the 'Soprassindaci' were more often than not related to the accountants they were supposed to be investigating. Lorenzo Ubaldini, a *soprassindaco*, was the brother of the *camerlengo* at the 'Monte redimibile'. Niccolò Compagni, deputy employed in the 'Soprassindaci', was the brother-in-law of Francesco Manetti, *camer-*

lengo at the 'Parte'. The brother of *sindaco* Domenico Maria Niccolini, Averardo, was in charge of the cathedral fabric. Giovanni Pitti, *provveditore* at the Leghorn customs station, where he was responsible for the levying of meat taxes in that town, had a nephew, Luca di Roberto Pitti, who was employed as deputy by the 'Soprassindaci'. Carlo Alamanni was cashier at the lazaretto in Leghorn and his brother Adamo was first deputy at the 'Sindaci'. Lastly, senator Gaetano, *provveditore* at the 'Abbondanza', and senator Alberti, *protettore* of the same, were both *soprassindaci*. Braccio Degli Alberti was even in charge in 1747, the year in which the embezzlement was discovered, of the auditing work on the so-called fine bread service which was actually dependent on the 'Abbondanza'.

Whether or not the parental links I have just mentioned were the root of the ineffectiveness of the inspection bodies remains to be seen. What is certain is that neither the 'Sindaci' nor the 'Soprassindaci' fulfilled their functions very efficiently.

A more careful examination of the inspection procedures shows that the inefficiency was not insignificant. They were too slow, too superficial and not sufficiently systematic. Whereas the audits carried out by the 'Sindaci' were fairly rapid, the 'Soprassindaci' varied quite considerably in speed. Delays of up to several years were not uncommon. Some accounts were not audited on a regular basis but in stops and starts, several years' takings being examined in one session following a long period of negligence.

Because they did not make in-depth checks, the auditors did not always discover the fraud committed by the most brazen of *camerlenghi*. In fact, the 'Soprassindaci' failed to notice the three false money orders drawn up by the military treasurer Malegonelle and thus allowed him to increase his spending by more than 10,000 *scudi*. Ascanio Teri, *camerlengo* at the Pisa customs office, managed to conceal more than 1,000 *scudi* received in taxes during his management. Once the embezzlement was declared, it took two years for the accountants in charge of auditing the accounts to put their fingers on this piece of dishonesty. Besides this, most checks were concentrated on previous operations which were long since closed, without the balance of the account being drawn up to the day of the audit. This meant that if, at the end of operations, the books showed a deficit, the accountant could always pretend that since then the situation had been reversed and that, in reality, on the day of the audit, he had a positive balance.

Lastly, audits were not carried out systematically. Some accounts were never inspected either by the 'Sindaci' or the 'Soprassindaci'. The impunity they enjoyed sometimes called the validity of the other audits into question. The treasurer Malegonelle not only administered the coffers of the military bank but also that of the 'Giubbe', which probably dealt with the supply of uniforms to soldiers. Whereas the bank's accounts were inspected regularly, those of the 'Giubbe' were never visited. In consequence, when the auditors visited the bank, 'Giubbe' funds 'were used to complete those of the bank'. More generally, the inspections performed by the 'Sindaci' took into account only a part of the accountants' incomes. Therefore, if the audit only considered part of the elements forming the financial situation, there was no way that it could be reliable.[29]

Be that as it may, these means of inspection were not totally ineffective. The overwhelming majority of the cases of embezzlement mentioned so far were in fact revealed by the 'Sindaci' and 'Soprassindaci'. They were not then to be taken too lightly by officials. Although they may not have been widespread enough to catch all embezzlers, they certainly sufficed to confound a number of them.

*   *   *

Claims of innocence, social rites, spontaneous or imposed laws of silence, none of these factors, therefore, could guarantee impunity to officials whose administration was liable to be inspected at any time by auditors who were sometimes completely devoid of indulgence. It was necessary to take a leap forward, that is to say to falsify entries on balance sheets.

It made it possible to engage in particular forms of corruption, either using false money orders or duping the more credulous citizens by false entries. Falsifying was also used for other purposes, either to camouflage embezzlement or to re-establish on paper an order and regularity which no longer existed in reality.

I have just mentioned that Malegonelle and Teri were guilty of this crime, but there are many other examples of such practices. At the time of Buonaventuri and Benini, the entries in the books of the 'Monte redimibile' had been altered.[30] The same could be said of those of the Florence fortresses when it was discovered that the deputy cashier, a certain Pietrozzi, had been pilfering funds.[31]. Gherardi, employed at the 'Monte Pio' in Pistoia fiddled the books to cover up his crime.[32] The *camerlengo* of the direct property tax office in Florence was sent to the gallows at the end of the sixteenth century by the *auditore* Cavallo for the same practices.[33] Here again, however, these cases were overshadowed by the 'Abbondanza' affair which provides us with the most evocative examples.

At the 'Abbondanza', falsifying accounts was almost part of daily life. If, for example, the official in charge of retail grain sales pocketed the returns from these sales in order to hand them over to knight Borgherini, those sales did not appear in the books, as if the grain had remained in the storehouse without ever having been sold. False money orders, on the other hand, were carefully inscribed in the register of money orders even though they did not correspond to any amount of grain deposited in the 'Palco' silos. Expense accounts showed imaginary overheads which in any case would have been spent had the silos been full. As for the annual balance drawn up at the end of August, it was a work which reflected, systematized and summarized all these tricks. It took into account stocks that had never existed, but which had been entered in the register of money orders. It did not take into account, on the other hand, grain sales which had been omitted from the books. It gave figures relating to stocks that were infinitely higher than those really contained in the 'Uccello'.

Lastly, there were the weekly reports on the state of stocks drawn up by Lorenzo Rossi for the *protettori* so that the latter could decide on quantities of grain to be purchased. The former guard of the storehouse explained that those documents were to be 'accorded no value, for they were drawn up without checking receipts or money orders; and since these weekly reports did not render me debtor nor creditor, and were drawn up for the sole purpose of informing the *protettori*, I did them from memory and I even tried to minimize stocks; considering that stocks were depleted, endeavoured to induce the *protettori* to purchase and order grain provisions. But no value could ever be accorded to those balance sheets.'[34]

Thus, as grain provisions at the 'Abbondanza' became more and more depleted, the magistracy's accounts gave the impression of an ever-growing prosperity or, at the most, a slight strain on stocks. Embezzlement itself was completely dissimulated. Although the grand embezzlement of the 'Abbondanza' was well and truly a given fact, there was no sign of it in any accounts book.

*   *   *

Putting the naive off the scent, silencing the inquisitive, falsifying entries, these were all techniques used by defrauders to evade prosecution and escape the censure of public opinion. They made it possible for even the most corrupt officials to be regarded as perfect judges and model administrators. Indeed, they opened the way to all types of effrontery.

Vincenzo Degli Alberti, for example, while carefully pilfering from the 'Abbondanza' storehouse, had the audacity to talk about himself in the most flattering terms, indeed, presenting himself as a paragon of administrative virtue. On 6 August 1736, he sent to the sister of the reigning Grand Duke a note which read as follows:

> The disorder that reigns in the administration of public bread supplies is on the increase and the disadvantages resulting from it grow daily. A few days ago, Your Highness, the 'Grascia' . . . withdrew bread from the market, for they deemed it to be of poor quality and inferior to standard weight. Most of the time it is difficult to find bread at midday, a situation unheard of in the past, and that confirms what I said. HRH should also know that

a number of people have an interest in impeding justice. Without the intervention of HRH, I can foresee a thousand conflicts, the first of which will be addressed against myself, I who have acted loyally and duly informed the *protettori* not only of what is happening to the detriment of the public and the glory of HRH, but also of the responsibilities of those who occupy the magistracy. However, without any fear whatsoever, I shall always be honoured to serve the public and HRH to whom I owe all.[35]

More claims of loyalty were made a year or two later, after the Lorraines came to power. This time Alberti, addressing Count Richecourt in French, presented himself as 'always a very loyal subject and eager to honour the prince'. In 1720 he had been designated deputy to the *provveditore* of the 'Abbondanza', whom he had hoped to succeed, but 'missed his chance'. However, 'as he had done his duty adequately and could be reproached for nothing, he was kept in the same post.' Then, 'the same Alberti was requested to introduce order into the deregulated administration. He must therefore obey, changing the ways, and discharging the more undesirable people, at which the people rejoiced, the prince was enchanted and the administration saved. . . . Since then, his decisions have always been contended. Nevertheless, he continued without paying heed, wishing only for the public good.'[36]

Thank heaven for lies! Without them these two radically opposed universes could not have coexisted: on the one hand, the secret world of corruption, venal officials and the prince who was deceived or robbed; on the other hand, the soothing empire of a public discourse founded on auto-celebration, self-satisfaction, adulation by courtiers and the systematic elimination of wrong notes. These lies did not, however, provide a completely satisfactory solution. They left two problems unresolved. For all the falsifying of accounts, the silencing of the inquisitive, the suppressing of the indiscreet and the pretending to be virtuous, the fact remained that the stolen money was still missing and that sooner or later a tardy, but thorough, inspection would probably shatter a reputation that had long been sheltered by lies. Dissimilation certainly delayed punishment, but it could not eliminate the risk. What is more, masking reality could disincriminate the guilty in appearance only. It did not suffice to clear their own consciences. Sheltered from all external censure by lies, the sinner was still at war with his conscience and his worries were made even more acute by the idea that, on Judgement Day, a cruel and powerful God would mercilessly tip the scales with sins that had been hidden from human eyes. It was therefore not enough to lie. To be perfectly at peace with oneself, the sin had to be cancelled out. It was necessary to disassociate corruption, or at least the acts committed personally, from the notion of guilt. It is the methods used to exculpate corruption that we shall now examine.

SAVED BY REASON

Nobody questioned the fact that corruption, in all its forms, was a serious offence. A rather austere jurist, don Garcia Mastrillo, even went so far as to state that men who committed extortion were guilty of a crime more detestable than those committed by highwaymen.[1] Berart y Gassol proclaimed that 'anyone who accepts bribes cannot be on good terms with the law.'[2] Bonifacio, in his essay on theft, placed embezzlement on the same level as sacrilege and held that corruption in judges was near to simony and crimes of lese-majesty.[3] 'Of all the crimes that can be imputed to the magistrate', echoed Jousse, 'the most serious and most infamous is that of letting oneself be corrupted by money: as a consequence it is among the most severely punished crimes, for it is among those that most dishonour the dignity and sanctity of the profession.'[4] In Germany, Lyncker thought along the same lines: 'Anyone who receives gifts', he explained, 'jeopardizes the health of the Republic, conspires against its liberty and integrity, neglects justice, perverts judgement, corrupts the just cause of honest men, the innocent and defenceless', and he went on to talk about lese-majesty and murder, the only crimes he felt fit to follow the abomination he had just denounced.[5] Lastly, Savelli did not hesitate to qualify all these criminal practices as 'very serious, encompassing counterfeit, theft, brigandry, sacrilege, simony and murder, which are all the more injurious . . . when committed under the veil of public authority, at the expense not only of the criminals who are victims of extortion but also of the poor innocent . . . in such a way that these crimes are justly compared with crimes of lese-majesty, in that they consist in deceiving the prince by abusing the power and confidence he has given to them for dispensing justice.'[6]

Thus, from the north to the south of Europe, and from the Renaissance to the Enlightenment, a unanimous chorus rose to denounce traitors, scoundrels and murderers who, as if possessed by their vile passions, deceived their masters. What is more, no one doubted that these infamous crimes were also dreadful sins. Even the most liberal of Christian moralists were convinced of this fact. Escobar, for example, the doctor of theology criticized by Pascal in his *Provincial Letters*, included in his *Liber Theologiae Moralis* an examination of the mortal sins that could be ascribed to public servants. In this work, imaginary culprits confessed their crimes. 'I sold public offices without the authority to do so', confessed a judge. 'I received some money to buy grain' admitted a senator, 'and I bought nothing'. 'I withdrew grain from the public cornhouse', he continued 'and I did not replace it when the poor needed it; I did not distribute public alms to real paupers, but to my servants and relations.' And the official in charge of the public Treasury added, 'To settle what I owed, I demanded payment, despite the fact that I should not receive anything for carrying out my duties apart from voluntary contributions without any constraint or obligations attached. In exchange for having settled a debt early, I received a gift from someone, but this meant that another of my creditors received a late payment.'[7]

Was it possible for culprits to take these crimes lightly and to live in sin with impunity? Not at all, because, as Gerson wrote, 'it is wicked, condemnable and dangerous to neglect one's sins.'[8] Prudence, on the other hand, was advisable since 'before the tribunal of the eternal judge who watches and sees all the innermost reaches of the heart . . . we will have on Judgement Day to account for the slightest superfluous word.' Judges, in particular, 'are accountable to God for their judgements, and the glory or punishment they are to receive depends on the quality of these judgements.'[9] This God of Judgement was not at all a forgiving God but a terrifying one, with not an ounce of clemency left in him. When brought before him, the most minor sins became enormous. The horrors of Hell, such as preachers described calmly to the Christian population, were awaiting sinners in general, and in particular corrupt officials.[10]

Corruption was therefore a crime. Crimes were sins, and sins led to the damnation of their authors. This time, moralization held a noose around the consciences of sinners. To escape from that noose, it was no use calling into question the certitude of the ultimate Judgement. That would have been pointlessly to attract the thunderbolts of the Church. It was hardly more expedient to pretend that sins did not lead to Hell. No one would have believed it. It was far more cunning to begin by playing on the difference between human laws and the divine commandments, thereby insinuating that not all crimes punished by the prince were sins punished by God. It was much more advantageous to reflect on the scope of laws and on the nature of human actions.

Cases of conscience originated in the feeling of having broken the law – human or divine – by committing a particular action. However, was this sentiment justified? Was it not, on the contrary, the result of an over-rigorous interpretation of texts. To have things clear in one's own mind, it was necessary to make a thorough examination of what one had done and to ask the question if, in doing so, one had in effect engaged in an act sanctioned by the law. This reflection comprised two aspects. Firstly, it meant defining the conditions for a crime or a sin to have been committed in the eyes of the law: premeditation, the rank of the person involved, time, place and so on. The second aspect looked at the character of each incriminated action: purety of intent, effects of coincidence, cases of absolute necessity and so forth. This led to a distinction between crimes punishable by law – and which had not been committed – and actions carried out in reality – and which were not outlawed. Thus, claims of innocence could be made, thereby completely ruling out the danger of damnation.

If an official was to clear his conscience, he could therefore adopt, indeed combine, two tactics. He could either take the line that what was condemned by human law was not necessarily punishable in divine law, or else he could claim that what he had done was far from the activities these laws, in any case, most wisely punished. In both these hypotheses, he could only gain from backing up his arguments with casuistry and probabilism.

*   *   *

I use the term casuistry here in its widest sense. It designates here an art of thought or a method of reasoning which, being founded on the examination of concrete situations or individual cases, establishes the extent to which individual actions are permissible by human and divine law. This intellectual technique was adopted by theologians, who used it for centuries to resolve the problems that arose when divine law was applied to human actions. The most famous, but by no means the only, expression of this religious casuistry was the moral theology of the confessors – Jesuit and others – who, after the Council of Trent, wrote heavy treatises for tormented souls, in which it was explained how they could settle every point of conscience more effectively. I shall quote, here, from three of these theologians: Antonio Diana, Lodovico Molina and Antonio de Escobar y Mendoza.

Casuistic reasoning was also used by lawyers. In legislative systems with little or no codification and with many different interpretations of the law, it was applied almost without limits. As far as penal matters are concerned, for instance, legislation was substantially based on Roman law, which was supplemented by other texts such as the criminal ordinances introduced by Charles V, French or foreign royal ordinances, customs, and the municipal laws of Italian towns. However, neither Roman law nor later legislation, taken individually or combined, constituted an organic system that provided definitive solutions for all practical cases. On the contrary, uncertainty and the finding of loopholes were frequent. Scholars tried to come up with solutions to problems through endless reasoning, leading to the formulation for each case of an 'opinion'. They made use of a formula for reasoning, that is to say, they began with a general rule (*regula*) from which they established the consequences (*ampliationes*), of which they then defined the limits by examining exceptions (*limitationes*) in order to arrive at a solution that was generally founded on Roman law: the *opinio.*[11]

For corrupt officials, casuistry proved to be a useful tool. Its juridical version provided them with comforting interpretations which limited the scope of human laws by disincriminating a number of criminal practices. Its moral version taught them, as well as all sinners, 'how to cavil with God, by showing them up to what point they could offend Him without His having the right to punish them.'[12]

* * *

Let us take a first example, that of the crime of embezzlement which, as we have seen at the beginning of this book, had devastating effects on the financial institutions in the Grand Duchy of Tuscany.[13] We will define it and then, with the help of the doctors, we will provide a more precise meaning, probe its mysteries and perhaps limit the extent of its scope.

According to the famous jurist Loyseau, embezzlement was 'theft or transposition of public funds.'[14] Jousse goes into more detail, defining it as 'theft or defalcation of royal and public money committed by tax collectors, or other officials responsible for it or to whom deposits have been entrusted, or by magistrates responsible for its use.'[15] Lastly, Savelli explained that the 'officials and administrators in charge of money who hid, stole or converted it for their own gain, or that of their friends, are liable to be charged under *lex julia* for embezzlement or defalcation.'[16]

Roman law, therefore, was the foundation of legislation relating to embezzlement. In fact, it distinguished two crimes. Embezzlement in the true sense of the word was the theft of public money. The crime of defalcation, on the other hand, consisted in retaining or misappropriating public money which the culprit had received, had been responsible for or had had entrusted to him. Authors of these two crimes could be prosecuted in both civil and criminal courts. In criminal courts, the crime of embezzlement by public servants was punishable by a death sentence, and that of defalcation by a criminal punishment left to the discretion of the judge. In civil courts, the judge could order the person accused of embezzlement to restore a capital equal to four times the misappropriated sum or only double if the money had been appropriated before being in the possession of the state. Anyone found guilty of defalcation was liable to restore a capital amounting to one and a third times the sum in question.[17]

These principles gave rise to contradictory interpretations. More severe commentators tended to extend their scope. Berart and Mastrillo, for example, condemned anyone who had happened to trade with public funds in a fortuitous way, as well as those who appropriated the money entrusted to them without any hope of redeeming it.[18] Berart also considered it to be a criminal offence to use state money for ends which, although they may well have been in the interests of the public, were not what it was originally meant for.[19] This view was shared by Bonifacio.[20] As for Cavallo, he had drawn very firm conclusions regarding a specific case. He stated that defalcation was more serious than theft. He pointed out that only three cases of larceny deserved capital punishment. He asserted that accountants had to be able not only to pay the sums entered in their books, but also to produce exactly the same coins they had originally received. For this reason, he concluded, they were strictly forbidden to indulge in any form of trade. Cavallo, in a word, preached severity.[21]

Not everyone, however, adopted such a severe line. For Menochio, another commentator, it was important to make the distinction between the treasurers in ancient Rome and those of modern times. *Lex julia*, he explained, had been conceived for the former, who handled public money but did not secure it at their own risk. It cannot, therefore, be applied to the latter who were personally responsible for their cash. 'Nowadays', he commented, 'the prince's treasurers are very different from the tax collectors, cashiers and other accountants of Antiquity. . . .

They do not commit the crime of embezzlement or defalcation.'
Did they not commit theft? Not at all, retorted the scholarly
judge, for when treasurers conserve funds at their own risk 'the
dominium of this money is supposedly transferred to them.'
According to Menochio, cashiers were therefore free to do as
they wished with the contents of their tills. They could place the
money in commerce, trade in any way, and even benefit from
any profits made. All that was expected from them was that
they honour their commitment to pay back the money when
payment was due. Their responsibility was, nevertheless, purely civil: it was limited to their goods and securities.[22]

This constituted a total reversal of ideas. The one-time
criminal about to be sent to the gallows was now a cashier
exposed at the most to civil court action, and even then only in
the event that his juggling made him insolvent. A loophole (and
what a comforting one for dishonest accountants!) had opened
up in the penal system.

One of the best lawyers of the Grand Duchy, the auditor
Savelli, was clearly aware of this evolution. When called upon to
give his opinion in a case of embezzlement, he recognized that
the accused well and truly 'merited punishment', but he added
that 'nowadays it is difficult to charge such administrators with
embezzlement, because they are not debtors of the actual coins
they received, but of an amount of money for which they are
personally responsible, and also because they offer securities
for their administration.' Moreover, he continued, if the accused man had omitted to enter the sums he received in the
books, then he was guilty of falsifying and not theft. False
entries made by the culprit could, of course, always be put
down to errors. As for the missing money, said Savelli, as the
sums omitted in writing were never cashed materially, there
was nothing to be said. In effect, he observed, 'to miss something presupposes prior possession': *privatio praesupponit habi-
tum*. In this specific case, as the till had never been filled, it
could not have been emptied.[23]

This subtle way of disincriminating the authors of embezzlement did not escape the vigilant attention of the Tuscan
legislator. In fact, in 1681 the Grand Duke made a law in which

the misappropriation of public funds was assimilated to theft. This law also contained the measures to eliminate all the exceptions indicated by Menochio. It specified that charges were applicable even if the cashier conserved the money at his own risk, and even if he 'owed an amount of money and not the exact coins he received'.[24]

It would be interesting to know if in other states the dangers created by this disincriminating casuistry generated similar reactions. In France, it is true, new measures which were more rigorous than previous texts were decreed against embezzlement around the 1700s. But Jousse, who describes these measures,[25] does not analyse their origins. These may be explained as much by the desire to limit the excesses of casuistry as by the need to stamp out illicit practices which, during the war years and the subsequent commercial speculation, had become rife in the kingdom. It is important to note, however, that in Tuscany itself, despite all the imaginable precautions included in it, the 1681 law did not discourage efforts to disincriminate embezzlement. Towards 1750, the officials accused in the 'Abbondanza' affair still defended themselves by stating that their administration was not a public service but a 'commercial affair' to which the rules and privileges of the treasury could not be applied.[26]

All the possibilities offered by 'reason' were therefore explored and used to distinguish the crime of embezzlement, of which neither the reality nor the abomination was denied, from the acts for which accountants were criticized and which apparently had nothing in common with the practices punished by Roman law. Therefore, juridical casuistry tended to create a 'zona franca', in which anyone who dipped his fingers in the coffers of the state, in any way whatsoever, without permission, was wise to remain.

*   *   *

Let us now leave human laws aside in order to define the extent to which divine laws forbad accountants from using the money in their accounts for their personal gain, and at what point these misappropriations constituted mortal sin. This time, it is the turn of the theologians to speak.

'Does a depositary have the right to use what has been deposited?' Escobar asked gravely. He provided the answer himself: 'He does sometimes,' especially 'if he sincerely believes that the owner permits him to do so.'[27] A reply as concise as this did not, however, cover the entire subject. Thus the famous theologian developed, a few pages further on, 'a practice relating to the subject of the free contracts drawn up from the authorities of the Society of Jesus'. Here again, he posed the question 'does a depositary have the right to use what has been deposited and to transfer it without the express or presumed permission of the owner?' He answered first that the person responsible for such practices was 'considered to be guilty of theft'. But he immediately limited the scope of that statement by adding that, according to Laymann, another casuist, a depositary was allowed 'to transfer oil, grain and other consumer goods, if he was certain of being able to return them, in the same quantity and quality when requested to do so by the owner.' Escobar then gave an example: 'An administration ... forbids the extraction of grain from public storehouses without permission; the keeper can extract some if he is certain to have the same quantity when it is requested.' Escobar posed another question: 'Does a treasurer have the right to trade to his own profit with somebody else's money without that person's knowledge?' 'He does', he answered, 'according to Lessius, provided that it is without prejudice or risk to the owner.'[28]

These reflections were obviously welcomed by the men accused in the 'Abbondanza' affair. They were also echoed in the works of another author, the Theatine Diana, to whom the souls of sinners owed the aid of a particularly monumental treatise on cases of conscience. Diana took up the question posed by Escobar and invoked the expertise of half a dozen theologians to conclude that a treasurer could 'trade with his master's money ... and use the profits for his personal gain.' This liberty, he specified, was particularly valid as far as grain deposits were concerned, on which it was perfectly licit to speculate between two harvests.[29]

Not all casuists therefore forbad accountants to make the money in their accounts work for them. But they all forbad them to steal that money. On this subject, they established several opinions likely to calm the conscience of a guilty official. Firstly they posed the very tricky problem of knowing from what point theft constituted a mortal sin. Escobar believed that the quantity varied with the quality of the victim. The richer the victim, the more considerable had to be the theft.[30] This idea resulted in the notion – an advantageous one for officials – that the person who could be robbed most copiously without going beyond the limits of venial sin was the prince.

There was not, however, far to go before the border line with mortal sin was reached. Indeed, a cashier who helped himself to small sums on a daily basis was in danger of reaching that fatidical threshold very rapidly. The question that was then raised was whether or not the effects of a series of petty crimes could be accumulative. Did they add up to one big mortal sin? Were they not separate venial sins which, however numerous, could not be counted together to make one major sin? Escobar, on this subject, made some relatively consoling remarks. He explained that a multitude of petty thefts did not necessarily produce the same consequences as one major theft – for example, if these crimes were committed 'on rare occasions, by chance and without the intention of being repeated', or if they were separated 'by long intervals . . . in such a way that previous thefts had been forgotten'.[31]

What should be thought, then, of petty thefts committed following the perpetration of another, more serious theft which constituted a mortal sin? Did they make another mortal sin? This issue was violently debated. Diana, basing his theory on the ideas of several doctors, recognized that the most 'probable and sure opinion in practice' was the most indulgent one. According to this opinion, 'petty crimes which are committed after a previous crime involving a more considerable quantity are not in themselves mortal sins. The reason for this is that they do not constitute that considerable quantity (without which there is no mortal sin) but simply increase it.'[32]

The next issue was whether or not the accused man was

guilty of another sin if he kept the fruits of his theft over a number of years. A great number of theologians replied in the negative, pointing out that keeping stolen goods did not constitute a new sin, but was the continuation of a previous sin. The fact of continuing a sin could, however, be seen to make that sin more serious. The casuist Tanner affirmed this, but was contradicted by Diana, who stated that 'the penitent satisfies the requirements of confession if he only admits to not having restored someone else's goods, and it is not necessary to interrogate him on the date or duration of this retention.'[33]

The consciences of accountants therefore found some relief in the reasoning of jurists and theologians. They could begin by adopting Menochio's line and by trying to convince themselves that dipping one's fingers in the till did not constitute the crimes of embezzlement or theft, but was no more than the most legitimate of business. They could then opt for the consoling lessons of Escobar or Diana rather than the maxims of the more severe theologians and claim, in consequence, that it was morally licit to make someone else's money work for one's personal gain. Moreover, an accountant could multiply mis-appropriations without ever falling into the abyss of mortal sin. The important thing was always to steal in small quantities. And if by misfortune he committed a mortal sin, the culprit was free to add a few petty thefts to his first crime and to keep the bounty for years without further burdening his conscience.

* * *

Bribes, or to use a more delicate term, gifts, were also the object of some interesting speculation. They were, of course, strictly forbidden. 'An officer guilty of having lowered himself or of accepting presents' explained Conti, for example, 'is dismissed.'[34] This salutary and severe maxim was developed fully by the auditor Savelli, who wrote:

> Any officer or public minister who by reason of his office or ministry accepts money or the promise of money, or any advantages other than his due fixed salary, in exchange for

carrying out or neglecting to carry out one of his duties, even if
the donation or offer is spontaneous, or does not infringe on the
law, or ... even if it is given in the aim of quickening the
proceedings ..., he is, in all cases, guilty of prevarication [in
Italian *baratteria*], which derives its name from barter [in Italian
baratto], by using Holy Justice iniquitously for money or other
gain.[35]

The crime was committed, Savelli continued, even if 'the
minister receiving the money promises nothing or fails to do
what he promises, because the crime consists in the minister, in
his position as minister, accepting the money.'

As was the case for embezzlement, several commentators
called for a rigorous application of these principles. Jousse's
opinions on this subject were very resolute. He pointed out that
the decree pronounced by the *Conseil* on 28 February 1682 had
outlawed all gifts, and forbad all *seigneurs* to offer venison to
officers. Judges were to refuse any presents, even after the
sentence had been pronounced and even in the absence of any
presumption that the judgement had been made with a view to
obtaining a gift.[36] Such strict ideas were not new. They echoed
those which, at the end of the seventeenth century, had been
defended in Germany by Lyncker. For this jurist, even the
smallest amounts of money implied the crime of corruption. It
appeared to him equally unacceptable to receive gifts in kind
from litigants. Lyncker, in effect, criticized those commentators, such as Menochio, who suggested that a gift of a pheasant
could not stir the heart of a magistrate. He was convinced, on
the contrary, that 'these things could blind the eyes of a judge.'
He did not admit that a gift could be given in order to speed up
a trial and believed that, by accepting such a gift when he had
left office, a magistrate cast a shadow of doubt on the integrity
of his past actions.[37]

Here again, however, there was no perfect unanimity between jurists. Menochio, as I have already mentioned, considered that *esculenta* and *poculenta* – that is, food and drink –
were not enough to corrupt a judge.[38] Bonifacio thought that
they could be accepted, as long as they were offered spon-

taneously by the litigants and were in modest quantity. In his thesis, he invoked the authority of the Emperor Antoninus, who apparently believed that it was absolutely inhuman to refuse everything.[39]

The issue was also taken up by theologians. They underlined a number of exceptions. So many, in fact, that they tended to become the rule. Firstly, Molina upheld that it was admissible, although not recommendable, to reward a magistrate if, by doing so, the duration of a trial could be reduced and on condition that other people's cases were not delayed in the process. He explained: 'When the servant of a public minister arranges for his master to receive a litigant before the due time, or when he brings a certain case before his master to be examined earlier than the due time, without delaying other cases, but rather in view of forwarding to the public minister more cases than the latter was supposed to examine ... then that servant may, with a clear conscience, accept a modest price for services rendered.'[40]

Diana, for his part, posed the following question: 'Is it a sin for a judge to accept a fee for dealing with one case before the others, if the litigants have the same rights of precedence?' The answer he provided is based on the following logic: 'Let us suppose that many people have the same rights, so that a judge is free to choose where to start. Is the judge committing a sin if, for money, he deals firstly with the case of one rather than another?' No, is the Theatine's answer for, under natural law, the judge 'does not inflict any injustice on the others; on the contrary, he contracts, in favour of the person who offered him remuneration, the new obligation to deal with his case before that of the others.'[41]

This was not, however, the only case in which a judge was allowed to receive ready cash. Diana, echoing Molina, stated that a judge could receive gifts from litigants on condition that the gifts be offered spontaneously, without scandal and without the risk of doing injustice, and 'so that he may take greater care over the case than he is either used or obliged to do'.[42] The clever Theatine, former consultant for the Sicilian Inquisition, then became more adventurous. He envisaged a situation in which a magistrate, having to pronounce judgement on an affair, saw two equally lawful solutions, one of them being favourable to one of the contestants and the other to his adversary. Would it be a sin for this magistrate to act in favour of the one who had paid him? The casuist Tanner had formerly replied in the affirmative to this question. According to Tanner, a practice such as this would not be in line with justice. Diana, however, proffered the opposite opinion, proposed by the Fleming Lessius.* This doctor stated that the judge was 'free to chose the opinion he wished'; thus, 'if he accepts something to follow his own opinion rather than another, he is doing no wrong to anybody.' Moreover, 'when nothing is due, it is not unjust . . . to demand a price, if, at least, that price can be fixed. In a case such as this, then, the price should not be paid in order to obtain a fair sentence, but because in that particular trial that opinion is preferred to another, to which the judge has no commitment.'[43]

Many other situations could be envisaged. What, for example, could be said of judges whose salary was fixed by old tariffs, which, owing to inflation, were no longer in proportion to the cost of living? Were they supposed to respect those obsolete measures, or could they receive gifts as compensation? If so, could they still accept them if they had vowed to respect the tariffs? Diana, on this point, had no hesitations. He stated that a bonus could be accepted as long as it was within the limits of the 'fair price'. Even their promise should not burden their conscience, for 'the oath to respect a statute is valid only to the extent that the statute is just and compulsory: it will therefore not oblige the judge to respect an unjust tariff.'[44]

Molina cleverly turned to good account the notion of intent. He admitted that it was legitimate to offer a judge gifts if there was no intent to corrupt him. He gave, as examples, gifts offered to a magistrate freely, liberally, 'in friendship' and 'as if he were not a public minister'. He did not condemn the judge who was recompensed by the litigants 'through gratitude for the benefits they received and through the joy of having

---

*   Leonard Leys: another casuist in the Society of Jesus.

obtained a just outcome'. Likewise, it was permissible to offer a present to a magistrate in order to 'incite him to behave in the future in the same way that he had behaved in the past and so that the case of the person sending the gift be dealt with carefully'. Molina also deemed that a case did not deserve censure if the judge received something 'so that, within the limits of justice, he decides on the case in favour of the person sending him the gift.'[45]

*   *   *

At the end of the seventeenth century, the Florentine Savelli summed up, in a brief essay, the doubts held by jurists and the reasoning of theologians on the question of gifts. He accepted the most severe propositions and condemned outright the practice of offering presents to judges. He based his argument on divine law, on canon law, on ancient and modern civil law and on municipal law in Tuscany. But he immediately recognized that in practice these principles included a certain number of restrictions.

Firstly, a magistrate could receive presents from his relatives. He was also permitted to accept gifts from friends, not of course by reason of his office, but as marks of affection and goodwill. This liberty, however, was not to be taken too broadly. Savelli, following here the jurist Farinacci as well as Tuscan law, limited it to food and drink. It seemed to him to be admissible, however, for a judge to accept presents when the tariffs fixing his salary were too low. Nobody could have criticized an office-holder for wishing to guarantee his livelihood. However, the 'fair price' should not be exceeded, nothing should be demanded forcefully and no injustice should be committed in exchange for the presents received. Moreover, a judge could receive a gift if it was in exchange for extra work, or if the donor had no suit pending. He was even allowed to accept something after the sentence as long as no prior agreement had been made.

Savelli then tackled a problem which recurs frequently in such works: the question of *xenia, esculenta* and *poculenta*, that is to say, small gifts offered to magistrates by litigants, especially in the form of food and drink. This issue, to which Savelli had already alluded, is developed here in full. The space dedicated to the matter is, in all evidence, proportional to the extent to which this practice was widespread in the tribunals, as well as to the severity of laws that sanctioned it. To solve the problem, Savelli put to full use his skill in dialectics. He quoted the liberal declaration of the Emperor Antoninus. He pointed out that divine law did not condemn gifts themselves but that which could corrupt the human spirit. Besides this, he said, divine law contained no more than 'advice for perfecting oneself' and not 'legislative precepts'. He outlined the limits of canon law and of civil law in this field. He invoked the liberal customs practised in Rome and in Piedmont. He pointed out, as is written in chapter 19 of Genesis, that the angels sent to Sodom did not refuse the gifts offered to them by Lot. He ruled out the objections raised by the great medieval commentator Accursio. Indeed, the only obstacle he accepted was that of the prohibitive laws promulgated in Tuscany by the Grand Dukes.

Was it a sin, however, to violate the laws of the Medici family? To answer this new question, Savelli posed a more general problem: that of ascertaining the extent to which God would be offended by a breach of laws which, like Tuscan laws on gifts, were devoid of any foundation in divine law.

Several restrictions, observed Savelli, limited the scope of these civil laws. Firstly, they had no hold on consciences, unless the legislator had expressly specified that it should be so. This was not the case, fortunately, for Tuscan laws relating to *esculenta* and *poculenta*.

It was not the Prince's intention, then, in forbidding one practice of another, to condemn the act itself, but rather to prevent its pernicious effects: cases of *esculenta* or *poculenta*, for example, were not condemned for themselves, but for the trouble they could introduce in the souls of judges. It sometimes happened, however, that a magistrate received such presents without his objectiveness being affected. The truth of the facts, then, contradicted the motives of the law. In fact, the law had been infringed, since a gift had been handed over, but no fault had been committed. There was no way, under these conditions, that the person who received the gift could be considered guilty of a sin. Consciences, in this case, were not bound by law.

Moreover, some of these laws had been revoked in reality by customs that contradicted them. There was, therefore, no more reason to respect them. Nobody, claimed Savelli, committed a sin by infringing a human law that was devoid of divine foundation and was contradicted by customs.

Savelli was now near to his conclusion. He had begun by suggesting that natural law and divine law did not forbid, *stricto sensu*, the acceptance of *esculenta* and *poculenta*. He then argued that there was no sin in violating a human law that was contradicted by custom and that was not based on any divine precept. In Tuscany, he noted, custom contradicted the measures of prohibitive laws, since it was customary for judges to accept *esculenta* and *poculenta*. He thereby inferred that the laws drawn up by the Grand Dukes had no hold on consciences and that in consequence it was not sinful for a judge, in the Grand Duchy of Tuscany, to receive a pheasant or a pint of Chianti.

Savelli, however, had no intention of opening the door to abuse. This is felt very strongly in his conclusions which, in their very expression, are cautious and full of reserve. 'To conclude ... it seems that, without there being any risk or threat of corruption or injustice, judges are allowed, despite municipal law, according to custom and for the reason given above, to accept and keep, with a clear conscience, small gifts of food and drink offered to them by litigants, as long as the gifts were offered freely, were of modest value, consumed within a few days ... and there were no obligations attached.' One *scudo* per affair, specified Savelli, was the limit beyond which it was forbidden to go.[46]

*　　*　　*

Judges and accountants alike could therefore find in casuistry indulgent opinions which, without questioning the strictness of principles, enabled certain actions to be disincriminated. That does not mean, however, that casuistry offered only indulgent opinions. In fact, to those soothing ideas expressed by Menochio, Escobar or Diana, could be opposed the far less comforting maxims of Cavallo or Lyncker. Countless contradictory opinions were the rule, for instance in the field of law, 'Juridic knowledge encompasses many differing opinions', said, for example, Muratori; 'that is to say, it is full of confusion.' In law books, he added, 'the prosecutor as well as the accused can find arms with which it is possible both to attack and to defend either side.'[47] These statements, made for civil tribunals, could easily have been applied to that of the confessional. On this subject, the criticisms of Pascal are well known. Addressing his Jesuit adversaries in his *Provincial Letters*, he said: 'Does anyone wish to kill? Let him repair to Lessius. If the reverse, let him apply to Vasquez, that no one be discontented and have no grave author on his side. Lessius will discourse of homicide like a heathen and of almsgiving perhaps like a Christian. Vasquez will discourse of almsgiving like a heathen and of homicide like a Christian.'[48]

It was therefore not possible for an official to adopt at the outset the most indulgent opinions. Indeed, he had to choose between severe opinions which, although they rendered him guilty, were perhaps the more solidly founded, and more lenient ones which, although in his favour, risked being without foundation. Could he, in all consciousness, opt systematically for the indulgent opinions?

In order to sort out the most severe positions from the most liberal ones, the prince's servants, like all Christians, could rely on the moral system of probabilism. A few explanations on this subject are needed.

Probabilism is founded on the observation that ethical codes were not clear and that consequently anyone who had to follow a course of action was plunged into doubt. Doubt nurtured reflection and reflection in turn reproduced diversity of opinions. Some opinions, however, had no foundation and could not be accepted. Others were probable: these were known as *opiniones probabiles*. Others again possessed a higher degree of probability: these were called *opiniones probabiliores*. Sure opinions, or *tutae*, were those which extended the scope of application of the law to the detriment of human liberty.

Probabilism was based on the idea that, when faced with many opinions apparently equally well founded, it was legitimate to follow a probable opinion. In this, it differed from laxism, which accepted as a behavioural norm opinions which were not even probable. It stood a little behind probabiliorism, which admitted only the most probable opinions, and behind tutiorism, which recommended choosing, when in doubt, the sure opinions.

The application of probabilism implied the ability to recognize probable opinions. The casuist Sanchez provided a definition of a probable opinion as being one which was supported by the authority of one honest and learned doctor. One can be led to suppose then that there existed a remarkable quantity of these opinions and that it was even possible to find several conflicting opinions on the same case.

Probabilism, however, did not prescribe that all those opinions be followed. Neither did it make it obligatory to arrange them in order of probability and to opt for the most probable one. Nor did it hold that the opinion which truly appeared to be the most probable should be chosen. It simply recommended that as a maxim one of the numerous probable opinions proposed for the case in question should be chosen. This led to two important consequences. The first was that it was possible to adhere to an opinion even if it were less probable. The second was that it was legitimate honestly to adopt an opinion to which one did not fundamentally adhere, but which, because it had been defended by a learned doctor, was probable.[49]

With his usual clarity, Savelli summed up the issue: 'Judges', he explained, 'can adopt somebody else's opinion, even if it is less sure, as long as they deem it to be probable, and even if it goes against their own opinion that they believe to be more sure and more probable.'[50] Nothing, then, forbad the adoption of even the most indulgent of probable opinions. Thus, in probabilism, Christians in general and officials in particular found the means of adopting, with a clear conscience, the positions

which suited them the most. All that remains to be done now is
to define the period during which this moral system exerted its
influence.

*   *   *

Laxism, as I have already mentioned, involved considering as
probable opinions which were not necessarily so. It had been
repeatedly condemned by the pontiffs from 1665 to 1690.
Numerous propositions were censured during this period,
including the one according to which a judge, when litigants
had equally probable opinions, might receive money to pronounce a verdict in favour of one or the other. In 1679 the
pontiffs became even more severe. They condemned the
proposition that a judge could pass sentence according to an
opinion even less probable. This was how probabiliorism was
introduced into judicial activity.[51] A long time afterwards,
Muratori indicated this evolution in his essay on the defects of
the legal system when he said: 'The judge is morally obliged to
follow the most probable opinion; and he is not permitted to
hold a probable opinion if the opposite opinion is more
probable.'[52]

The condemnation of laxism coincided with the formulation
of an increasingly rigorous ethical code. In France, this culmin-
ated in 1700 with the condemnation of the most laxist propositions by the 'Assemblée du Clergé'.[53] In Italy, Genet's *Théologie*,
which was representative of the rigorist position, was published
in four different editions between 1702 and 1722. It was
recommended by Benedetto XIII himself.[54] As for the *Theolo-
gia moralis universa* by Antoine, another spearhead of austerity,
it was re-edited at least twenty-six times in the peninsula during
the period 1743 to 1789, in other words, about once every two
years.[55]

This condemnation of laxist propositions, however, was not a
condemnation of probabilism as a moral system. Nor was it
sufficient to guarantee rigorism an immediate triumph. Here
again, Tuscany provides us with an interesting case study.

Since the second half of the seventeenth century, Florence

had doubtless been the theatre for the sermons given by Father
Segneri. Most of these, it was observed, were characterized
chiefly by a strong tendency to culpabilize. Segneri stressed the
need for penitence, the gravity of mortal sin, the small number
of the chosen ones, the terrible nature of Judgement, and the
uncertainty of redemption. He did not hesitate to awaken
hardened souls by giving examples of self-punishment in
public, or by organizing flagellation sessions.[56]

Despite these warnings, however, probabilism and the lax
solutions it authorized seem to have prevailed in the Tuscan
capital for a long time. Again in 1723, the clergyman designated to occupy the strategic post of rector at the seminary was
defined by an observer as 'a good disciple of Busenbaum [i.e., a
good probabilist], a sworn enemy of the disciples of Genet and
other severe probabiliorists of the kind.'[57] Four years later, in
1727, a Dominican monk, Father Orsi from Florence, had a
dissertation published in Rome on mental reservations. The
rigorist position he defended was immediately criticized by two
Jesuits in the capital, Fathers Venturi and Lagomarsini, who
supported the opposite opinion.[58] The probabilists did not give
in. When in 1741 Monsignor Incontri, Archbishop of Florence,
published in Turin his essay on human acts, a Jesuit from
Pistoia launched an immediate attack on the severe position
defended in it.[59] The Jesuit, it is true, was discharged by the
Bishop of Pistoia, Monsignor Alamanni. But, as soon as he
arrived in his diocese in 1732, this prelate had himself come up
against several difficulties from supporters of probabilism who
did not appreciate his demanding and austere code of ethics.[60]

* * *

Casuistry and probabilism thus joined forces to offer relief to
consciences which would otherwise have been overwhelmed by
the rigorous principles that obviously conflicted with the administrative practices in force. Before concluding on the matter, a
summary of these systems of thought in relation to corruption
is needed.

At the beginning, as we have seen, there was a series of

propositions which made corruption into a crime, crime into sin and sin the route to Hell. Casuistry dealt with this difficult subject. It studied the ways in which principles – general principles and therefore ambiguous ones – could be applied to individual actions. It thus assessed, case by case, the possible degree of guilt of individuals in relation to human and divine laws. It then raised the question of the reciprocal relationship between crime and sin. This method, used by jurists and theologians alike, could be carried out in two very different states of mind. Practised in the sense of indulgence, it was the source of consolation. Serving rigour, on the other hand, it reached terrifying conclusions. The problem was whether or not it was legitimate to choose from this mixture of very severe or very indulgent opinions the latter rather than the former. Probabilism provided the ethical code to overcome this new difficulty. It authorized the following of the lessons of the most indulgent authors, on the sole condition that their opinions were probable. But this probability, as we have seen, could be rated very low.

These attitudes were gradually called into question as rigorism gained supremacy while laxism and probabilism lost ground. However, it would no doubt be erroneous to think that the papal condemnations of the second half of the seventeenth century could reverse overnight the thought habits of Christians. On the contrary, it is probable that the resistance of mental habits was strong enough to guarantee the long survival of any attitude that proved to be useful in a society besieged with sin. It is quite possible, in the case of Tuscany, that they continued to exert an influence right up to the mid-eighteenth century.

*   *   *

The processes I have just described present several characteristics. Firstly, they safeguarded the rigour of principles on which the juridic and moral condemnation of corruption was founded. At the same time, they limited the effects of these principles on practical life. By disculpabilizing acts without altering precepts, they enabled each individual to fear sin in general while offering him the satisfaction of feeling that, in his own case, he had not sinned. Thanks to them, judges and cashiers could denounce moral corruption while committing embezzlement or dishonest acts themselves. Casuistry and probabilism did not eliminate the moralization of corruption: they only rendered it compatible with the realities of life.

The effect of casuistry was not only on occasion to disculpabilize certain practices. It gave rise, in fact, to a more general consequence: that of relativizing principles. It substituted the universality of the norm with the omnipresence of doubt. This doubt, in turn, was very useful to sinners. It created fringes or margins where neither guilt nor innocence could be clearly established. It eliminated clear-cut oppositions, made simple solutions impossible, and facilitated shifts of position and hasty but pardonable assimilations. In short, it multiplied the chances of making sincere mistakes and distanced the certainty of guilt more and more.

Therefore casuistry and probabilism enabled the guilty to keep the ever-threatening spectre of Hell at bay. However, they did not remove the threat of human punishment. Judges, in fact, were not in the slightest way obliged to take into account the good reasons that officials, eager to justify their acts, found in the works of the most indulgent theologians. On the contrary, they were free to adopt the positions of the most severe, as long as the chosen opinions were probable. This contradiction was not without consequence. It meant worse problems for dishonest officials if, by misfortune, their actions were brought to the knowledge of stern tribunals.

The threat, albeit hypothetical, of a revengeful judge troubled the new-found peace of corrupt officials. It led to the need for lies, which enabled anyone who had slowly and patiently cleared his conscience to guarantee himself against any external questioning. Lies, such as I described in the last chapter, thus completed, consolidated and, in a certain way, made it possible for officials to make the heroic efforts to achieve inner rehabilitation. Without them, nothing could ever be obtained by defrauders, neither their innocence, nor their tranquillity, nor their reputation. With them, on the other hand, a re-found virtue could develop fully, sheltered from storms. By leaving the official face-to-face with his own conscience, lies afforded him the chance to rebuild it as he wished.

*   *   *

Moralization, lies and casuistry: these are the three columns on which the reality of corruption was built. Moralization, firstly, made it possible to individualize that which would otherwise have been the object of a collective interpretation and answer. It thus culpabilized corruption and called for penal legislation designed to punish offending subjects. At the same time, it also troubled the consciences of corrupt officials.

Faced with this increase in danger, officials defended themselves by lying and through casuistry. Lies, firstly, guaranteed them against external aggressions. They established a distinction between what was visible and honest and the reality that was not. Casuistry rehabilitated this reality with the aid of probabilism. It authorized a division between principles that were incessantly proclaimed and actions which, as was wisely explained, were not actually concerned with principles. The validity of principles produced by casuistry, however, were not universally recognized. Thus corrupt officials were not protected from the prosecution of human justice. Their rehabilitation, which was purely an inner rehabilitation, suggested the protection afforded by lies.

Moralization thus rendered corrupt officials guilty. Lies dissimilated that guilt and casuistry rehabilitated the culprits. The societies of the *ancien régime* were thus torn between two contradictory trends: on the one hand, the demand for rigour expressed by moralization, and, on the other, an inclination towards permissiveness supported by lies and reason. The problem which arose as a consequence was to ascertain which of these two tendencies was the stronger. Would moralization manage to gain supremacy in officialdom despite the reticence and the desires felt by officials? Or would permissiveness triumph and open up the way to violations? Where would the balance between indulgence and severity be placed? What would be, consequently, the effective spread of abuse?

To examine this last question, it is necessary to introduce a new personage: the prince. Indeed, it is within the framework of a dialectic between the sovereign and the officials that the balance of corruption was established in the monarchies of the *ancien régime*.

Part IV

THE JUSTICE OF THE LORD

Introduction

Of all the ministers that served Charles V in the vast Habsburg empire, Ferrante Gonzaga, governor of Milan, was far from being the most honest. Racketeering, venality and abuses of influence were more than familiar to him. Indeed, they played such an important part of his activities that the auditors sent by the emperor to investigate his administration and that of his subordinates had no trouble in collecting a large quantity of evidence against him. A short time later a commission met in Brussels, where the emperor resided, in order to examine the charges against the governor. Contrary to all expectations, it concluded that there was no 'malice' in his behaviour. The minister Granvelle, for his part, declared gravely that they had found 'not as many things as had been said against him'. On 19 June 1555, Charles V finally signed a solemn declaration of Gonzaga's innocence. In this document it was stated, among other things, that some of the accusations against the Milanese governor 'did not correspond to any form of crime, and indeed, the above mentioned Signor Ferrante would have admitted to them naively had he been interrogated on the

subject ... and others were of such little consequence that it
could not be and was not our intention to pursue the matter
further.'[1]

In England, at the same time, a trial opened against the
former general receiver of the 'Court of Wards'. His name was
John Beaumont, and he was guilty of embezzlement. He was
charged with having misappropriated £9,675 and of having
omitted to enter payments to the sum of £11,823 in the
accounts books, the total of which he apparently pocketed. If
the law was hard on him, it is because, apart from this most
reprehensible crime, he had the fault of being a friend of the
king's ex-favourite, Somerset, who had just been swept from
power and arrested. Indeed, it was this allegiance that the
judges wished to punish, as much as his fraudulent acts.
Punishment of embezzlement thus became a way of settling
political disputes.[2]

The examples of Beaumont and Gonzaga illustrate the fact
that the state's discourse was not necessarily the discourse of
equity. Monarchs knew full well, in fact, how to paralyse the
course of justice by adopting, as in the case of Gonzaga, a
hypocritical, lenient and redemptive discourse. They also knew
how to stimulate the zeal of tribunals when, as the Beaumont
affair illustrates, the rigorous application of laws enabled a
cumbersome adversary to be eliminated. Repression of corruption, then, was governed by political strategies which sometimes
called for leniency and at other times for rigour. The powers
that be thus sorted culprits into the good and the bad, institut-
ing a double truth according to which the same actions could be
treated with clemency or prosecuted with severity, depending
on the situation at the time. This inevitably calls to mind the
fates of Fouquet and Colbert in France. The former, whose
numerous financial operations made him extremely rich, was
condemned by history with the reputation of being a despicable
financier and corrupt minister. Although guilty of the same
misdeeds, the latter was treated with more indulgence and went
down in posterity as a hard-working and incorruptible minister
full of integrity.[3]

These huge injustices demand consideration. But the relationship between the prince and corruption did not end there. Indeed, the sovereign had to judge many affairs that did not directly concern either favourites or enemies. He had to pronounce verdicts on a number of cases dealing with individuals who were not involved in politics. In these cases, his decisions no longer had the function of protecting a courtier or crushing an agitator. His primary motivation lay elsewhere. Severity, for example, could originate from a resolute desire to guarantee the triumph of the monarchic order. It could also reflect the elevated conception the sovereign had of his duty as a judge. Moderation, on the other hand, was proof that the sovereign was vigilant not to upset a social body that had been used to indulgence and was therefore little inclined to accept repression. It could also be interpreted as the sign that it was impossible to force severity on a tribunal which had deep roots in the practice of benevolent clemency towards culprits.

The prince's action was not necessarily immediate. Various stages of jurisdiction intervened which had their own repressive policy. The balance between rigour and permissiveness, therefore, was often obtained in the form of a three-man game. Not only did it involve the prince and the culprit, but the prince, the culprit and the tribunal.

A global balance of corruption, beyond the political disputes and circumstantial protections, was then determined in each state by the more or less firm position of the prince, the more or less severe policies of the tribunals, the more or less high criminality rate. These factors determined empirically the continually moving boundary between that which in practice fell victim to the force of moralization and repression and that which, on the contrary, sheltered by lies and consoling philosophies, continued to prosper.

The kingdom of Naples provides an impressive example of this. Charles V and Philip IV both attempted to treat the problem of corruption energetically. This was an ambitious policy to put into practice. Their aim was not only to punish criminals but also, it seems, to strike by prosecuting abuses, the traditional autonomy of Neapolitan magistracies. The policy resulted, in both cases, in complete failure. By unwisely putting the problem onto political ground, the sovereigns came up against a head-on conflict with Neapolitan tribunals. Judges took advantage of the uncertainties in legislation that characterized the kingdom, and succeeded, by means of scholarly dissertations, in defending all the violations brought to court by the prince. They pointed out that Spanish legislation was, in fact, contrary to the law, that justice lay in what was customary, and that customs had never condemned anything that the Castilians denounced. All doctors, in a word, agreed to recognize that, between the essential integrity of judges and the daily actions of Neapolitan magistrates, there was, all things considered, no contradiction. Thus, in Naples, the *scientia juris* pardoned everything that the kings of Spain attempted to punish. In the name of customs, law and justice, it proclaimed the legitimacy of the majority of abuses and it authorized the most corrupt judges to consider themselves as honest. Arguments in favour of disincrimination finally prevailed over the moralizing lessons which the Habsburgs had unfortunately loaded with political significance, and permissiveness became the rule.[4]

Thanks to the work recently dedicated to it, the Neapolitan example demands attention. However, it is not certain that it has a universal value and that it is not necessary to compare it with other, different, situations observed in other social and political contexts. This is the exercise I would like to carry out now, taking examples, as in previous chapters, from the Grand Duchy of Tuscany.

THE GRANDEUR OF CLEMENCY

The story of Antonio Parrini is a very sad one. He was the only son of a small craftsman who had set up his business in the heart of Florence, near the cathedral. Thanks to his father's devotion, Antonio received a good education based entirely on honour and virtue. However, this education was completely wasted on him. He soon began to lead a life of debauchery and to frequent the company of highly undesirable people. His poor conduct had become so notorious that his employer, the *auditore* Ferrante Capponi, had him thrown into jail. He was released only to be banished to Leghorn, where he was unable to find employment. His father decided to send him to work on a galley. However, Antonio's supplications made his father change his mind. Trembling with fear, Parrini senior threw himself at the feet of the *auditore* Capponi, begging him to give his son an honourable job. The good-hearted *auditore* was moved by such a show of affection and resolved to offer a second chance. With a recommendation in hand, Parrini junior entered the salt tax office as a copyist.

The salt magistracy was responsible for handling taxes as well as for part of the public debt. It offered ingenious minds many possibilities for getting rich at the expense of the sovereign and the public. Two officials had tried their hand at this a few years earlier, but had been caught almost straight away. In 1677, the *cancelliere* Roncalli, who was one of the most important members of the service, had also fallen under the arm of the law after having engaged in various illicit practices. Antonio Parrini naturally followed this tradition. He joined up with two accomplices: an obscure doctor named Buattini and a priest who called himself Abbot Pergolini da Galeata. By using fake procurations, and with the help of Parrini, this pseudo-Pergolini managed on several occasions to receive improperly arrears from the salt magistracy, and even the capital of certain government bonds. The fruits of this activity were then shared among the three accomplices.

The secret was soon let out of the bag and Parrini was put in jail on 19 August 1684. He was tortured and made to stand trial where, it is said, his baseness and heartlessness made a very bad impression, and finally he was judged fit for the gallows. The execution was carried out with the greatest solemnity. Parrini, under heavy guard, was made to cross the town on foot, going through the cathedral square, the old market place and through Via di Calimala successively before reaching the Grand Ducal square, now known as Piazza della Signoria, where the gallows had been erected. Of course, he did nothing to speed up the process, in the hope that at the last minute the sovereign would have mercy on him and release him from the hands of the hangman. He requested that the chief of police walk slowly to the place of execution. He paused regularly, sometimes to beg people he knew to pray for him, and at other times to ask priests to celebrate a Mass for his soul. He even stopped in front of the archbishop's palace, until the prelate came out onto the balcony to give him the *in articulo mortis* blessing. When he finally reached the scaffold, he suggested that the executioner take his time, to which the latter consented. In the end, Parrini was hung as high as Haman.[1]

The Grand Duke of Tuscany could therefore be severe at times. This can be seen in the fate of the two officials employed at the salt magistracy who some years earlier had dared to misappropriate funds from this important branch of administration: Vanni died in the galleys, and the other, Pitti, died in prison in February 1674.[2] The prospects awaiting *cancelliere* Roncalli were not much brighter, and the same amount of publicity was given to his punishment as Parrini's. The former salt *cancelliere* was exhibited publicly in Florence

> shaved, with side-whiskers in Turkish style, a white beret and a galley slave's coat. Accompanied by four policemen, he was paraded around the streets of the town in an open cart so that everyone could have a good look at him. He was then led to the galleys, where he stayed no more than six days before being removed in the same way and led back to Florence, which inspired in him great fear; he believed he was to end his days with a noose around his neck, but instead he was thrown back into the 'Bargello' prison.

This happened in July 1678. Roncalli stayed in prison until 1705, when he died. Tuscan law had not been kind to him.[3]

This kind of severity was by no means rare. Another example is the case of two officials both called Del Buono employed at the 'Zecca'. In 1666 they were sentenced to life imprisonment because of their illicit production of copper coinage, although they had not even pocketed the mintage duties.[4] In 1679, following a case of embezzlement from the customs, two employees and two policemen were paraded around Florence on a donkey before being sent mercilessly to the galleys, where they were joined by another citizen of Florence involved in the same crime.[5] For all that, this kind of treatment was somewhat lenient in comparison with what happened at the beginning of the century when two other officials in the same division had been hung without trial for having dipped their fingers into the till of the toll house.[6] In 1692 an employee from the 'Monte Pio' in the small town of Colle, who had appropriated no more than 1,000 liras or so, was sentenced to death by the 'Magistrato dei Nove', the authority in charge of inspecting local communities.[7] Four years later, the bailiff employed at that same court was condemned to ten years at the galleys, which was then commuted into as many years of exile on the Island of Elba, for having pocketed the proceeds from taxes he had been in charge of levying.[8] Bronzuoli, from the 'Monte di Pietà' in Florence, who, in exchange for a fee, had increased the value of pawned objects, was simply dismissed,[9] whereas Doctor Benini, who, as the reader may recall, had taken part in the embezzlement of the 'Monte redimibile', had been tortured for several hours and sentenced to life imprisonment in the dungeons of a fortress.[10] Life imprisonment was, at the same time, the punishment inflicted upon the ex-cashier of the commune of San Sepolcro, Jacopo Grifoni, guilty of another case of embezzlement.[11] Last but not least, in 1737, at the time when power changed hands, Raffaello Amiconi, one of the culprits of the embezzlement discovered in 1729 following the death of the treasurer Malegonelle was already serving his eighth year in prison in the Belvedere fortress in Florence.[12]

These punishments were coupled with economic sanctions, the object of which was to repair the damages caused to the grand ducal treasury. Most of the trials for embezzlement thus opened with the confiscation of the goods and income of the accused. This indispensable precaution was sometimes followed by more radical action. In the case of Ascanio Teri, former cashier of the 'Dogana' in Pisa, all his furniture and government bonds were sold for the benefit of the Grand Duke; his lands were auctioned and it was only because no purchaser was found that in the end they were rented out.[13] In another affair, that of the embezzlement in 1713 by the *camerlengo* of Sestino in the Appenine hills, the culprit's possessions – a tannery, a house, a wine cellar, land – were sold and the proceeds were sufficient for almost the entire sum stolen to be redeemed.[14]

*   *   *

There were quite a few risks involved in defrauding the Grand Duke of Tuscany. Was the danger the same for everyone, however? The law indicated that it was, without exception. Jurists stressed this by insisting that neither the dignity of a doctor nor the rank of a nobleman could constitute the right to be treated less severely in court. Cavallo upheld that a nobleman convicted of having failed to carry out the duty imposed on him by his office should 'receive the same punishment as that which would be inflicted on a lower-ranking man.' The privilege of nobility, he explained, was not proof against the infamy brought about by crime.[15] The *auditore* Savelli express-ed an equally harsh point of view: the higher the status of the culprit, he stated, the more serious was the offence. *Dignitas aggravat delictum*: it was according to this maxim, in the eyes of the severe jurist, that high-ranking persons should be treated when they were found guilty of an infringement. Doctors and noblemen, he added, lost their privileges whenever they com-mitted an offence and could be hanged without controversy.[16]

These rigorous opinions, however, required some attenua-tion. Savelli, himself, envisaged the hypothesis according to which the inequality of persons called for different sentences. He underlined the fact that 'equality was the greatest form of inequality or inequity', and that 'nothing was so unequal as equality itself, as if inequality was a kind of equality and performed its function.'[17] The *auditore* Conti drew practical conclusions from this theoretical position. He sided with the opinion that a subordinate, for whom the slightest offence called for instant dismissal, cannot be treated in the same way as a dignitary whose crimes could be sanctioned only within the framework of a regular trial.[18] There was, therefore, no question of classing everyone under the same heading. The culprits, of course, took advantage of this notion in their defence. Vincenzo Gaspero Borgherini, one of the culprits of the 'Abbondanza' affair, had his lawyer plead that, 'since they were dealing with very noble people, their nobility should serve to make the punishment less severe.' The defence council backed up this argument with quotations from leading jurists and did not hesitate, at the same time, to mention a practice reputed to have occurred in Tuscan courts.[19]

The arguments used in Borgherini's defence were not com-pletely new. The idea was expressed in this aphorism of Tiraqueau, for example: 'The nobleman suffers more from a light corporal punishment than a low-class citizen from a heavy one.'[20] What is more, they were reinforced by a context in which the punishment of distinguished persons posed a few practical problems.

Firstly, culprits exploited their acquaintances in order to

avoid the worst. Giovanni Ubaldini, the former cashier of the 'Possessioni', attempted to influence the judgement of the Grand Duke by counting on Gian Carlo dei Medici, a prince of blood to whom he had handed a report presenting his crimes in a favourable light.[21] As for Alessandro Degli Alessandri, he sought the help of one of the *segretari di Stato*, Lorenzo Caramelli, to whom he wrote from the convent where he had taken refuge thanking him 'infinitely for the help afforded me in this time of adversity'. Caramelli had written a letter concerning Alessandri's case to the *depositario generale*, the Superintendent of Finances, as well as to the War Secretary, who was the culprit's direct superior.[22]

It must also be pointed out that the culprits were assisted by other factors. In particular, a certain sense of discretion dissuaded potential buyers from purchasing their possessions at low prices. I have already mentioned the case of Ascanio Teri's land, which even after seven attempts failed to attract a buyer. This is not a one off example: the goods belonging to Francesco Malegonelle, located in the region of Vicchio, north-east of Florence, were auctioned twenty-three times without any success, despite the fact that, on the last day of sales, a discount of 25 per cent was offered. Six years after the death of the treasurer there was still a large part of his land left unsold.[23]

To these social restraints – pressure exerted by influential people, reluctance to lay hands on the goods of culprits – other factors related to the legal status of family fortunes were added. Economic sanctions could be applied only to the extent that the culprit had the entire disposal of his wealth. This was far from the case in a society in which all possible measures were taken to guarantee the preservation and the handing down of family holdings. In many Tuscan households, the rule was that most of the wealth of the family be bound by a *fedecommesso*, that is to say, subject to a regime which governed the transmission of wealth from one generation to the next in the order desired by the author of the original will. In this case, the person holding the fortune was not free to distribute it as he wished, and the state, therefore, could not claim it as repayment. The measures taken by families to guarantee the transmission of their wealth thus enabled nobles to rob the state while running very few economic risks.

The untouchability of inheritances held up legal proceedings. For example, it was necessary to separate from the confiscated goods of Anton Maria Gherardini, the former cashier of the salt office, those which were covered by a *fedecommesso*.[24] Alessandro Degli Alessandri, for his part, was not the sole proprietor of his villa and six farms in Petriolo, just outside Florence. What is more, the ownership of a part of his other country properties was claimed by Senator Antonio Antinori on the grounds of a will made a long time previously.[25] The same situation occurred in the case of Giuseppe Verdi, the deceased cash clerk of the Iron Monopoly: his inheritance, being bound by a *fedecommesso*, could only be partially used to repay the deficit he had left.[26]

Apart from these social and legal restraints, there were also real problems of opportuneness which reduced even more the sovereign's margin of manoeuvre. Let us take for example the case of Cremoni, the *camerlengo* employed at the 'Monte Pio' in Leghorn, who had embezzled more than 100,000 liras. Of course, the Grand Duke had various means at his disposal to recover the sum due to him. Firstly, he could round on the guarantees provided by the accountant; it was also possible for him to sue the *auditori* of Leghorn who had not done their job correctly, or the commissioner of the 'Monte Pio', knight Bartolini, or even the accountants of the office of the 'Nove' in Florence who should have revised the entries made by the *camerlengo* more attentively. It was not opportune, however, to put all these measures into practice. It would, in fact, have ended up in 'punishing the majority of the most distinguished people of Leghorn who composed the magistracies'.[27] Repression, then, would have threatened social order.

Economic sanctions, therefore, were easy to apply only in appearances. Punishment without distinction of individuals was even more problematic. Corporal punishment as spectacular as that inflicted on Parrini or Roncalli, in fact, cast infamy not only on the culprit but on his entire family. The judge Santucci, who was called upon to give his opinion on the 'Abbondanza' affair, was perfectly sure of that. 'From the point of view of the Italians', he explained, 'the infamy ordinarily cast on an offender by an ignominious sentence extends to his innocent relatives. It is very difficult, therefore, for the latter to be able to maintain their status afterwards through the same kinds of alliance.'[28] Richecourt, the regent for the emperor, confirmed: 'It is true that infamy should be individual, but it is otherwise in this country; it is not entirely prejudice, since the law in the cases of fraudulent bankruptcy extends the infamy to all posterity.'[29]

The chronicler Bonazzini illustrated these principles with no less striking examples. Commentating, for example, on the fate of Ruberto Pitti, a patrician who died in prison before standing trial for his misbehaviour, he expressed the idea that this death had in fact come at the right time. Otherwise, he underlined, Pitti would have suffered a 'dishonourable sentence *for his household*.'[30] As for the punishment inflicted on Roncalli, according to Bonazzini, not only had it dishonoured the former salt chancellor, but also cast infamy on his wife, a Vespucci, whose father then 'found himself with his daughter at home neither widowed nor married and without a dowry, and, what is worse, sullied by a stain that was impossible to wash away.'[31]

Punishment was thus not so much a problem for the culprit as for his innocent family. The reaction of Antinori, the War Secretary, to the case of a patrician from Pistoia named Gherardi, was symptomatic. He spoke of the 'strange situation of the *innocent and noble relatives* of this miserable subject'. Antinori thereby placed the question not on the individual level of the offender but on the more general level of the repercussions that an infamous sentence would have on the culprit's family.[32]

In a context such as this, the discovery of embezzlement implied a veritable catastrophe for the people close to the official. Through alliances, the consequences of that catastrophe could reach a very wide circle of people. The temptation to hush up the affair and to block court cases was therefore great, even if it meant putting the misdeeds of the culprit down to insanity. This was, in effect, the price to be paid for the respectability of the families. It is clearly expressed in this letter from the governor of Pistoia, addressed to the War Secretary on the subject of the above-mentioned Gherardi:

> My duty obliges me with sorrow to inform Your Excellency of a shameful action committed here by a gentleman who is a kind of mad man and who should have been locked up long ago for his poor conduct. He is allied to the highest nobility of this town. His only daughter, of nubile age, is liable to become the sad and innocent victim of her wretched father, who has just committed a shameful deed in this 'Monte Pio'.
>
> The superintendent of the 'Monte', accompanied by one of the highest ministers of this charity, came to inform me of this misdeed, begging me not to bring it to court, saying they would find the means to make the culprit redeem the stolen money and to hush up this affair, if I would to consent, in consideration of his poor family and all his relatives.
>
> The 'bargello'* knew of it, but imperfectly, and so I ordered him to suspend his 'comparsa'† until he had more definite and clear facts.
>
> I beg Your Excellency to grant protection, since I am eager to save this poor family and a large part of this nobility from the unfortunate and dishonourable consequences that this affair would provoke. I implore the clemency of the Regency Council . . .[33]

Faced with an affair for which the laws provided an unacceptable solution in that it cast dishonour on innocent people, nobles as well as the governor were greatly troubled. This uneasiness was felt also by the sovereign, and therefore it took on a political aspect.

* * *

With some reservations, which will be dealt with later, the context outlined above lasted throughout the period in ques-

---

* Chief of local police.
† Report presented to the judge.

tion in this work. The prince commanded adequate legislative instruments to satisfy the need for repression, and he knew if need be, how to apply them rigorously. Complications set in, however, when the culprit was a person of distinction and in particular a member of nobility. Then justice came up against several stumbling blocks: interventions, reticence and legal complications transformed what should have been no more than a routine procedure into a tricky problem. Lastly, questions of opportuneness which arose from the need to preserve fortunes and not to plunge the most eminent familes into infamy, called for caution. An excess of repressive ardour could put social order at risk and stir up discontent among the prominent families who, at the same time, would have lost their resources and respectability. Repression thus reached far beyond the individual dimension. It became a political issue, the terms of which were clear. Should the prince adopt the logic of the solidarity of lineage, respecting at all costs the inviolability of fortunes and even abandoning court action against criminals in order to save their families? Or, should he, on the contrary, seek the interest of justice alone, which was an essential part of his sovereign attributions, by considering criminals as individuals and not in relation to their families, refusing thereby solidarities which brought an end to the repression of crimes committed by members of nobility, even if that meant alienating a social class he was supposed to rely on? Francis of Lorraine, as we shall see, opted for the second solution. In that, he did not imitate his Medici predecessors, who were far more flexible in their functions of sovereign judges.

*   *   *

'On 18 January 1641 ... the already dead body of Signor Filippo de'Nobili, Florentine gentleman, was hung beneath the Uffizzi, opposite the 'Nove', for having falsified the balance sheets of the office where he was employed as *provveditore*.' Hung, therefore, but hung when already dead and, according to another source, after having been poisoned in prison.[34] The fate of Filippo de'Nobili Valori seems to me to be symbolic for two reasons. Firstly, it resulted from a judicial system which, all things considered, did not always treat matters of corruption lightly. Secondly, it illustrates usages which distinguished between different classes of culprits: those who were paraded through the town with their head covered with a galley slave's bonnet, and those who were executed in secret and exposed to general infamy only in the form of a dead body. The fate of Valori, besides this, seems to me to be particularly harsh. I know of no other condemnation so radical as this inflicted on a member of nobility during the years up to the end of the Medici principality. On the contrary, the Tuscans seem to have been in the habit of making the distinction between culprits liable to be reprimanded ferociously, and those with whom it was not such a bad thing to show lenience. Thus, whereas Vanni, who was an obscure functionary employed in the salt magistracy, was sent to the galleys, his accomplice, the patriciate Pitti, awaited in the seclusion of a prison a verdict which curiously never arrived.[35] A few years later, in 1679, a citizen named Ducci who, as I have already mentioned, had been involved, together with several other people, in professional misconduct in the 'Dogana', was sadly sent to the galleys with his companions of misfortune. His accomplice Galilei, on the other hand, was simply banished to Portoferraio. The reason given: 'he was a member of the very noble Galilei family.'[36]

State pardons for members of the nobility were not rare. Commander Petrucci, guilty of embezzling the 'Monte dei Paschi' in Siena of a huge sum, benefited from special treatment. As a knight of *Santo Stefano*, he was liable to life imprisonment and confiscation of his knight's coat. He was spared the latter mortification and, in fact, even the prison sentence was somehow avoided.[37] Antonio Maria Gherardini, who, as we know, stole from the salt magistracy in Florence, never suffered anything more than economic sanctions.[38] No infamy, apparently, recoiled on him, and he was able to marry some time later. Antonio Malegonelle, the culprit of the famous embezzlement from the 'Dogana' in Florence, fled to Venice. But when he returned, he was not troubled at all. On the contrary, he was even on the official list of candidates for public office and, in a report written in 1735, the *auditore* Luci mentions the 'gracious intentions of His Excellency towards him.'[39] Lastly, Ascanio Teri had undoubtedly had to cut into his personal fortune to redeem the funds he had appropriated from the 'Dogana' in Pisa. But, despite the falsifications discovered in the entries he made in the books, he was never made to stand trial. Moreover, the confiscation of his goods was annulled before the amount owed to the Grand Duke had been entirely paid off. Ascanio Teri attracted the interest of Violante de Bavaria, the widow of Prince Ferdinando de Medici and daughter-in-law of the reigning Grand Duke. This princess most charitably encouraged the new career which, contrary to all expectations, her protégé had undertaken in the government of the provinces. In the letters of recommendation addressed under the signature of her personal butler, she evoked 'the need to assist this family who try had to conform to the arrangement that HRH has accorded them to pay back their debts.' The 'compassion' and the 'pious sentiments' expressed by Violante were not left unsatisfied. In 1722, Teri had already been named *podestà* of the Chianti area, and two years later he was honoured with the same title in Figline, in the Val d'Arno. In 1726 he was made *capitano di giustizia* at Marradi in the Appenine hills and in 1728 *vicario* at Vicopisano. Finally, in 1729, he was named *capitano di giustizia* at Pietrasanta, near the border with the republic of Genova. His official biography, handed to the Grand Duke in view of his nomination, made no mention whatsoever of his previous misconduct.[40]

Thus, there was a double-sided system of weights and measures. What is more, this differentiation was not limited to penal proceedings. The same kind of arrangements were made in the field of economic sanctions. The prince renounced the use of all the possibilities offered to him by the law. By contenting himself with a few payments, which were modest and more or less spontaneous, he demonstrated a benevolence to which he was all the more inclined, in that severity would be met with problems of dowries and possessions bound by a *fedecommesso*. Thus, the confiscation of goods was quickly abandoned and the culprit was made to promise to pay his debts gradually by means of annual instalments.

Ascanio Teri, for example, was able to recover his personal effects in 1719 in exchange for a covenant to pay sixty *scudi* per year until the complete redemption of his debt.[41] Anton Maria Gherardini benefited from the same treatment: in 1732, twelve years after the event, he was allowed to recover goods that had been confiscated on condition that he promise to pay the same amount, sixty *scudi* each year: a very modest annuity, considering the fact that he still owed 6,382 *scudi*.[42] Antonio Malegonelle, who, as I mentioned before, enjoyed the favour of the prince, repossessed a part of his fortune in exchange for 150 *scudi* per year: his outstanding debt amounted at the time to 4,400 *scudi*.[43] In 1718 the heirs of the deceased knight Pandolfi, the former *sotto-provveditore* of the Pisa fortress, obtained permission to pay back the 2,194 *scudi* of the good man's debt, in yearly instalments of sixty-five *scudi*.[44] Last but not least, Orazio Guidetti, who in 1618 had been named pay clerk of the grand ducal household, left the post with a deficit of 9,949 *scudi*. It was agreed in 1632 that he pay back the sum in the form of annual payments of one hundred *scudi*, reduced in 1651 to fifty *scudi*.[45]

These arrangements did nothing to speed up the recovery of the money owed to the Grand Duke by his former servants. At the rate of sixty *scudi* a year, the balance on Ascanio Teri's debt would have taken twenty years to redeem. This period would have amounted to more than thirty years for Antonio Maria Malegonelle and around a century for the debts of Guidetti and Gherardini. But years often passed without the sum owed being paid, and therefore affairs of embezzlement were frequently postponed to a non-immediate future, which meant that they would drag on for years, even decades. The affair of the Malegonelle brothers, which had begun under Cosimo III, ended only after the cessation of the Medici dynasty and by a *coup de force* of the Lorraine government. The case of Anton Maria Gherardini had still not been resolved even after thirty-five years. In fact, the person in question had paid nothing at all before 1748. In 1688, fifty-six years after the debt of Orazio

Guidetti had been scaled down to one hundred *scudi* per year, his son Tommaso died leaving behind him three years' arrears, with the debt still exceeding 6,000 *scudi*. As for the money pocketed by Vittorio Nelli from the Siena treasury in 1666, it was still being debated in 1768, that is, 102 years later, between ministers of the Grand Duke Peter Leopold.[46] The disloyalty of accountants, then, defied the centuries.

These facilities, both penal and economic, benefited first and foremost members of the nobility such as Malegonelle, Teri, Alessandri and Gherardini. Representatives of the lower echelons of society were nevertheless also allowed to benefit. Here, for example, is the case of a minor judge who, in the exercise of his functions, felt authorized to capitalize on favours granted to certain parties. The *auditore* Savelli, who was to give a ruling on his case, was overwhelmingly harsh and systematically overruled all the exceptions brought to light by the defence council. However, as he noted himself in his *Summa*, 'following his long imprisonment of eighteen or twenty months', it was resolved 'to free him on bail, and to assign him a forced residence in his own house and later on his land. To date, his case, a voluminous file of more than 1,700 pages of investigations, has not been mentioned again.'[47] The case of Luigi Mercianti, the former cash clerk at the 'Monte Pio' in Leghorn, is also revealing. The proceedings taken after his flight were abandoned by an express order from the Grand Duke which was addressed to the commissioner of all the 'Monte di Pietà' in Tuscany. The order read as follows: 'with relation to the case of Signor Luigi Mercianti, His Excellency decides that the tribunal of the "Nove" will have all procedures against him stopped in Leghorn once the accounts of the "Monte Pio" have been reimbursed, HRH having various reasons which lead him to this decision.'[48] Lastly, a chronicler reported the example of a 'certain Bettazzi, *camerlengo* at the magistracy that levied flour taxes in the town of Prato, brother of doctor Domenico Agapito Bettazzi the secretary to the *auditore fiscale* [who], having caused a debt in the above mentioned till of 4,500 *scudi*, obtained from [the Grand Duke] permission to pay yearly instalments of 150 *scudi* until its extinction, and was reconfirmed in his office.'[49]

Why, in the case of Bettazzi, so much indulgence was granted is fairly obvious. It emerged from the actual report of the chronicler, who called the *auditore fiscale* into question. However, whatever motivated the prince to spare Mercianti or to leave the judge denounced by Savelli is less clear. It can only be supposed that it was thanks to some timely intervention from influential people that these wretches escaped the fate normally reserved for people of their kind. There are insufficient sources, however, to invalidate or confirm this hypothesis.

'Laws', declared solemnly the jurist Bonifacius, 'are often compared to spiders' webs, which trap flies, but are destroyed by bigger birds.'[50] He thereby expressed a truth which could more or less be applied to Tuscany under the last of the Medici. In the states of the Grand Duchy, in fact, justice does not seem to have been applied with equal rigour to all the functionaries who were guilty of fraud. In a regime where social pressure, juridicial constraints and political needs made it unwise to treat members of the aristocracy harshly, it was admissible to differentiate between condemnable criminals and pardonable ones. Executions, outrageous punishments and long prison sentences continued, of course, to be inflicted. But they tended to avoid privileged culprits, who were spared not so much for themselves but in consideration of the damage that a confiscation of their goods and the subsequent infamy could have for their innocent relatives. These happy beneficiaries of grand ducal pardons were frequently prominent citizens. But there were also among them some people of more modest extraction, who had miraculously escaped the clutches of the law. The nobility therefore did not have the monopoly on indulgence. However, it seems to be the only class that, after a certain date, did not suffer the rigour of the courts.

This situation can be historically dated. It corresponds to a certain balance of social and political forces in which, at the end of the seventeenth century and the beginning of the eighteenth, the monarchy and Tuscan nobility became partners apparently condemned to live – and to govern – together. It is not certain that it existed in previous times during which the relations between nobility and the Grand Duke were more

strained. To condemn an official from the noble classes guilty
of corrupt practices was, at that time, probably easier than
under Cosimo III. The question that could then be raised was if
the execution of Filippo de'Nobili-Valori, far from constituting
an exception to the rule, did not rather mark a turning point
between a situation in which punishment of the aristocracy paid
off politically, and another in which it no longer did so. This
question merits deeper analysis.

*			*			*

The last Grand Dukes of the House of Medici seem to have
been mixed up in a contradiction between principles and
practice which was difficult to resolve. On the one hand, they
were the guarantors of a legislative order founded on the
moralization of corruption and the punishment of abuses. On
the other hand, they met with a political and social situation
which actually made it difficult to apply the laws rigorously.
Thus, despite the fact that the official line was to incriminate
the guilty, the Grand Dukes often had to pardon misdoers who
were manifestly guilty. They were therefore often obliged to
suffer the very practices they condemned. All they could do,
under these circumstances, was try to attenuate the negative
impression left by their renouncement by giving it a tint of
heroism. Clemency then became, in the rhetoric of the court,
the only concept that was politically and psychologically accept-
able to account for what was in fact no more than a necessary
resignation. The funeral speech for Cosimo III, as composed
by one of the most remarkable personalities of the eighteenth
century in Tuscany, Monsignor Bottari, is very instructive on
this subject.

Bottari, having exalted the sense of justice of the deceased
Grand Duke, added that this eminent virtue was, in Cosimo III,
'accompanied by a pleasant and sweet clemency of gold, which
was no less heroic in him than his sense of justice. The two
qualities combined to perfection in his great heart.' Everybody
had witnessed the effects of this clemency, for 'whoever had to
resort to the clement prince was always relieved and helped by

the kind words and even more powerful action.' For example, Cosimo III did not hesitate to sacrifice the claims of the treasury against the culprits. But there was no political strategy behind his actions. Unlike Caesar, the Grand Duke was moved only by 'love of virtue'. If he was merciful, it was 'only through his heroic magnanimity and in order to demonstrate, as it is befitting for grand princes, that in his soul he encompassed all moral virtues to a sublime degree and far more perfect than the rare demonstrations of virtue in other men'. 'Oh how supreme, generous and precious is the clemency of our prince!' concluded Bottari, 'What abundance, what flood, what inspiration, what volubility, what eloquence could suffice to express our praise of you?'[51]

The eulogy given by this excellent prelate was significant for more than one reason. Bottari firstly recognized that Cosimo III had not always applied laws rigorously: the Grand Duke had even gone so far as to sacrifice tax dues in order to spare culprits. That renouncement, added Bottari, was nevertheless devoid of political significance, because the Grand Duke was not acting out of self-interest. Nor was it a manifestation of individual weakness. It offered, on the contrary, an example of edifying heroism, that is to say, of love of virtue. Bottari thus totally wiped out the political problem inherent in repression and shifted the question onto an ethical ground. He then substituted the false ideas of weakness or resignation by the concept of clemency. Finally, he succeeded in presenting the behaviour of the Grand Duke as a series of virtuous actions and great works. Thus, Cosimo III was not discredited by not having punished the guilty. On the contrary, it was added to the list of great achievements that enabled him to be inscribed in the gallery of heroes.

The concept of clemency alone appeared to be able to overcome the contradiction existing between the principles that were constantly repeated and a political situation that did not allow them to be put into practice. It enabled a political dimension to be veiled which, if explicitly formulated, would have been unacceptable. It made it possible to present in a favourable light that which otherwise would have been seen as a form of abasement. Thus, the fact that he did not punish culprits meant that the prince could surpass himself in the exercise of virtue.

*   *   *

At the beginning of this work, I showed how moralization and the punishment of corruption prevented the collective political implications from being perceived and how it transformed the phenomenon into a strictly individual form of criminality. This culpabilization, in its turn, provoked a response in the employees which was based on lies and deculpabilization. The arbiter between these two tendencies was the prince. But it was not merely a confrontation between two ethical choices, one being rigorous and the other laxist. The political dimension that had been wiped away by moralization was in fact reintroduced by the same moralization at the punishment stage. In a state like Tuscany, the prince's choice was more than one of rigour or leniency. Very often he had to pronounce a rigorous verdict at the risks of provoking certain political consequences, or, on the contrary, he had to choose leniency for the sake of social peace. It is precisely for that reason that, without repudiating the principles of rigour, he tended to practise leniency. But since this despicably political choice was morally unacceptable, it was necessary to invoke clemency in order to shift onto virtuous ground what was actually more of a cold calculation. Moralization, casuistry, and clemency had complementary functions: moralization culpabilized, casuistry deculpabilized and clemency made it possible to tolerate disculpabilization without going back on the principle of culpabilization. The resulting discourses combined in an organic way: they enabled the removal of the political dimension of abuses, left a certain freedom for officials, especially those who came from leading families, and at the same time, preserved, at least officially, the dignity of the prince.

This moral system of corruption was perhaps not exempt from a certain amount of hypocrisy. What is more, not everyone was a dupe. In fact, in the advice given in 1723 to the

Grand Duke Gian Gastone, an observer had pointed out the negative effects produced by the fatherly benevolence with which the late Grand Duke had treated dishonest officials. 'For some years', he wrote,

> we have observed important occasions of embezzlement committed by *camerlenghi* who helped themselves to the contents of the coffers entrusted to them, thereby causing damages for considerable sums of money. This was heard of far less in the past, because the punishment was more severe. But the clemency of the late prince, whose memory is glorious, had led the second citizen to expect the same leniency that was granted to the first one, and so on for all the others. They saw that not only did people escape punishment and the confiscation of their possessions, but that they were also granted the mercy of the fines and were allowed to pay back their debts over a long period. Within a few years, such cases numbered thirteen or fourteen.[52]

There was, no doubt, some truth in those statements. The reasoning suffered, however, from the fact that it is not complete. It took into consideration only the unfortunate consequences of clemency without considering the positive ones. Cosimo III, the clement prince, was inevitably a prince who was robbed. But he gained in political tranquillity what he lost in cash. Of course, he was sad that the 'Abbondanza' and the 'Gabella' were despoiled. But it would have been very foolhardy of him to send to the gallows the representatives of a Florentine aristocracy that the Grand Dukes had firstly feared, and then managed, not without some difficulty, to tame and who still nurtured some republican feelings. Clemency, therefore, was part and parcel of a political stability which it accepted and at the same time concealed. It could not survive, as such, in the new climate that presided during the government of Francis of Lorraine.

8

THE GOOD OF PUNISHMENT

These few lines, written in the midst of sighs and tears, ask for pardon. They were written by the hand of a repentant sinner who throws himself at your feet and implores your clemency concerning his punishment for an abominable affair. In my affliction, I console myself by remembering that, from the beginning, Your Excellency had promised me your protection.... I also remember that I begged you to consider me as your son, and that is why I implore Your Excellency to grant me the mercy befitting of a father full of love for his son.[1]

Senator Alberti, former *protettore* at the 'Abbondanza', had therefore changed his tone. He no longer boasted of his merits. He no longer protested his zeal. He pitifully begged Count Richecourt, the destinee of this letter, to show leniency in this painful affair[2] of which he was the protagonist. From the prison, where he had been vegetating for more than a month, he invoked that magic word: clemency, a word that had the power instantly to restore his reputation.

His 'innocent relatives', of course, reinforced the supplication. The Alberti brothers, the senator's sons, wrote to Richecourt ensuring him that they were ready to sacrifice their entire fortune in order to avoid their father being condemned ignominiously. They asked for nothing else, in fact, but the 'grace to live without shame in the country where they were born'.[3] Friends of the family added their voices to this plea. Cardinal Corsini intervened in favour of knight Borgherini or, more precisely, of his unfortunate relatives bound for disgrace if the former *provveditore* of the 'Palco' were to be convicted. 'I recognize that there was abuse of authority', he admitted, 'but, on the other hand, I see a young wife and a decrepit mother who ask Your Excellency to be tenderly compassionate, as well as His Imperial Majesty* to practise the clemency that is natural to him'. 'I am also concerned', he continued, 'for Messrs Alberti, who most certainly deserve the goodness you have shown them [and] whose grandmother was of my family if not my household.'[4]

Throughout the 'Abbondanza' trial, the spectre of the innocent relatives was brandished by the culprits. Alberti humbly begged 'His Holy Majesty for a generous pardon and for the most special mercy, in proportion to His great clemency, and moreover justified by my large family.' And just to make sure that everybody should know, the former *prottetore* placed a footnote to his petition giving 'a partial list of the most closely connected families of the supplicant'. The list included the names of Cardinal Corsini, Cardinal d'Elci, Monsignor Torrigiani, Baron Del Nero, senator Guadagni, Duke Salviati, Count Bardi, the Marquis Alamanni, the bailiff Del Rosso, Count Strozzi and many others.[5] The pride and joy of Florentine nobility, in short, had his honour at stake in Alberti's trial.

The situation was the same for the other three culprits. Borgherini, Libri and Gaetani followed the example of their companion and set out as a footnote to their petitions the list of the innocent people who were likely to be dragged down with them if they fell. Vincenzo Gaspero Borgherini, for example, quoted about thirty names, most of which were those of the most illustrious families of Florence: Pucci, Capponi, Antinori, Medici, Ricasoli, Cerretani, Salviati, Vettori, Albizzi, Strozzi, Pecori, and so on. The relations of Lorenzo Libri and Francesco Gaetani were of the same order.[6]

---

* Francis Stephen of Lorraine, ex Duke of Lorraine (1729–37), Grand Duke of Tuscany (1737–65), Emperor of the Holy Roman Empire (1745–65). Married to Maria Teresa of Austria, which made him the founder of the Habsburg-Lorraine dynasty, Francis Stephen resided in Vienna. He went to Florence only once, where he was represented by a regency. The regency was presided over successively by Prince de Craon, Count Richecourt and finally by the Marquis Botta-Adorno.

The court, during this time, pursued its activities. On 6 October 1747, Doctor Santucci, the *assessore* of the tribunal of the 'Otto', the main penal jurisdiction in Florence, presented a preliminary report in which the crimes of each culprit were scrupulously listed in detail. It cannot be said that the list exalted the four leaders who had fallen into the hands of the law, nor, for that matter, Lorenzo Rossi, the former, now absent, *custode*. Santucci, however, did not preach rigour. He recognized the gravity of the crimes committed by the managers of the 'Abbondanza', but he pointed out that, since they were knights of the order of *Santo Stefano*, neither Alberti nor Borgherini could be sentenced to capital punishment. That made it difficult to inflict that same punishment on Gaetani and Libri, who were less guilty. Economic sanctions thus seemed preferable to any other type of punishment, and all the more so in that, as Santucci underlined, 'the generous nobility of a large number of families would [thus] be ... preserved.'[7]

In short, the affair turned out for the good. Nobody, of course, denied that the culprits were in effect guilty. But everyone agreed that the guilt of four individuals was not a sufficient motive to cast infamy on many innocent people of distinction. There remained, however, a difficulty: it lay in the head of the Florentine government, Count Richecourt, who was trusted totally by the emperor and whose recommendation was thus essential to obtain a pardon. Nobody was unaware of the terrible harshness with which the count had treated the nobility of Florence. The obstacle, therefore, was considerable and the worst could be feared. However, attempts were made to sway the uncompromising Lorraine. In the month of August, even before the culprits were arrested, a foresighted hand proposed that he sign the draft of a letter to the emperor which ended with a vibrant call for clemency. The text, handed to the minister for approval, had the following conclusion:

I find some solace in seeing His Imperial and Holy Majesty freed from the extreme rigour of laws on delinquents and, in consequence, in a position, if His Majesty would consent (after having clarified the crime and the culprits), to resort to economic punishments which could better serve as a sufficient example to the others, while sparing as far as possible the guilty (all the more necessary in that there could be some who had relatives who are honest and worthy of attention). Such punishment, above all, would make the ineffable and compassionate clemency, one of the most remarkable qualities of His Imperial and Holy Majesty, to shine forth all the more, and, confident of your unique and glorious kindness, I do here and now implore your clemency in their favour.'[8]

Richecourt, however, did not let the author have his way. He crossed the text out and the dispatch left for Vienna with this laconic conclusion: 'I shall have the honour to render account to His Imperial Majesty of the development and outcome of this trial.'[9] But nobody was discouraged by this. In fact the regent himself ended up by pleading his master for clemency. On 19 December 1747 he sent a dispatch to Vienna in which, having outlined the events, he persuasively resumed the ideas developed in the note written by the *assessore* Santucci. He underlined the fact that the four guilty men came from the most prestigious families of the state and that Alberti, Borgherini and Gaetani had among their relatives not only two-thirds of the nobility, but also cardinals. It followed, he continued, that 'an ignominious punishment inflicted on these four men would affect, in one way or another, the prominent subjects of His Majesty.' Richecourt thus opted for economic sanctions. He pointed out, on this subject, that the families of the culprits had declared themselves to be ready and willing to pay. 'The brothers', he stated, 'promise to pay more than they are obliged, the wives offer their dowries and renounce the advantages of their marriage settlements, the sons stand security for their fathers and renounce the trust (*fedecommessi*) guaranteeing the substance of their family.' The arrest of the guilty men, esteemed Richecourt, had sufficiently served as an example. The Emperor, now, could close the proceedings and be content to have damages paid to the 'Abbondanza', to dismiss the culprits and to banish them for a certain period. He could thereby satisfy his sense of justice and clemency at the same time. His approach would consist in 'penalizing the guilty without including in their punishments such a large number of leading subjects of his States'.[10]

The trial of the 'Abbondanza' affair was typical. The problem, from the outset, had been transferred from the guilty to their innocent relatives. In this way, rigour had no more purpose and clemency took its place. Relatives, friends, judges and the regent implored the emperor in unison not to commit irreparable damage and not to sacrifice the Florentine nobility to the errors, however abominable they may be, of just four of its representatives. The social logic inherited from the Medicis was given full reign. It seemed capable of saving the guilty by curbing a judicial system which, by its rigorous approach, had become subversive.

*   *   *

The affair, however, had not been clinched. In fact, the emperor showed great severity. In the month of October 1747 he had made notes in the margins of a report of his council relating to the 'Abbondanza' embezzlement: 'Je veut et croy très nesesere que l'on allé aveque tout la rigeur nesesere contre ces coupable.' 'Je veux', added Francis of Lorraine, 'qu'en Tosquan l'on voye que c'et de tou de bon que je soutien la justis.'*[11]

These statements were not a good sign and indeed the dispatch in which Richecourt asked for clemency was received coldly in Vienna. In the sitting held on 24 January 1748, the council expressed the opinion that the file was being handled very lightly by the regent in Florence and that, moreover, the line suggested by Count Richecourt went 'directly contrary' to the orders decreed by His Imperial Majesty. Thus, it proposed to 'order the trial to be continued and that the case be investigated with exactitude and celerity until a fully definitive

---

* Quotations from Francis Stephen have been left in French in order to appreciate the strange spelling used by the emperor. Where spelling conformed more to the purity of the French language, texts were dictated, recopied or corrected by editors. The translation of the emperor's words will be given as footnotes. Here, 'I wish and deem highly necessary that all due rigour be used against these guilty men', and 'I want the people of Tuscany to see that I maintain justice firmly.'

verdict be sent to His Imperial Majesty. If His Imperial Majesty esteems it appropriate to be lenient, it must be in full knowledge of the facts.'

The Emperor then burst out: 'Je ne conpran pas comen un chose de cet importance et treté si legereman; ensi je *veut et ordone* que la prosedur criminel soua fete *osi prompteman posible* et pourtan aveque tout la rigeure posible. . . . Les proposition de diminué la pene en remetant les some volé pare les coupable ne m'a fet d'otre efet que de m'étoné que Richecour i et apuié. . . . En un mot, Richecour me deveret conetre poure savoy conbien j'ay a coueure que mes etta vent un foua en régle et que le crime n'i soua pas com si-devan enpuni.'*[12]

After this warning shot, the 'Abbondanza' trial took on a new look. Richecourt was eager to justify himself by alleging that if he proposed economic sanctions it was only 'to guarantee the patrimony of the poor and to save the innocent by punishing the guilty.'[13] The judges, of course, were less eager and even let Alberti die in prison before pronouncing their verdict.[14] But, with a sovereign on their heels who was demanding rapid and severe justice,[15] they ended up by complying and in November 1749 proposed a harsh sentence. Lorenzo Rossi, the former *custode* of the 'Uccello' storehouse, was sentenced to death *in absentia*, and his effects were to be confiscated. Knight Borgherini, the former *provveditore*, had his knight's coat of the order of *Santo Stefano* confiscated, was dismissed from all his charges and dignities and condemned to life imprisonment. Francesco Gaetani and Lorenzo Libri, the former *provveditore* and former *sotto-provveditore* of the 'Abbondanza' respectively, were dismissed, discharged from all their public duties and dignities and condemned, the first man to five and the second to seven years' exile in Volterra. *Cavaliere* Borgherini and Rossi, besides this, were condemned to pay indemnities to the 'Abbondanza' for the total of the sums embezzled with compensation and interest.

---

* 'I fail to understand why an affair of this importance be treated so lightly. Thus, I wish and order that the criminal proceedings be made as promptly [as] possible and with as much rigour as possible. . . . The proposition to diminish the punishment by giving back the sums stolen by the guilty only surprised me that Richecourt could support such an idea. In a word, Richecourt should know me well enough to know how eager I am for my states to get back into order and for crime not to be as previously unpunished.'

The heirs of Gaetani, Libri and Alberti were also hit by economic sanctions which, applied fully, would have left them with absolutely nothing.[16]

This verdict was all the more severe in that it was added to the two years and three months of prison that the three main culprits had already undergone. Thus Richecourt took the risk of intervening once more. He pointed out again to the emperor the fact that the culprits belonged to the 'leading noble families of his state'. 'The zeal with which I have handled this affair from the beginning', he continued, 'leads me to hope that His Majesty will not disapprove if I now solicit his clemency.'[17] This time, the Council of Vienna agreed to satisfy the regent's request. It 'took the liberty of bringing His Imperial Majesty's attention to a last observation which is that today this affair is brought before him and in consequence before the tribunal of the prince, which is always considered to be the tribunal of mercy.' It suggested, at the same time, that Borgherini's prison sentence be reduced to five years and that Gaetani and Libri be granted a pardon in consideration of the long prison term they had already served.[18]

The emperor was presented with the report and had the task of confirming or vetoing the sentence proposed by the Florentine judges. The file was returned with the following note: 'Je confirme en tout la santan ci-desu et elle doua être publié et exécuté.'*[19]

This caused a great deal of consternation in Florence: 'I am grieved . . . to see that His Majesty has confirmed the verdict of the judges',[20] confessed Count Richecourt in a letter. The grief was also shared by the culprits as well as their relatives who, of course, made several attempts to make the emperor change his mind. Indeed, the Council of Vienna was bothered for a number of years by appeals. For all that, the emperor was very reticent in departing from his initial rigorous line. However, in November 1750 he substantially moderated the sentences of Gaetani and Libri, who were far less guilty than the others and had already been harshly punished by their preventive deten-

* I confirm the entire sentence above and it must be made public and carried out.'

tion. The two men, in effect, had their banishment reduced by half and, what is more, they were allowed to carry out the rest of the sentence in one of their country estates instead of Volterra. Borgherini, on the other hand, had to wait longer. Of course, he was spared the public confiscation of his knight's coat, a ceremony which was particularly humiliating, but the emperor refused to answer a supplication to have him released from prison. It was only in 1752, and in consideration of his seventy years of age, that he was allowed to withdraw to a country house far away from Florence. All the other requests for pardons, from Borgherini or from his colleagues, were overruled.[21]

*   *   *

Rigour, in fact, was part of the Emperor's habits. In 1737 Count Richecourt had laid his cards on the table, ensuring the Florentine magistrates that they would be supported by a prince who was eager to 'punish vice and to recompense virtue'.[22] It was doubtless necessary, in the beginning, to keep the judges inherited from a regime which was more noted for its clemency than for its severity. These magistrates, however, were not eternal, and their replacements were often very harsh. The new *auditore fiscale* Bricchieri-Colombi, nominated in 1747, had the reputation of being 'fiery and cruel' and of causing a massacre in the ranks of offenders.[23] Ten years later the emperor himself ordered his new representative in Tuscany, the Marquis Botta-Adorno, to observe 'un *justis* exaquet, courte et sever, lorsqu'i en et besouen'*, for, he added, 'ille fau dans un bon gouverneman des example pour en anpéché un enfinité d'otre.'†[24]

No pity, therefore, was granted to swindlers. Francis of Lorraine, on this point, was intransigent. When informed of the alleged fraud committed by a certain Fei, *provveditore* of the fortifications of Portoferraio on the Island of Elba, he ordered

---

*   'Justice that was exact, brief and severe, when needed.'
†   'A good government needs examples to prevent an infinity of others.'

de lesé allé le proset *à la dernière rigeur* tan contre le provéditeur que contre les entrepreneur et *en lésé allé l'exécusion sa leur acordé le recour hisi*, le ca n'étan pas grasiable et vouslan que de parellieu friponeri soua puni publiqueman pour par là doné un tereure et enpéché des crime qui ne son que trop comeun en Toscane. Ensi j'ordone que ce proset soua fet à la dernier rigeur et les condanation exécuté san nouvel ordre le ca étan trop grave pour ne pas mérité la corde.*[25]

In conditions such as this, it was hardly very wise to deceive the prince. Senator Uguccioni, patrician and *provveditore* of the silk guild in Florence, lost his job in this way, for having accepted a bribe. At the same time he was exiled to one of his villas.[26] Lucatelli, *segretario delle Finanze*, was dismissed for abusing his influence and was exiled from the states of his Imperial Majesty; he was only allowed back in 1764 after twenty years' absence.[27] Benzoni, former corporal of the police force in Lari, in the region of Pisa, was sent to the galleys for life charged with extortion and in 1748 was refused a pardon.[28] In the 'Monte di Pietà' affair which broke out during the same year, one of the culprits, Simone Varrochi, was condemned to death *in absentia*. The other culprit, Anton Francesco Durazzi, saved his neck by taking refuge in the Republic of Venice. The Venetians only returned him to Tuscany on the condition that he would not be executed. He was nevertheless condemned to life imprisonment and died in jail fifteen years later. Lastly, in 1752, Jacopo Marini, another employee of the 'Monte di Pietà', but of 'lower social extraction', was purely and simply hung for his fraud.[29]

This break with the past, of course, was not radical. During the first years of his reign, Cosimo III had also shown harshness and was criticized later for having changed his attitude.[30] Secondly, the ministers of Francis Stephen often intervened in

---

* To pursue the trial with the utmost rigour both against the *provveditore* as against other contractors and to carry out the execution without granting any appeal here, the case being unworthy of a pardon, and wishing that such trickery be punished publicly so as to inspire terror and thereby to prevent crimes which are already too frequent in Tuscany. Thus, I order that the trial be pursued with the utmost rigour and the sentences be executed without new order, the case being too serious to merit not the rope.

order to curb the repressive ardour of their master.[31] Lastly, the graduation of punishment according to status did not disappear entirely. The bribe accepted by the senator and Florentine patrician Uguccioni was thus punished with three years' banishment from the capital, while that of Lucatelli, the secretary employed at the Finances, meant twenty years of expatriation. With these reservations, certain features of the Lorraine regime were specific to the reign of Francis of Lorraine. Firstly, the repressive will of the master was clearly defined. Secondly, nobles were more threatened than ever. Finally, the new government took measures to make economic sanctions more effective.

In fact, in 1748, just when the affair of the embezzlement from the 'Abbondanza' had demonstrated the extent to which *fedecommessi* could protect the possessions of culprits, the ministers in Florence sent their master a bill on the subject which would modify the law in favour of the state. In substance, the bill declared that, in the event of a debt to the state, any of the culprit's possessions bound by *fedecommesso* could be sold, like any other, for the benefit of the sovereign. These measures constituted a full-frontal attack on an institution which, for several centuries, had been the pillar of patrimonial inheritance and of the preservation of the economic foundation of prominent families. This made the emperor hesitate before passing a ruling: 'Cela', he observed, 'fera bocoup de brui.'* He nevertheless agreed to sign the bill, and on 23 January 1749 the new law was promulgated in the states of the Grand Duke of Tuscany.[32]

* * *

The case of the 'Abbondanza' affair, as, in fact, that of the *provveditore* Fei, leaves no room for doubt: it was the emperor and the emperor alone who was behind the new repressive rigour applied in sentencing culprits. Thus it is Francis Stephen

---

* That would cause a great stir.

of Lorraine, his idea of justice, and more widely his religious convictions that must be examined to assess the exact value of the policies adopted by the Lorraine government.

First of all, the emperor claimed the right to punish culprits regardless of their social origins or their families. In the 'Abbondanza' affair, he ordered that the trial be carried out 'sans le mouendre égare ni à paran, ni au ran des person, leur crime ne tomban par sure leure famillieu et ettan personel et ces même crime fesan avoyre peu d'égare à leur ran.'* He added, 'que l'on et égare que au crime et non au famillieu, la justis n'i devan jamet avoyre égare.'[33]† These opinions were also expressed with regard to other cases. Faced with a considerable affair of contraband discovered in Pisa in 1749, the emperor manifested his will to see the culprits punished according to the rigour of the law, 'san la mouendre considération poure le ran de qui que se soua et seuleman prandre ceux que l'on trouvera les plus coupable.' And he specified once more that 'en fet d'otre procet criminel on doua toujours opéré san la mouendre considération pour les famillieu.'[34]‡

Francis of Lorraine thus proclaimed several truths. The behaviour of judges should be based on the crime alone, and not on the social origins of the culprit. Crime, then, was strictly personal and, for that reason, the infamy that resulted from it could in no way affect the families of the culprits. Finally, punishment did not undermine the honour of the nobleman, who in any case was already dishonoured by his crimes, nor that of the families who were not concerned by the crimes of their relative. It could therefore be inflicted in all circumstances.

The emperor thereby overturned the perspectives to which Tuscany had become used under the last of the Medici. He repudiated the logic by which the respect of innocent relatives could spare a culprit who, on the sole grounds of his nobility,

---

* Without the slightest regard to the relatives or the status of the persons, since their crime does not fall on their families, and is an individual matter, and these same crimes lead to little consideration for their status.
† 'that the crime and not the families be considered, since justice is never concerned with the family'.
‡ 'without the slightest consideration of the status of anyone and only to catch the most guilty'; 'as far as other criminal trials are concerned, no consideration should be given to the relatives.'

merited some kind of consideration. He put aside aristocracy, he put aside lineage, he wanted to see only the crime. Francis of Lorraine did not stop here, however. Not only did he claim the right to punish, he regarded it as his duty.

In the emperor's eyes, the sovereign was obliged to punish the wicked. Punishment was first and foremost exemplary. It was 'nesesere poure retenire pare la peure ce que le pouen d'oneure ne peut pas'.*[35] Not to punish, on the other hand, was detrimental to justice, and made it 'suffer'[36] whereas, for the prince, justice was a lordly duty, 'un artiquel qui intéres la conscience.'†[37] Indeed, Francis Stephen was very scrupulous about this point. As was expressed by one of his most intimate collaborators, justice was a responsibility 'that His Imperial Majesty holds dear to his heart'.[38]

Francis of Lorraine's attitude, therefore, was not only a break with the Medici way. It was also very demanding, both for his subjects, and for himself. This was not without cause. It was explained by the religious fervour of the sovereign, and resulted from the idea he formed of man, of God and of the prince.

In the eyes of Francis Stephen, man was naturally inclined to sin, for which he himself was responsible and from which he had to defend himself through examining his conscience and through confession. 'It is necessary', wrote the emperor to his son Peter-Leopold, the future Leopold II, 'to warn you of a thing on which few people reflect; one's own self. It is this which makes us lose our soul and our body: it is this which causes so much evil . . . which makes us do so much wrong.'[39] And again, 'Reflect on yourself, and you will easily find these types of *inspiration*, the one which pushes you towards evil . . . and the other of the good spirit which acts in the opposite direction.'[40] This 'cross examination' of oneself alone, however, was not sufficient. According to the emperor, it was also necessary to go to confession once a week.[41]

Faced with this man who was responsible for his own

---

* 'necessary to maintain through fear that which honour cannot do'.
† 'a matter of conscience.'

damnation, was the brilliance of God. Apart from being
almighty, He was endowed with 'goodness without equal, never
failing in gentleness and infinite patience, listening to all those
who address Him'.[42] This goodness, however, did not exclude
justice, nor punishment, for God, 'apart from being the best
master, is also the most just, and punishes the slightest faults.
And it is always a favour when He punishes us in this world,
where the greatest suffering and the worst sorrows are mere
trifles in comparison to the slightest ones in the other world.'[43]
God, in a word, was 'good, but just, and inflicts small punishments on those whom He wishes to bring back to Him in order
to oblige them to reflect and to avoid committing in the future
the same deeds for which they deserved these punishments.'[44]

Between this fallible man and his benevolent, albeit repressive God, the prince occupied an intermediary position. As a
man, he was subject to sin. He had, however, to be even more
wary in that he was responsible not only for his own faults but
also those he could inspire by his bad conduct. 'You should
render yourself responsible in your conscience', he wrote in his
instructions to Peter-Leopold, 'not only for your personal sins,
but also for those that were authorized and caused by your
example.'[45] The prince, in fact, had to be perfect.

The exemplary role of the prince conferred upon him a
similarity to God. In fact, the good prince shared certain
attributes with divinity. He cultivated, like God, gentleness and
goodness. Francis Stephen never ceased to eulogize gentleness.
'In all conditions', he explained 'it is the most necessary virtue,
the most worthy, and the most sought after by everyone.'[46] The
prince, more than anyone else, had to practise it. That did not,
however, mean that he could not inflict punishment. On the
contrary, the moral perfection of the sovereign gave him
particular right to punish: 'Someone who is irreproachable',
observed the emperor, 'can punish others with more justice,
without fear and without regard to anybody.'[47] The sovereign,
like God, was thus both gentle and repressive, and his justice,
like that of his creator, was above all punitive. The sentence
'God is good, but also just, and punishes those he wishes to
bring back to Him' can be answered logically by another,

likewise from the hand of the emperor, 'Je doua la justise et punision à tout mes suget.'*[48]

These moral ideas can be summed up in a few words. Firstly, men had to be punished. The condition of the prince, then, implied the absolute obligation to punish, in the very interest of the subjects. The sovereign thus cleared his conscience. He showed his moral perfection. Finally, he behaved as God himself would behave. Punishment, in this system, therefore carried out a double function: it was beneficial for the subject who underwent it, and, for the prince who inflicted it, it was the condition and the expression of his perfection. In this light, the repressive ardour of Francis of Lorraine is not surprising.

* * *

The emperor's ideas were therefore clear cut. They were not, however, particularly new. They doubtless echoed, as has been mentioned,[49] the lessons of Fénelon and Muratori. More generally, they were penetrated by a religious sense which made sin and examination of conscience the major preoccupation of the faithful.[50] Lastly, these ideas were full of commonplaces on the art of ruling.[51]

The theme of the prince's responsibility and the necessity of punishment can be found, for instance, in the classic work *De l'art de régner* by the Jesuit Lemoyne. Like Francis Stephen, this Jesuit scholar stressed the fact that the prince was heavily responsible not only for his own sins but also for those of his subjects: 'The sins of princes', he wrote, 'cannot be small. . . . They are transferred from them to their subjects and with them go punishment and torture.' 'Whatever good or evil princes may do', he added, 'everything is in proportion to them.' Thus, 'a prince can never fall without a whole world falling with him.' Lemoyne also underlined the need for punishment, to which he opposed the dangers of clemency: 'Although recompense and punishment are both part of justice, it nevertheless seems that punishment has more impact

---

* 'Justice and the punishment of all subjects is my duty.'

and more effect, and is more demonstrative and stronger than recompense.' Clemency, on the other hand, was no more than 'honest languor' or 'specious laxity'. 'It deprives laws of vigour and magistrates of credit. . . . Sooner or later, it destroys the government by loosening authority and fear, which are equally necessary to the preservation of political harmony.'[52]

Eighty years later, another author, Duguet, in his *Institution d'un prince*, developed some ideas which are very close to those of Francis of Lorraine. He evoked the figure of a prince 'highly persuaded that he is charged with the task of representing in his conduct the behaviour of God himself.' Such a prince had to be perfect. In fact, he gave the example to his people, who based their behaviour on his. For this reason, he was 'entrusted with everything that is done and everything that is not done'. It was therefore up to him to do the impossible in order to shelter his conscience from 'the consequences of impunity'. This 'minister of God' ruled in a very similar way to that of the emperor. He paid no heed to individuals. Having in mind only the observation of laws, he refused to resort to clemency to the detriment of justice. He believed in the exemplary nature of punishment. He therefore gave few pardons and punished corrupt officials without pity. Duguet, on this subject, was more than clear: 'When their offences are definite and proved, there is no punishment that offers a better example than a dismissal, without giving in either to prayers or to repentance, if the offence is serious or if it is not the first offence and previous counsel has not been followed. . . . A weaker attitude would lead to a multiplication of culprits and would mean also multiplying punishments.'[53]

The prince, therefore, rendered God visible in his person, and approached Him by his perfection. He was responsible for his own shortcomings as well as those of his subjects and was authorized, without contradiction, to punish criminals without any consideration for their status or for their rank. Finally, people were to be punished for their own good and for that of the state. None of these ideas, in fact, were original to Francis Lorraine who, far from conceptualizing and formalizing them – he was incapable of that – did no more than develop them in an abrupt way according to the affairs presented to him. The originality of the emperor lay elsewhere, namely, in the will to transform these austere principles into actions.

Politically, this choice was not opportune. The relationship between the monarchy and the aristocracy in Tuscany had became very strained following the arrival of Francis of Lorraine to the throne in 1737. The first ten years of the new regime, in fact, were marked by a conflict that became more and more intense between the Lorraines, the faithful executants eager to carry out the will of their master, and the champions of an equilibrium which, inherited from the Medici, was also advantageous to the nobility. This conflict began during the first years of the Regency. It crystallized little by little in a radical opposition between two leaders; the Lorraine Richecourt, on the one hand, and the Florentine Ginori, on the other, the first being the incarnation of the absolute devotion to Francis of Lorraine, and the second, the resolute will to perpetuate the situation that had existed under the last of the Medici. The crisis finally reached a peak during the War of Austrian Succession, when a large part of the Florentine nobility was suspected of taking sides against Francis Stephen. It came to an end in 1746-7 with the concentration of power in the hands of Richecourt and the downfall of Ginori, who was sent to Leghorn as governor.[54]

In 1747, the very moment that the affair of the grand embezzlement from the 'Abbondanza' broke out and when the emperor began to tighten up his rigorous policies, Florentine nobility had been reduced to a battered elite class, aware of having been excluded from political power. On the whole, they remained profoundly hostile to the newcomers, whom they held in contempt while at the same time envying their power. Finally, they could not cast off the yoke that had been imposed on them. For all that, nothing authorized the Lorraines to abuse their victory. On the contrary, it was all the more advisable to calm the atmosphere, in that Count Richecourt, now master of the situation, had begun preparing some structural reforms that the traditional elite could only receive with defiance: a new law on nobility, new regulations on inheritance, a new organization of jurisdiction.

It thus becomes easy to understand the calls for clemency launched by a minister who, being in Florence, had to restore confidence with his main interlocutors.[55] The disadvantages of excessive rigour, on the other hand, were obvious: in order to make the glow of his justice shine more brightly, Francis of Lorraine ran the risk, very ill-advisedly, of increasing the rancour of a nobility he could not get rid of.

It would be tempting, at first sight, to read into the verdict of the 'Abbondanza' trial a political decision and to recognize in it a judgement meant to affect, by means of corruption, a social elite with which the new regime was not on friendly terms. This interpretation, in fact, would not be justified. Nothing in the trial would support it, whereas the main protagonists in this affair, and the emperor in particular, left much written evidence of their intentions. It seems to me to be much more accurate to say that the noblemen involved in these proceedings were not hit because they were nobles, but because they were guilty, and not for political reasons but by virtue of the moral principles highly proclaimed by the emperor. They were not condemned because of their nobility, but in spite of it. Of course, the political situation was favourable to the Lorraine authority, but there was the risk of having the punishments regarded, in the eyes of those who could not perceive the moral justifications, as perfectly wanton victimization.

*   *   *

The ideas developed by the emperor were therefore in no way original and the application of them was not very opportune. But they included deeper implications from a social point of view. In fact, they fundamentally changed the relationships between the sovereign and the aristocracy.

Under the Medici the punishment of a corrupt official of noble extraction was not only a matter between the prince and the culprit. It brought together the sovereign and a lineage the honour and wealth of which it was necessary to defend, no matter what the price. Francis Stephen, as we have already seen, radically changed the terms of this problem. By declaring that infamy was strictly personal, he broke the link that existed between punishment and the honour of families. By decreeing a law which did away with *fedecomessi* in favour of the state, he prevented the nobility from blocking the repayment of debts to the state. In a word, the emperor refused to consider his employees in relation to the interests of their households, and treated them as isolated individuals, responsible for their own transgressions, on their persons, as well as their possessions. Lineage thus ceased to form a barrier between the sovereign and his servants. The policies of Francis Stephen tended implicitly to mark a threshold between two opposing situations: the one, inherited from the Medici era, in which the prince collaborated with the representatives of families; the other, in which he dominated from high above and exercised his authority over individuals considered independently from their social sphere.

This evolution was probably not provoked deliberately by a sovereign whose intentions, there is no need to repeat, lay elsewhere. But was in keeping with the general pattern of events, and came very opportunely to the aid of important institutional transformations.

The government of Francis Stephen, in effect, was noticeably different from that of his predecessors. In the field of finances the last of the Medici had counted on loans and taxes much more than on the control of expenditure or on administrative rigour. Pressure from the sovereign on institutions had thus remained relatively limited and the rationalization of procedures had never been a vital objective for an administration that was more inclined to create new resources for itself than rigorously to exploit the tools of which it disposed. This situation was called into question by the Lorraines. Francis Stephen counted neither on the creation of new taxes nor on new loans: he resorted to these facilities only in the case of absolute necessity and in a way which, all things considered, was rather marginal. The Lorraine policy, on the other hand, was geared to a tighter control of public liquidities, a more rigorous administration of expenditure and the methodical exploitation of the existing fiscal resources.

These financial politics were shown in the establishment of a farm-general of taxes. This new institution, created in 1741, was a new administrative melting pot. It replaced what was a rather nebulous and poorly structured system by one more formally centralized under the dual control of the general board of the farm and the new 'Segreteria di Finanze'. The offices, in the provinces, were grouped into branches, the directors of which were flooded with instructions and the employees with rules. The management of business, because of this, became more and more centralized and impersonal and was less and less suited to the presence of potentates who were used to dealing with all matters alone, limiting, as far as possible, interference from central power. This led to a new type of official: a dependant and flexible employee, subject to the undisputable will of an omnipotent authority.[56]

The repressive policy of Francis of Lorraine, in this context, was very timely. On the one hand, it created a climate of insecurity which incited officials to be more rigorous. The principles on which it was founded, on the other hand, tended to modify precisely the relationship between sovereign and servants and to substitute the prince–lineage relationship with a prince–individual relationship. In that, they were exactly in line with an administrative reorganization, the implication of which for the staff was to transform gradually an administration of prominent citizens into a bureaucracy of 'functionaries'.

Here again, errors must be avoided. The repression and doctrinal declarations that accompanied it were concomitant with a certain evolution within the institutions. It does not, however, seem that they had as main objective to facilitate this evolution. If they seconded it, it is through consequences, admittedly of great importance, not explicitly planned by the sovereign.

*   *   *

After 1737, the repression of corruption followed a specific route in Tuscany. It first grew stronger when relations between the monarchy and the traditional elites were not very good and when more centralized and more impersonal administrative procedures were established. This accentuation of repression was doubtless facilitated by the loss of power of the aristocracy. Equally, it supported the administrative reorganisation led, in particular, within the farm-general. It did not, however, constitute the intention to undermine, in the guise of corruption, members of aristocracy. Neither could it have as an objective to create through greater rigour and a modification of the sovereign–employee relationship the conditions for a new institutional balance.

The problem of corruption was treated fairly independently. It would be excessive, doubtless, to wish to link the conflict with nobility, the institutional reforms and the struggle against corruption within a perfectly organic system. The attitude of the Lorraines with regard to corruption depended firstly on certain religious and moral conceptions which, although completely unoriginal, had been adopted by the sovereign and put to fervent use in his actions. Francis Stephen, thus, stayed well within that universe where corruption was seen as a moral failure. But he resolved the problems posed by this moralization in a different way to that used by his Medici predecessors. By ruling out clemency, he pushed the system which until then had managed to conciliate rigour with permissiveness into a crisis. He caused a stir within consciences. He substituted a stable situation, founded on artificial compatibility between opposites, a regime of competition between two effective contradictory discourses: on the one hand, that of culpabilization, of which the sovereign made himself the apostle, and on the other, that of lies and disculpabilization, to which officials seemed to cling.

Corrupt officials did not, however, relent. In the previous pages I outlined a chronicle of the cases of embezzlement from Tuscan financial insitutions. I was thus able to show that embezzlement was still committed during the reign of Francis Stephen.[57] Other types of abuse were also rife. Indeed, the formation of a Tuscan regiment for the war against the Prussians in 1757 was punctuated by a scandal in the supplies of the troops.[58] As for the foreigners – Lorraines or otherwise – that Francis Stephen had taken into service, they did not always shine forth for their integrity. A certain Rautvich, who commanded the fortress of Pisa, had fled following the announcement of the arrival of an inspector, having previously embezzled the funds entrusted to him.[59] Joseph-Charles de Poirot, *segretario di Guerra*, paid the price of several months' imprisonment for having traded passports.[60] The representative of the Grand Duke in Paris, the Marquis de Stainville, father of Choiseul, purely and simply stole 100,000 *livres* from his master in order to pay off his debts.[61] The imperial treasurer at Nancy, Felix-Yves de Toussaint, brother of the closest financial adviser of the emperor, died in 1760 leaving behind him almost 25,000 *livres* in outstanding debt. The affair, at first, was not taken any farther and the son of Félix-Yves, Joseph, succeeded his father. However, with the death of his uncle in May 1762, things turned sour. Indeed, in July of the same year Joseph de Toussaint found himself in prison. He was released a few years later thanks to a pardon granted by Joseph II.[62]

There was thus an evolution but an evolution which was doubly limited, both in its concept, which was still that of the traditional moralization of corruption, and in its practical implications, since violations did not in fact stop. Francis Stephen thus met with enormous difficulty. It was fairly easy to put aside clemency and the permissiveness it seemed to allow. It was far more difficult, on the other hand, to build on the ruins of clemency a new equilibrium, founded on virtue and of which punishment would have been the supreme regulator. The route taken by the Grand Duke, in fact, was unilateral. It lay in an ostensible will to be firm. However, his subjects had not the desire nor were sufficiently educated to satisfy his will. Francis Stephen decided, on his own initiative, to have virtue reign. But had this decision any sense? Was it possible in reality to decree a new order of things?

The reply to this question is undoubtedly negative. It follows then that the repressive policy pursued by the emperor could not lead to a new equilibrium of corruption. It rather replaced the existing equilibrium by a conflictual situation to which there were only three ways out: terrorism, renouncement or persuasion. Whether to impose by force a rigour that officials did not want, or to return, willy-nilly, to the past situation, or else to succeed in convincing officials of the cogency of moralization.

It is up to the historians of the Enlightenment to show whether or not, under the enlightened reign of Peter-Leopold, this third hypothesis succeeded and if the young Grand Duke was able, in the end, to place Tuscany on the road to rigour – a road which during the following century Puritan England was to follow. This reaches beyond the subject here, which is rather to underline that the effort made by Francis Stephen was, as such, condemned to failure. In that sense, his effort was typical of despotic *coups de force*, of those reactions by which monarchs attempted, once and for all, to stamp out corruption, without noticing that, because their rigour was not understood by officials, it ran the risk of falling flat and of succumbing very quickly to the sea of interventions, recommendations and justifications. Tuscany in the seventeenth and eighteenth centuries, thus, seems to me to have presented two of the three attitudes that a sovereign of the *ancien régime* could, a priori, adopt faced with the problem of corruption. The first, based on punishment, was founded a little ambitiously on the incompatibility between rigour and its opposite, while the other, centred on clemency, defended culpabilization while tolerating disculpabilization. As for the third situation, it seems to have been put into practice in the kingdom of Naples, where permissiveness remained the name of the game.[63] This may not be the complete range of possibilities, for we lack systematic historical studies on corruption.

THE FRAGILITY OF THE STATE

Throughout this work I have been concerned with a small state which was governed by a pious and peaceful prince. This virtuous monarch lived in the midst of his courtiers: he was represented abroad by ministers, and he entrusted the administration of his subjects to a body of hard-working officials. In his tribunals, judges actively defended the weak and the oppressed in his name. At the gates of the towns and the frontiers of his state, customs officials collected the duties owed to the sovereign and handed the money to cashiers who deposited it in coffers which were reputed to be inviolable. Lastly, administrators took care of the smooth running of offices where functions essential to the tranquillity of the population and to the glory of the monarchy were carried out. Thus, to the satisfaction of the ruler and for the well-being of his blessed states, the capital city was supplied with foodstuffs, the roads were kept in good condition and the waterways under control; bridges could be built, the public debt and taxes could be managed correctly and epidemics were kept at bay.

For all that, government administration suffered from some strange goings-on. The coffers of the state, which were believed to be brimful of money, were discovered to be totally empty at the most inopportune moment. There was no other possible answer to the mystery than the hypothesis that they had been pillaged by the very people to whose care they had been entrusted. High-ranking officials, in whom the prince had had confidence, had been insolently engaging in abuse of their positions. Subordinates had been assuming a little more authority than that warranted by their positions in order to commit extortion. Even judges defiled the temple of equity by succumbing to the temptation of bribes.

These defects did not enter the regime from outside. On the contrary, they originated well within the machinery of the state, where they recurred regularly in an all too familiar form. They thereby constituted a threat to the favourable realization of the beneficient intentions of the monarch.

Not everyone, however, was harmed by these dysfunctions. The authors of the crimes, for example, gained certain advantages from them. Not only did they obtain the financial means to lead the ostentatious lifestyle they believed suited to their social status, but they also provoked an evolution in which power shifted surreptitiously from the hands of the sovereign to those of his servants.

Corruption therefore fulfilled a double function. It shared out money, which public servants, being for the most part from noble extraction, needed badly. At the same time it redistributed power in favour of a born elite class who had never completely accepted the fact of its deprival.

Neither the monarch nor his subjects, however, regarded corruption as a permanent *coup d'état*. They saw it simply as a series of individual although regrettable incidents. They considered it as another form of moral deregulation. They put it down to the natural defects of a depraved human nature which only punishment could remedy. Malversation, therefore, in this state, was subject to harsh laws similar to those which condemned thieves, traitors and murderers.

This moral interpretation of corruption and its penal implications were not without effect. The less audacious officials were discouraged and the spread of the curse was thereby kept under control. At the same time, its political implications were dissimulated, and corruption, while it was seen as a purely individual phenomenon, became tolerable. The law thus carried out the twofold function of punishing misbehaviour and ensuring that it was limited to simple misdeeds.

The moralization of corruption imposed certain obligations on offenders. Firstly, lies became essential to keep up an appearance of honesty despite the most illicit practices. The law of silence, then, provided liars with a security which was further guaranteed by the fact that it was not considered the done thing to denounce one's neighbour.

Lies, however, did not suffice to allay the consciences of the more sensitive souls. The latter could then resort to casuistry and probabilism, which offered corrupt officials a glimmer of hope. Both made them feel that their much criticized actions were in fact honest and that they would not fall under the censure of either divine justice or human laws. With his innocence intact, the most reprobate of judges could furnish himself with the esteem his excess of scruples had denied.

Punishments, both terrestrial and celestial, could therefore be avoided. Despite the rigour applied by the law, an underlying permissiveness gradually enlarged the circle of justifiable acts.

Was the prince, that virtuous guardian of justice who was responsible for the sins of his subjects, going to tolerate that ever-increasing laxism? That was impossible and the severity with which he would have punished culprits would have been applauded by the good and feared by the wicked. However, punishment often came up against obstacles. Indeed, when it concerned prominent families, it even posed a delicate problem of appropriateness. The question was raised as to the legitimacy of plunging a member of nobility into infamy if that meant dragging with him his family. In a society in which honour was collective and fortunes belonged to entire families, was it appropriate to cast infamy on innocent people for the sake of punishing one culprit?

One sovereign answered these questions in the negative. This prince thus pardoned nobles and thereby granted impunity to subjects, an impunity moreover reinforced by the defence offered by lies and by theological and legal reasoning. He did not, however, give up his principles. He did not adopt the line of casuists. He contented himself quite simply with making exceptions. His courtiers were thus able to observe the exemplary clemency and heroic love for the nobility that he manifested. This clemency also made it possible to overcome the contradiction between rigour and permissiveness. It shed a moral light on a pardon, the motivation of which was, in reality, political.

This heroic weakness was not in the character of all the sovereigns who succeeded to the throne of this state. One of them, in particular, rejected that stand and insisted on fighting against all corrupt officials, no matter what their social origins, whom he regarded as individual sinners. Consciences were deeply shaken by these politics, and even the prince's ministers felt it was their duty to remind their master that a representative of the upper classes could not be punished with the same harshness as a low-class citizen. The sovereign was inflexible, but nevertheless he did not succeed in stamping out abuse.

The repressive discourse therefore came to nothing. It did not sufficiently move officials who ought to have been terrorized by it. Admittedly the sovereign was right in proclaiming that rigorous principles were incompatible with lax customs. But he was not able to decree the reign of virtue. His initiative was bound to fail, and clemency seemed likely to return in the long term.

Admonitions, therefore, did not suffice to resolve the moral questions. For that, it would have been necessary to convert subjects who were as used to regarding corruption as a sin as they were to engaging in corrupt practices while relying on lies and casuistic logic to save their souls. But that conversion must have seemed, to many, all the less urgent in that the triumph of morality, by leading to a wave of punishments, would have opened the way to the worst kind of subversiveness. Virtue, as always, could wait.

*   *   *

The system I have just described would have worked in seventeenth- and eighteenth-century Tuscany. Its limits should be clearly outlined. Firstly, in time, because there is nothing to indicate, *a priori*, that the situation would have been the same during the Renaissance[1] or during the Age of the Enlightenment. Secondly, the social context, since there is far more documentary evidence concerning corrupt nobles and town-dwellers than their obscure emulators in the country.[2] We must therefore be wary of attributing a universal value to the model I have outlined. Some aspects, such as the secondary role played by the tribunals, would not exist in a monarchical regime as judicial as the kingdom of Naples. Moreover, the culture to which it refers is obviously not that of contemporary democracies and any kind of transposition would be erroneous.

These limits, real as they may be, do not make it impossible to make some general remarks. The method I have used is founded on a few basic principles which are liable to be extended to other studies related to the same subject and which, once more, I would like to stress.

Whoever studies this problem cannot stick to a purely anecdotal approach consisting in gathering information on affairs, preferably scandalous ones, in order to recount them without investigating their meaning. That would teach us nothing. What is more, it would lead to a narration of the facts based on today's standards, that is to say, to a perfectly artificial view of the issue.

It would be just as erroneous to take the initiative to explicitly make this distortion. Nothing would be easier than to apply criteria currently in use in different political orders to the events described in historical sources. The originality and the specificity of the phenomena being studied would be veiled by an absolutely specious moralization.

There is one more danger to be avoided – less obvious, but no less pernicious than the preceding ones: that of social determinism, which, by making short work of what the people concerned really felt, would establish an arbitrary link of cause and effect between corruption and certain structural aspects of the society being observed. This link may well have existed, but it would not have been strong enough to condition radically the behaviour of individuals who, after all, also had a conscience. It is precisely that conscience which should be the main object of a history of corruption.

Corruption, therefore, cannot be tackled as an insignificant and disconnected series of minor events, nor as the ground of a purposeless declamation on the vices of Babylon, nor as the terrain of a social automatism in which the individual would vanish behind all-powerful structures.

That individual, however, acted in a system of values and standards which was not ours. Thus, the first aim which should be fixed is to reconstruct the way, or ways, in which contemporaries interpreted their relationship with power. Corruption, finally, is only a historical object in that it was, for those who lived with it, an object of perception and discourse. It is on those discourses, and their implications, imbrication and conflict, that no doubt the future of this type of behaviour depended and depends.

The state thus appears in all its fragility. It is not free to carry out a unilateral elimination of corruption. Anathema may well be reassuring, but integrity will never be imposed. As for the rules the state decrees, they may fail to attain their aim by modifying the framework of corruption, leaving corruption itself intact. The eradication of evil, in fact, does not fall within the scope only of public authority. It also depends on employees, and in the end it is they who must penetrate the meaning of transgression and of duty. From this point of view, the state is at the mercy of those who serve it.

Does that mean that there is no remedy to corruption? It does not. History has taught us that, between the end of the eighteenth century and the beginning of the twentieth, a small part of mankind was gradually converted to integrity. Nevertheless, that integrity is not a given fact, and may even appear in today's world as a curious exception to a completely different rule. A question can then be raised: why, and by what means, did corruption for the citizens of some nations go from being condemnable to impracticable? How did interdictions become veritable bars? Are we naive enough to put this evolution down to proof of the inexorable advances made by hypothetical Progress? Should we be more lucid and interpret it as the last effects of a religious culpabilization which finally extends to relationships with the state? It then remains to be seen whether or not, within a given period, the integrity of public servants depends, chiefly, on a kind of sacralization of institutions.

This problem doubtless deserves a book to itself. By posing it, however, we bring to light a simple fact: the integrity of functionaries is not natural – no more, that is, than their corruption – and the progress of the former will never rule out the possibility of the return of the latter. The state is always under threat.

NOTES

Abbreviations
ASF Archivio di Stato di Firenze
BNF Biblioteca Nazionale di Firenze

INTRODUCTION THE STORY OF CORRUPTION

1 R. Mousnier, *Les Institutions de la France sous la Monarchie absolue* (2 vols., Paris, 1974, 1980).
2 R. Mousnier, *La vénalité des offices sous Henri IV et Louis XIII*, 2nd edn (Paris, 1971), p. 151ff.
3 Y. M. Bercé, *History of Peasant Revolts* (Cambridge, 1990).
4 F. Bluche, *Les magistrats du Parlement de Paris au XVIIIᵉ siècle* (1715–1771) (Besançon, 1960), p. 277ff.
5 M. Antoine, *Le Conseil du Roi sous le règne de Louis XV* (Geneva, 1970), p. 266.
6 J.-C. Waquet, *Les grands maîtres des eaux et forêts de France de 1689 à la Révolution* (Geneva, 1978), pp. 32ff, 36, 263n, 310.
7 D. Dessert, *Colbert contre Colbert*, unpubd paper presented at the Colbert Congress, Paris, 1983.
8 There is, however, an exception: the remarkably penetrating essay, which is nevertheless very far from our period, by P. Veyne, 'Clientèle et corruption au service de l'Etat: la vénalité des offices dans le Bas-Empire romain', *Annales E. S. C.*, 36 (1981), pp. 339–60
9 J. Van Klaveren, 'Die historische Erscheinung der Korruption, in ihrem Zusammenhang mit der Staats- und Gesellschaftsstruktur

betrachtet', *Vierteljahrschrift für Sozial- und Wirtschaftsgeshichte*, 44 (1957), pp. 289–324; 45 (1958), pp. 433–504; 46 (1959), pp. 204–31. Study contd in 'Fiskalismus – Merkantilismus – Korruption: drei Aspekte der Finanz- und Wirtschaftspolitik während des Ancien Régime', ibid., 47 (1960), pp. 333–53.

10   For a rapid but evocative summary of Weberian thought on bureaucracy: M. Albrow, *Bureaucracy* (London, 1970).

11   J. C. Scott, *Comparative Political Corruption* (Englewood Cliffs, NJ, 1972), p. 4. Scott takes here the definition provided earlier by J. S. Nye, 'Corruption and political development: a cost-benefit analysis', *American Political Science Review*, 61 (1967).

12   Scott, *Comparative Political Corruption*, p. 7. For a more factual but more substantial approach to the question, see G. E. Aylmer, *The King's Servants: the civil service of Charles I, 1625–1642* (London, 1961), p. 179ff.

13   He thus uses the expression 'protocorruption' to designate the behaviour in question ('we will refer to pre-nineteenth-century practices which only became "corrupt" in the nineteenth century as "protocorruption"'; ibid., p. 8).

14   On the relationship between corruption and modernization, see, apart from Scott, *Comparative Political Corruption*, S. P. Huntington, *Political Order in Changing Societies* (New Haven, CT, and London, 1968), pp. 59–71, and A. J. Heidenheimer, *Political Corruption: readings in comparative analysis* (New York, 1970), p. 479ff.

14   Van Klaveren, 'Die historische Erscheinung', p. 224.

16   G. C. S. Benson, *Political Corruption in America* (Lexington, MA, and Toronto, 1978), pp. 29–30

17   T. Barker and J. Roebuck, *An Empirical Typology of Police Corruption: a study in organizational deviance* (Springfield, MA, 1973), p. 18.

18   R. Wraith and E. Simpkins, *Corruption in Developing Countries* (London, 963), pp. 47, 50.

19   H. Sarassoro, *La corruption des fonctionnaires en Afrique: étude de droit pénal comparé* (Paris, 1980), p. 11ff (quotation from p. 24).

20   F. Chabod, 'Usi et abusi nell'amministrazione dello Stato di Milano a mezzo il' 500', *Studi storici in onore di G. Volpe* (Florence, 1958), 1, p. 181.

21   C. Mozzarelli, *Per la storia del pubblico impiego nello stato moderno: il caso della Lombardia austriaca* (Milan, 1972), p. 116.

22   J. Hurstfield, *Freedom, Corruption and Government in Elizabethan England* (London, 1973), p. 159.

23 Van Klaveren, 'Die historische erscheinung', p. 204ff.

24 Heidenheimer, *Political Corruption*, p. 13.

25 Chabod, 'Usi et abusi', p. 110.

26 U. Petronio, *Il senato di Milano: istituzioni giuridiche ed esercizio del potere nel Ducato di Milano da Carlo V a Giuseppe II* (Milan, 1972), p. 177.

27 See, for example, J. P. Lynckerius, *Tractatio de barattaria* (Jena, 1684), p. 4; J. Bonifacius, *Liber de furtis* (Vicenza, 1619), p. 89, etc.

28 These measures were in fact modified rapidly, but that is another problem (P. L. Rovito, *Respublica dei togati: giuristi e società nella Napoli del Seicento, 1: Le garanzie giuridiche* (Naples, 1981), p. 20ff).

29 On which see D. Jousse, *Traité de la justice criminelle de France* (Paris, 1771), 4, p. 29ff.

30 On these affairs, Hurstfield, *Freedom, Corruption and Government*, pp. 145, 167, 183ff.

31 Heidenheimer, *Political Corruption*, p. 5.

32 Reported by Duval, the imperial librarian of the time, and quoted in M. Payard, *Mémoires de Valentin Jamerey-Duval* (Tours, 1929), p. 387.

33 Jean-Claude Waquet, *Le grand-duché de Toscane sous les derniers Médicis. Essai sur le système des finances et la stabilité des institutions dans les anciens Etats italiens*, Rome, Ecole française de Rome, 1990, (Bibliothèque des écoles françaises d'Athènes et de Rome, 276).

34 Rovito, *Respublica dei togati*, pp. 63, 68.

35 Chabod, 'Usi et abusi', p. 182.

36 On this point, see chapter 4.

37 Refer to J. Delumeau, *Le péché et la peur: la culpabilisation en Occident (XIIIᵉ–XVIIIᵉ siècle)* (Paris, 1983).

38 Sarassoro, *La corruption des fonctionnaires en Afrique*, p. 33. See also Wraith and Simpkins, *Corruption in Developing Countries*, p. 45, on the subject of corruption that 'has nothing to do with traditional values, with the African personality, or with the adaptation to western values; those responsible for it have no difficulty in adapting to western values if they want to. Its simple cause is avarice; the wrong that is done is done in the full knowledge that it is wrong.'

39 Wraith and Simpkins, *Corruption in Developing Countries*, p. 33.

40 Hurstfield, *Freedom, Corruption and Government*, p. 159.

41 R. Merton, 'Functional analysis in sociology', *Social Theory and*

Social Structure (New York, 1968). Merton's analysis will be developed further on.

42 Richecourt to Francis of Lorraine, 2 Nov 1738 (ASF, 'Reggenza' 13, fo. 428).

43 Idem, 11 Oct 1737 and 2 Nov 1738 (ASF, 'Reggenza' 12, fo. 77; 13, fo. 427ᵛ).

PART I THE SOUND OF MONEY
INTRODUCTION

1 On functional analysis, R. Merton, 'Functional analysis in sociology', in *Social Theory and Social Structure* p. 59, from which quotations are taken.

2 G. C. S. Benson, *Political Corruption in America* (Lexington, MA, and Toronto, 1978), pp. 17–56, 89–118, offers an analysis of machine politics, with bibliography.

3 Merton, 'Functional analysis in sociology', p. 119, from which quotations are taken.

CHAPTER 1 THE GRAND EMBEZZLEMENT FROM THE 'ABBONDANZA'

1 On the Buonaventuri affair, see the 'Diario fiorentino' of A. Squarcialupi (BNF, II, III, 457, 21 Sept 1731, 14 Oct 1733, 20 Jan 1734); the 'Diario' of C. Settimanni (ASF, MS 144, fo. 624–637ᵛ); the private archives of the Corsini family (St. 2a, Arm. A, 16: correspondence of C. Ginori with B. Corsini, 13 Oct–3 Nov 1731); 'Difesa della buona fama dell'illustriss. signor Tommaso Buonaventuri . . .' and 'Informazione a difesa del sig. dottor Bartolommeo Benini' (BNF, Palat. (11) C.9.5.6. LIVm and b); and 'Buonaventuri', in *Dizionario biografico degli Italiani*, 15 (Rome, 1972).

2 BNF, II, III, 457 (21 Sept 1731).

3 'Diario' of C. Settimanni, fo. 624ᵛ.

4 On the grand embezzlement from the 'Abbondanza', see essentially: the dispatches from Count Richecourt, regent in Florence (ASF, 'Reggenza' 21, fo. 91, 136, 140, 201; 22, fo. 186, 326, 354; 23, fo. 459; 'Finanze' 75, fo. 99); the deliberations of the Council of Vienna and the notes added by the emperor (ASF, 'Reggenza'

357); the transcription of the proceedings contained in ASF, 'Reggenza' 206–209; the report of the judges and the sentence conserved in ASF 'Reggenza' 736; various letters and evidence contained in ASF, 'Abbondanza' 124–128, 'Miscellanea di Finanza' A, 217, and 'Miscellanea di Finanza' B, 'Abbondanza' 15. Unless otherwise indicated, the facts described were taken from these files.

5 R. Del Bruno, *Ristretto delle cose più notabili della città di Firenze*, 6th edn (Florence, 1757) pp. 146–7.

6 On the 'Abbondanza' in Florence, the history of which cannot be given here, see A. M. Pult Quaglia, 'Controls over food supplies in Florence in the late XVIth and early XVIIth centuries', *Journal of European Economic History* 9 (1980), pp. 449–57, and, for the eighteenth century, M. Mirri, *La lotta politica in Toscana intorno alle 'riforme annonarie'* (n.p., n.d.). On the sales from the 'Abbondanza', there is an interesting dispatch from Richecourt in ASF, 'Finanze' 75, fo. 99ff (15 Aug 1747). For a more international approach on the techniques used for conserving grain: M. Gast and F. Sigaut, *La technique de conservation des grains à long terme: leur rôle dans la dynamique des systèmes de cultures et des sociétés*, 2 vols. (Paris, 1979, 1981).

7 Inventory of the building in ASF, 'Abbondanza' 124, no. 272.

8 G. A. Farulli, *Cronologia dell'antichissima e nobilissima famiglia de' Gaetani di Firenze, che è la medesima di Pisa, di Napoli, di Roma, di Anagni, di Gaeta, di Siracusa e di Palermo* (Florence, 1722), esp. pp. 5, 13.

9 Quotation taken from a report of the Council of Vienna of 5 Oct 1747 (ASF, 'Reggenza' 357).

10 The best narrative of this arrest is the 'Diario fiorentino' of Squarcialupi (BNF, II, III, 457, 24 Aug 1747).

11 Quotation taken from the testimony of L. Rossi, 26 Aug 1747 (ASF, 'Reggenza' 206, fo. 416ᵛ).

12 ASF, 'Reggenza' 206, fo. 212 (letter dated 8 July 1747).

13 ASF, 'Reggenza' 208, fo. 1265 (letter dated 23 Oct 1747).

14 Summary of these operations in dispatch from Richecourt; see note 6.

15 ASF, 'Depositeria generale' 1473, and 'Miscellanea di Finanza' B, 'Abbondanza' VI.

CHAPTER 2   JUST ONE OF MANY CASES OF EMBEZZLEMENT

1   See sources given in note 2.
2   Apart from the cases of embezzlement mentioned in the text, others included: G. Gasperi (1618, 'Possessioni' in Pisa, 1,585 *scudi*); O. Guidetti (1632 at the latest, grand ducal household, 9,949 *scudi*); A. Melari (1636, 'Monte Pio' in Siena, at least 2,716 *scudi*); A. Martellini (1636, 'Abbondanza' in Florence, 8,866 *scudi*); G. Ubaldini (1637, 'Possessioni', at least 2,000 *scudi*); P. Panizzi (1650, 'Abbondanza', 1,525 *scudi*); J. Guglielmi (1663, 'Abbondanza', 2,052 *scudi*); V. Nelli (1666, Siena Treasury, 34,280 *scudi*); A. Parri (before 1670, 'Possessioni', 1,337 *scudi*); L. Rossiroti (1671, 'Gabella dei Contratti', 6,000 *scudi*); M. A. Sostegni (1675, 'Dogana', Florence, about 10,000 *scudi*); I. Niccolini (1688, 'Gabella dei Contratti', 3,245 *scudi*); F. Della Rena (1689 at the latest, 'Fortezze', amount unknown); T. Massi (1690, Commune of Galeata, 1,800 *scudi*); C. Spigliati (1694 at the latest, 'Gabella' and 'Monte del Sale', 1,681 *scudi*); G. Verdi (1699, 'Magona', 9,405 *scudi*); V. Borghigiani (1733, 'Magona', 17,428 *scudi*). For all these cases, and for the ones quoted in the text, the following sources were used: ASF, 'Depositeria generale' 278 (Del Pugliese), 1242 (Bonsi-Bucetti, Mancini), 1473 (Paoli, Venturi-Gallerani) and 1475 (Mancini); 'Fabbriche' 1940 (Pandolfini), MS 142 (Del Pugliese) and 143 (Grifoni, Bettazzi); 'Mediceo' 1670 (Del Pugliese) and 1798 (Rustici); 'Miscellanea di Finanza' A, 477 and 497 (Paoli); 'Miscellanea Medicea' 365 (Ubaldini) and 366 (Mercianti); 'Monte delle Graticole' 401 (Guidetti), 402 (Bindi), 403 (Verdi), 404 (Teri), 405 (Alessandri), 407–409 (Malegonelle, Amiconi, Bussotti) and 411 (Bati, De'Luigi); 'Nove' 767 (Massi) and 1268 (Chiti); 'Reggenza' 189 (Ghezzi, Melari, Rustici) and 744 (Del Turco); 'Finanze' 453 (Borghigiani); 'Sindaci' 137 (Ambrogi, Parri, Sostegni, Zampogni), 140 (Catignani, Chivani, Guidetti), 166 (Bussotti, Della Rena, Gasperi, Gherardini, Guglielmi, Martellini, Nelli, Niccolini, Panizzi, Rossiroti, Spigliati, Teri, Verdi), 668–669 (Alessandri), 722 (Fioravanti), 723–725 (Gherardini), 727–733 (Malegonelle), 734 (Mearelli, Del Feo) 736–738 (Nelli); private archives of the Corsini family, St. 2a, Arm. A, 16 (Buonaventuri-Benini, Capei); Milan, Ambrosian Library, X 249 inf. (Chiti-Cremoni).
3   ASF, 'Conventi soppresi' 84/73 fo. 3.
4   ASF, 'Reggenza' 866, no. 9 (1744).

5   ASF, 'Reggenza' 357.
6   ASF, 'Reggenza' 210 (12 Feb 1745) and 738, file 'seta'.
7   BNF, II, III, 457 (the 'Diario fiorentino' of Squarcialupi, 15 June 1748).
8   ASF, 'Nove' 1169 (17 Aug 1696).
9   ASF, 'Regia Consulta' 293 (29 July 1748).
10 BNF, Magliab. XXV, 42 ('Diario' of F. Bonazzini, 31 Aug 1680).
11 ASF, 'Archivio Gondi' 95.
12 ASF, 'Carte Strozziane', V, 1259, 9 Nov 1722 (I owe the indica-tion of this document to the kindness of Adam Manikowski, of the University of Białystok, Poland.) At the end of the Medici era the average annual product of the 'Gabella dei Contratti' was 200,860 liras (ASF, 'Finanza' 23, no. 17).
13 See sources given in note 2.
14 Idem.
15 Idem.
16 Idem.
17 BNF, II, III, 457 (7 July 1748).
18 ASF, 'Reggenza' 744, file 4 (the events occurred in 1743).
19 G. Conti, *Decisiones Florentinae, Tomus secundus, Pars prima* ... (Florence, 1775), p. 173ff. (the events occurred in 1713).
20 Private archives of the Antinori family, correspondence of the War Secretary G. Antinori, vol. XIV (4 Feb. 1757).
21 ASF, 'Nove' 1160 (22 May 1692).
22 M. A. Savelli, *Summa diversorum tractatuum, II* (Bologna, 1685), p. 325ff. (quotation on p. 331).
23 ASF, 'Reggenza' 189.
24 Private archives of the Da Verrazzano family, 103 (20 June 1736).

PART II   DISSOLUTE MORALS
INTRODUCTION

1   F. Chabod, 'Usi et abusi nell'amministrazione dello Stato di Milano a mezzo il '500', *Studi storici in onore di G. Volpe* (Florence, 1958), 1, p. 142.
2   W. Paravicini, *L'émergence des bureaucrates*, report presented to the XIV Settimana di Studio organized by the Istituto internazionale di storia economica Francesco Datini, Prato, 1982, p. 8.

3 J. Hurstfield, *Freedom, Corruption and Government in Elizabethan England* (London, 1973), p. 155.
4 P. L. Rovito, *Respublica dei togati: giuristi e società nella Napoli del Seicento, 1: Le garanzie giuridiche* (Naples, 1981), p. 137.
5 J. C. Scott, *Comparative Political Corruption* (Englewood Cliffs, NJ, 1972), p. 13.
6 H. Sarassoro, *La corruption des fonctionnaires en Afrique: étude de droit pénal comparé* (Paris, 1980), p. 28.
7 F. Chabod, 'Stipendi nominali e busta paga effettiva dei funzionari dell'amministrazione milanese alla fine del cinquecento', *Miscellanea in onore di Roberto Cessi* (Rome, 1958), p. 204.
8 S. Huntington, *Political Order in Changing Societies* (New Haven, CT, and London, 1968), pp. 63–4.
9 J. Scott, *Comparative Political Corruption*, p. 20ff., and 'Corruption in underdeveloped countries', *Cultures et développement*, 5 (1973), p. 107 (quotations).
10 These two hypotheses can in fact be combined: it is perfectly plausible to imagine a case in which corruption satisfied both a political demand from excluded minorities as well as an economic demand from civil servants.

CHAPTER 3 APPROPRIATING THE STATE

1 See sources given in chapter 1, note 4, and chapter 2, note 2.
2 ASF, 'Archivio Gondi' 95, 1 March 1743.
3 I will publish the results of the survey in a more extensive work on Tuscany in the seventeenth and eighteenth centuries.
4 Here, I refer to a study currently being prepared (in collaboration with Adam Manikowski) on prices and salaries in Florence.
5 ASF, MS 142, fo. 345, and 'Sindaci' 723–725.
6 Benini: 'Difesa della buona fama dell'illustriss. signor Tommaso Buonaventuri' (BNF, Palat. (11) C.9.5.6. LIVm and b); Teri: ASF, MS 142, fo. 22 (Sept 1713); Durazzi: BNF, II, III, 457 (7 July 1748).
7 ASF, 'Reggenza' 206, fo. 382, 395ff, 431, 432 (Borgherini); ibid., fo. 522ᵛ (Gaetani). For Roncalli, see source given in chapter 2, note 22.
8 ASF, 'Reggenza' 206, fo. 1128ff.
9 P. Cavallo, *Resolutionum criminalium . . . centuriae duae* (Venice, 1644), p. 152.

10 To the Grand Duke, 29 Aug 1747 (ASF, 'Reggenza' 21, fo. 137ᵛ).
11 See source given in chapter 2, note 2.
12 On the mint, Richecourt's dispatch to the Grand Duke in ASF, 'Reggenza' 17, fo. 681ff; 19, fo. 221ff (11 Sept 1742 and 5 June 1744).
13 On the Paoli affair, apart from dispatches contained in ASF 'Reggenza' 16–19, see the very important judges' report conserved (unfortunately incomplete) in ASF, 'Miscellanea di Finanza' A, 477 and 497.
14 ASF, 'Archivio Gondi' 95 (1 March 1743).
15 ASF 'Parte', 'numeri neri' 2047 (defence presented by Guadagni, 3 Sept 1767). The judges claimed in a report dated 2 Oct 1768 (ibid.) that 'the authority of the *provveditore* in this administration is at the most equivalent to that of an administrator'. The *provveditore*, they added, did not have the authority to 'do as he wished concerning the repaving'.
16 On all these affairs, see sources given in chapter 2, notes 5, 11, 12, 19.
17 On this point, G. Brucker, *Dal Comune alla Signoria: la vita pubblica a Firenze nel primo Rinascimento* (Bologna, 1981), p. 40ff.
18 P. Malanima, *I Riccardi di Firenze: una famiglia e un patrimonio nella Toscana dei Medici* (Florence, 1977), p. 212ff.
19 Buonaventuri: see sources given in chapter 1, note 1. Malegonelle: ASF, 'Sindaci' 733.
20 ASF, 'Miscellanea di Finanza' A, 217 (concerns assets that are 'liberi', that is, not bound by *fedecommessi*). Quotations from ASF, 'Reggenza' 206, fo. 210, 423, 481.
21 ASF, 'Miscellanea di Finanza' A, 217, and 'Reggenza' 206, fo. 224ᵛ, 522ᵛ.
22 F. Diaz, *Il granducato di Toscana: i Medici* (Turin, 1976), p. 471.
23 R. B. Lichtfield, 'Office-holding in Florence after the Republic', *Renaissance Studies in Honor of Hans Baron* (Florence, 1971), pp. 531–55.
24 F. Duffo, *Un voyage en Italie au XVIIe siècle* (Paris, 1930), p. 78.
25 ASF, 'Archivio Antinori' 25, file 288.
26 J.-C. Waquet, 'La gestion des finances toscanes des Médicis aux Lorraine (vers 1700–1765); le sens d'un changement de dynastie', 1979, unpubd.
27 ASF, 'Reggenza' 18, fo. 61 (15 Jan 1743).
28 Richecourt to Pecci, director general of finances, 1 and 30 April 1753 (ASF, 'Miscellanea di Finanza' A, 290).

29 Milan, Ambrosian Library, X 223 inf., fo. 304 (24 April 1758).
30 File on this affair in ASF, 'Parte', 'numeri neri' 2047–2050, and 'Miscellanea di Finanza' A, 494.

CHAPTER 4 THE MISFORTUNES OF VIRTUE
1   M. A. Savelli, 'Compendium de qualitatibus judicis perfecti', *Summa diversorum tractatuum*, 1 (Florence, 1677), p. 26.
2   G. Berart y Gassol, *Speculum visitationis* (Barcelona, 1627), p. 133.
3   L. A. Muratori, *Dei difetti della giurisprudenza* (Venice, 1742), p. 93 ('questi non sono giudici cristiani, sono assassini della giustizia').
4   Berart y Gassol, *Speculum visitationis*, p. 134; M. A. Savelli, 'Discursus de prohibita munerum et praecum datione', *Summa diversorum tractatuum*, 1, p. 5; G. Mastrillo, *De magistratibus* (Lyon, 1621), p. 173; Muratori, *Dei difetti della giurisprudenza*, p. 91.
5   P. Guyot, *Répertoire universel et raisonné de jurisprudence*, XVI (Paris, 1777), pp. 238–9.
6   Aristotle, *The Nicomachian Ethics*, ed. H. Rackam (Cambridge, MA, and London, 1982), pp. 111, 259, 269, 277.
7   Aristotle, *The 'Art' of Rhetoric*, trans. J. H. Freese (London, 1967), p. 7.
8   Mastrillo, *De magistratibus*, p. 170; Muratori, *Dei difetti della giurisprudenza*, p. 49.
9   Deuteronomy 16: 19; Exodus 23: 8; Ecclesiasticus 20: 29; Isaiah 5: 23, and 33: 15–16; Psalms 15: 1 and 5; Job 15: 34.
10 'Corruption', in *Le dictionnaire de l'Académie françoise* (Paris, 1694).
11 'Corruzione', in *Vocabolario degli accademici della Crusca*, 5th edn (Venice, 1741).
12 All quotations, as those of the preceding paragraph, are taken from J. Delumeau, *Le péché et la peur: la culpabilisation en Occident (XIIIᵉ–XVIIIᵉ siècle)* (Paris, 1983), pp. 137, 277, 301, 315, 523, 526 and 557.
13 *Encyclopédie ou dictionnaire raisonné des sciences, des arts et des métiers*, IV (Paris, 1754), p. 278.
14 Aristotle, *The Complete Works*, ed. J. Barnes (Princeton, NJ, 1984), p. 520.
15 A. Bonadeo, *Corruption, Conflict and Power in the Works and Times of Niccolò Machiavelli* (Berkeley, Los Angeles and London, 1973), pp. 3–28.
16 Montesquieu, 'The Spirit of the Laws', in M. Richter, *The Political Theory of Montesquieu* (Cambridge, 1977), pp. 224–5.

17 Private archives of the Da Verrazzano family, 51 (Aug 1738).
18 Richecourt to Pecci, the general manager of finances, 23 May and 20 June 1753 (ASF, 'Miscellanea di Finanza' A, 290).
19 Richecourt to Francis II, 2 Nov 1738 (ASF, 'Reggenza' 13, fo. 431).
20 Law of 12 Feb 1550 and 19 Dec 1576 (L. Cantini, *Legislazione toscana*, II (Florence, 1800), p. 151; VIII (Florence, 1803), p. 315).
21 For the statute of 1415, A. Pertile, *Storia del diritto italiano*, V: *Storia del diritto penale* (Turin, 1892), p. 657; 'ordine' of 26 Sept 1622 and the law of 9 Sept 1681 in ASF, 'Monte delle Graticole' 402; law of 15 June 1562 in Cantini, *Legislazione toscana*, IV (Florence, 1802), p. 370.
22 The declared object of the law of 12 Feb 1550, cited in note 20, is to avoid gifts being able to 'corrompere gl'animi' of judges.
23 One could object, following the line taken by M. Foucault (*Surveiller et punir: naissance de la prison*, Paris, 1975, p. 52ff) that, in the penal system of the *ancien régime*, all criminals were considered as rebels; it follows then that any crime and any punishment had political implications. Be that as it may, however, the moralization of corruption enabled the collective threat to be transformed into an insubordination which, being limited to the individual, could not represent a serious danger to the state.

Is THERE A UNIVERSAL MODEL?

1 See Introduction, note 42.
2 I. Zemtsov, *La corruption en Union soviétique* (Paris, 1976), p. 73.
3 Ibid., p. 98.
4 See Introduction, note 18.
5 Zemtsov, *La corruption en Union soviétique*, p. 67ff.
6 P. Veyne, 'Clientèle et corruption au service de l'Etat: la vénalité des offices dans le Bas-Empire romain', *Annales E. S. C*, 36 (1981), p. 351ff.
7 C. Simis, *La société corrompue: le monde secret du capitalisme soviétique* (Paris, 1983), pp. 43–4.
8 A. Besançon, 'Eloge de la corruption en Union soviétique', in Zemtsov, *La corruption en Union soviétique*, p. 17ff.
9 Great Soviet Encyclopedia: a translation of the third edition, XIII (New York, 1976), p. 165.

10 Ibid., V (New York), 1974), p. 53.
11 Zemtsov, *La corruption en Union soviétique*, pp. 60ff, 98; Simis, *La société corrompue*, p. 91.
12 Zemtsov, *La corruption en Union soviétique*, p. 145.

PART III   CONSCIENCES AT PEACE
INTRODUCTION

1 G. Conti, *Decisiones Florentinae, tomus secundus, Pars prima* ... (Florence, 1775), p. 174.
2 See p. 49.
3 See p. 93.

CHAPTER 5   ON THE STRENGTH OF LIES

1 P. L. Rovito, *Respublica dei togati: giuristi e società nella Napoli dei Seicento*, 1: *Le garanzie giuridiche* (Naples, 1981), p. 68.
2 F. Chabod, 'Usi et abusi nell'amministrazione dello Stato di Milano a mezzo il '500', *Studi storici in onore di G. Volpe* (Florence, 1958), 1, pp. 177, 184.
3 See p. 150ff.
4 A. Pertile, *Storia del diritto italiano*, V: *Storia del diritto penale* (Turin, 1892), p. 656.
5 Florence, Library of the Accademia Colombaria, MS II, I, 28 (8 Oct 1773).
6 ASF, MS 142, fo. 22.
7 Sources: see the observation made in the Introduction, note 33.
8 Ubaldini: ASF, 'Miscellanea Medicea' 365, file 32 (1637); Malegonelle: ASF, 'Sindaci' 728.
9 J. K. Campbell, *Honour, Family and Patronage: a study of institutions and moral values in a Greek mountain community* (Oxford, 1964), p. 235.
10 Conti: see p. 49. Gondi: ASF, 'Archivio Gondi' 95.
11 ASF, 'Reggenza' 206, fo. 200 (quotation), 542^{v}ff.
12 Private archives of the Corsini family, St. 2a, Arm. A, 16 (Carlo Ginori to Bartolommeo Corsini, 16 Oct 1731).
13 ASF, 'Reggenza' 357 (5 Oct 1747).
14 ASF, 'Reggenza' 206, fo. 243ff (quotation at fo. 251).
15 See p. 106.

16 BNF, MS II, III, 457, 7 July 1748.
17 Chabod, 'Usi et abusi', pp. 117, 119, 124.
18 M. A. Savelli, *Summa diversorum tractatuum*, III (Bologna, 1683), p. 371.
19 Advice of 12 Feb 1745 (ASF, 'Reggenza' 210).
20 ASF, 'Reggenza' 206, fo. 447^{v}ff.
21 Ibid., fo. 557.
22 Ibid., fo. 417^v.
23 Ibid., fo. 237^v.
24 See p. 35.
25 By means of what were known as nominations *a mano*.
26 ASF, 'Reggenza' 206, fo. 100, 236, 476^v, 545, 561, and 'Reggenza' 21, fo. 203 (Richecourt to the emperor, 19 Dec 1747).
27 ASF, 'Reggenza' 206, fo. 75–75^v.
28 Ibid., fo. 84, 150^v, 267.
29 All these matters have been discussed in a work yet to be published: 'La gestion des finances toscanes des Médicis aux Lorraine (vers 1700–1765): le sens d'un changement de dynastie'. This topic is also discussed in my thesis, *Le grand-duché de Toscane sous les derniers Médicis*. On the Gaetani and Alberti situation: ASF, 'Miscellanea di Finanza' B, 'Abbondanza' 15 ('ricordo' of 15 July 1747 and letter of the 'Soprassindaci' to the emperor dated 7 July 1747).
30 Private archives of the Corsini family, St. 2a, Arm. A, 16 (attached to a letter from C. Ginori dated 3 Nov 1731).
31 ASF, 'Reggenza' 127, 2 May 1740.
32 Private archives of the Antinori family, correspondence of the War Secretary G. Antinori, vol. XIV, 4 Feb 1757.
33 P. Cavallo, *Resolutionum criminalium ... centuriae duae* (Venice, 1644), p. 152.
34 ASF, 'Reggenza' 206, fo. 170^{v}ff, 198^v, 359, 512ff, 533^v, and 'Reggenza' 207, fo. 620, 664ff, 851^v, 1169 (quotation).
35 ASF, MS 173, no. 10 (diary of G. F. Dei, 24 Augt 1747: contains a copy of Alberti's note).
36 ASF, 'Miscellanea di Finanza' B, 'Abbondanza' 15, undated letters (around 1737).

CHAPTER 6   SAVED BY REASON

1 G. Mastrillo, *De magistratibus* (Lyons, 1621), p. 264.

2   G. Berart y Gassol, *Speculum visitationis* (Barcelona, 1627), p. 134.
3   J. Bonifacius, *Liber de furtis* (Vicenza, 1619), pp. 194, 199.
4   D. Jousse, *Traité de la justice criminelle de France* (Paris, 1771), III, p. 778.
5   J. P. Lynckerius, *Tractatio de barattaria* (Jena, 1684), pp. 3–4.
6   M. A. Savelli, *Summa diversorum tractatuum*, III (Bologna, 1683), p. 369.
7   A de Escobar y Mendoza, *Liber theologiae moralis* (Lyon, 1659), pp. 308–311.
8   Quoted by J. Delumeau, *Le péché et la peur: la culpabilisation en Occident (XIIIe–XVIIIe siècle)* (Paris, 1983), p. 227.
9   Berart y Gassol, *Speculum visitationis*, pp. 2–3, 133.
10 Delumeau, *Le péché et la peur*, pp. 416ff, 447ff.
11 A. Laingui, *La responsabilité pénale dans l'ancien droit (XVIe–XVIIIe siècle)* (Paris, 1970), p. 6ff.
12 B. Lamy, *Entretiens sur les sciences . . .*, ed. P. Clair and F. Girbal (Paris, 1966), p. 289.
13 See above, chapter 2.
14 C. Loyseau, *Cinq livres du droit des offices* (Paris, 1610), p. 167.
15 Jousse, *Traité de la justice criminelle de France* IV, p. 26.
16 Savelli, *Summa diversorum tractatuum*, III, p. 365.
17 P. Cavallo, *Resolutionum criminalium . . . centuriae duae* (Venice, 1644), p. 152ff.
18 Berart y Gassol, *Speculum visitationis*, p. 149 (proposition no. 8); Mastrillo, *De magistratibus*, p. 273.
19 Berart y Gassol, *Speculum visitationis*, p. 149 (proposition no. 6).
20 Bonifacius, *Liber de furtis*, p. 197 (proposition no. 76).
21 Cavallo, *Resolutionum criminalium*, pp. 150–62.
22 J. Menochio, *De arbitrariis judicum quaestionibus et causis* (Cologne, 1672), p. 994ff.
23 Savelli, *Summa diversorum tractatuum*, III, p. 452ff.
24 Law of 9 Sept 1681 in ASF, 'Monte delle Graticole' 402.
25 Jousse, *Traité de la justice criminelle de France*, IV, p. 30ff.
26 ASF, 'Reggenza' 209, fo. 329, 404^v; 'Reggenza' 736.
27 Escobar y Mendoza, *Liber theologiae moralis*, p. 371.
28 Ibid., p. 378ff.
29 A. Diana, *Resolutiones morales*, I (Anvers, 1637), I, VIII, 32.
30 Escobar y Mendoza, *Liber theologiae moralis*, p. 152.
31 Ibid.
32 Diana, *Resolutiones morales*, I, II, XVII, 43.
33 Ibid., I, I, VII, 58.

34 G. Conti, *Decisiones Florentinae, Tomus secundus, Pars prima* ... (Florence, 1775), p. 183.
35 Savelli, *Summa diversorum tractatuum*, III, p. 368.
36 Jousse, *Traité de la justice criminelle de France*, III, p. 786ff.
37 Lynckerius, *Tractatio de barattaria*, pp. 39–43, 62, 67.
38 J. Menochio, quoted by Lynckerius, ibid., p. 43.
39 Bonifacius, *Liber de furtis*, p. 203.
40 L. Molina, *De justitia*, I (Venice, 1594), p. 374.
41 Diana, *Resolutiones morales*, I, III, V, 45.
42 Ibid.
43 Ibid., I, III, V, 55.
44 Ibid., I, II, XVII, 60.
45 Molina, *De justitia*, I, pp. 374–5.
46 Savelli, 'Discursus ...', in *Summa diversorum tractatuum*, I, p. 3ff.
47 L.A. Muratori, *Dei difetti della giurisprudenza* (Venice, 1742), pp. 8, 20.
48 B. Pascal, *Provincial Letters* (Griffith, Farran, Okeden and Welsh, 1889).
49 M. Petrocchi, *Il problema del lassismo nel secolo XVII* (Rome, 1953), p. 15ff; 'Probabilismo', 'Probabiliorismo', 'Tuziorismo', 'Lassismo', in *Enciclopedia cattolica*.
50 Savelli, 'Discursus ...', in *Summa diversorum tractatuum*, I. p. 22.
51 F. Delerue, *Le système moral de Saint Alphonse de Liguori* (Saint-Etienne, 1929), p. 19ff.
52 Muratori, *Dei difetti della giurisprudenza*, p. 110.
53 J. Guerber, *Le ralliement du clergé français à la morale liguorienne* (Rome, 1973), p. 1ff.
54 M. Petitdidier, *Justification de la morale et de la discipline de l'Eglise de Rome et de toute l'Italie* (Etival, 1727), pp. 61–9.
55 C. Sommervogel, *Bibliothèque de la Compagnie de Jésus* ... (Brussels and Paris, 1890–1900), see P. G. Antoine.
56 Delumeau, *Le péché et la peur*, pp. 373, 376, 423, 431, 437, 458, 467, 538.
57 E. Appolis, *Entre jansénistes et zelanti: le 'Tiers Parti' catholique au XVIIIe siècle* (Paris, 1960), p. 135.
58 Ibid., p. 139.
59 S. De'Ricci, *Memorie*, ed. A. Gelli (Florence, 1865), I, pp. 21–2.
60 R. Tanzini, *Istoria dell'assemblea degli arcivescovi e vescovi della Toscana tenuta in Firenze l'anno MDCCLXXXVII* (Florence, 1788), I, pp. xii–xiv.

PART IV THE JUSTICE OF THE LORD
INTRODUCTION

1 F. Chabod, 'Usi et abusi nell'amministrazione dello Stato di Milano a mezzo il '500', *Studi storici in onore di G. Volpe* (Florence, 1958), 1, p. 182ff.
2 J. Hurstfield, *Freedom, Corruption and Government in Elizabethan England* (London, 1973), p. 167ff.
3 D. Dessert, *Colbert contre Colbert*, unpubd paper presented at the Colbert Congress, Paris, 1983.
4 P. L. Rovito, *Respublica dei togati: giuristi e società nella Napoli del Seicento, 1: Le garanzie giuridiche* (Naples, 1981).

CHAPTER 7 THE GRANDEUR OF CLEMENCY

1 BNF, Magliab. XXV, 42 (8 Oct 1685).
2 Ibid. (14 Feb 1674).
3 Ibid. (2 July 1678; quotation); ASF, MS 141 (31 Jan 1705).
4 Affair quoted in ASF, 'Miscellanea di Finanza' A, 477 (13 Sept 1743).
5 BNF, Magliab. XXV, 42, 30 June 1679.
6 *Descrizione dei deliquenti stati condannati a morte in Firenze comincian-do dal 1328 fino al presente anno* ... (Florence, 1801), p. 14.
7 ASF, 'Nove' 1160 (report of 22 May 1692); the culprit, however, had fled.
8 ASF, 'Nove' 1186 (report of 6 Aug 1705 concerning events dating from 1696).
9 G. Conti, *Decisiones Florentinae, Tomus secundus, Pars prima* ... (Florence, 1775), p. 186.
10 See p. 25. ·
11 ASF, MS 143 (16 Oct 1728).
12 ASF, 'Mediceo' 1734 (26 Jan 1737).
13 ASF, 'Monte delle Graticole' 404.
14 ASF, 'Nove' 3500 (22 Dec 1736).
15 P. Cavallo, *Resolutionum criminalium ... centuriae duae* (Venice, 1644), p. 162.
16 M. A. Savelli, *Summa diversorum tractatuum* (Bologna, 1683), II, P. 341, and III, p. 376.
17 Savelli, 'Discursus de prohibita munerum et praecum datione', *Summa diversorum tractatuum*, 1, p. 19.

18 Conti, *Decisiones Florentinae*, II, 1, p. 174.
19 ASF, 'Reggenza' 209, fo. 386.
20 A. Tiraqueau, *De poenis* (Lyon, 1559), p. 133.
21 ASF, 'Miscellanea Medicea' 365, file 32.
22 ASF, 'Mediceo' 1683 (7 July 1716).
23 Teri: ASF, 'Monte delle Graticole' 404; Malegonelle: ASF, 'Monte delle Graticole' 408 and 'Sindaci' 732.
24 ASF, 'Sindaci' 725.
25 ASF, 'Monte delle Graticole' 405.
26 ASF, 'Monte delle Graticole' 403.
27 Milan, Ambrosian Library, X 249 inf., file 1 (undated report concerning events of 1745).
28 ASF, 'Reggenza' 21, fo. 244^v (report of 6 Oct 1747).
29 ASF, 'Reggenza' 22, fo. 187 (to the emperor, 23 March 1748).
30 BNF, Magliab XXV, 42 (14 Feb 1674).
31 Ibid. (11 Nov 1677).
32 Florence, private archives of the Antinori family, correspondence of the War Secretary G. Antinori, vol. XIV (to the governor of Pistoia, 8 Feb 1757).
33 Ibid. (to G. Antinori, 4 Feb 1757).
34 BNF, Magliab. XXV, 42 (18 Jan 1641); *Descrizione dei deliquenti*, p. 16.
35 BNF, Magliab. XXV, 42 (14 Feb 1674).
36 Ibid. (30 June 1679).
37 Affair quoted in ASF, 'Reggenza' 209, fo. 282^v, and 'Reggenza' 736 (reports of 1749; the events date from 1731 at the latest).
38 ASF, 'Sindaci' 723–725.
39 ASF, 'Sindaci' 732 (report of 1 Aug 1735: quotation) and 'Tratte' 700ff.
40 ASF, 'Monte delle Graticole' 404 and 'Tratte' 701–703; private archives of the Ginori-Lisci family; correspondence of the senator Giuseppe Ginori, 11 and 12 (the quotation is from the packet of letters 11, 6 Oct 1725).
41 ASF, 'Monte delle Graticole' 404.
42 ASF, 'Sindaci' 725.
43 ASF, 'Sindaci' 732 (the events are dated 1735).
44 ASF, 'Fabbriche' 1940.
45 ASF, 'Sindaci' 140, no. 555.
46 For Nelli: ASF, 'Sindaci' 738; for the others, see sources quoted in preceding notes.
47 Savelli, *Summa diversorom tractatorum*, III, p. 377.

48 ASF, 'Nove' 1160 (order of 23 April 1692).
49 ASF, MS 144, fo. 453^v (1729).
50 J. Bonifacius, *Liber de furtis* (Vicenza, 1619), p. 195.
51 G. Bottari, *Delle lodi di Cosimo III* . . . (n.p., n.d.). p. 37ff.
52 ASF, 'Miscellanea Medicea' 400, advice given to Gian Gastone de Medici by L. Fantoni (1723), p. 26.

CHAPTER 8   THE GOOD OF PUNISHMENT

1   Alberti to Richecourt, 6 Oct 1747 (ASF, 'Miscellanea di Finanza' B, 'Abbondanza' 15).
2   On the Abbondanza affair, see chapter 1.
3   ASF, 'Miscellanea di Finanza' B, 'Abbondanza' 15 (15 Sept 1747).
4   Ibid. (10 Oct 1747: autograph).
5   ASF, 'Miscellanea di Finanza' A, 217 (undated, but handed to the law courts on 22 Aug 1748).
6   Ibid.
7   ASF, 'Reggenza' 21, fo. 233–246^v (quotation fo. 244^v).
8   ASF, 'Miscellanea di Finanza' A, 217 (primary version of dispatch to the emperor dated 15 Aug 1747).
9   Ibid. (final version of the dispatch).
10 ASF, 'Reggenza' 21, fo. 201ff (quotations fo. 210–210^v and 213).
11 ASF, 'Reggenza' 357 (notes added to the Council of Vienna report dated 5 Oct 1747).
12 Ibid., 24 Jan 1748.
13 ASF, 'Reggenza' 22, fo. 187 (to the emperor, 23 March 1748).
14 He died on 7 Oct 1748.
15 The emperor even went so far as to threaten the regent in Florence with the sending of 'outside commissioners to bring [the trial] to an end and even to investigate the behaviour of those who had been handling the affair until now' (ASF, 'Reggenza' 357, 17 Oct 1749).
16 ASF, 'Reggenza' 736.
17 ASF, 'Reggenza' 23, fo. 459–459^v (10 Dec 1749).
18 ASF, 'Reggenza' 357 (5 March 1750).
19 Ibid.
20 Florence, private archives of the Antinori family, correspondence of the War Secretary G. Antinori, vol. XV (15 July 1750, Richecourt to the secretary of state Tornaquinci).
21 ASF, 'Reggenza' 357 (19 Nov 1750, 4 Feb 1751, 4 Feb 1752, 15 Dec 1752, 12 Oct 1753, 25 Oct 1754).

22 ASF, 'Reggenza' 12, fo. 8ᵛ (to Francis Stephen, 10 Sept 1737).
23 BNF, II, III, 457 (21 Oct 1747).
24 Milan, Ambrosian Library, X 134 inf. (18 Sept 1757).
25 ASF, 'Reggenza' 184 (margin notes in the report of the Council of Vienna of 3 March 1752. It came to light later that Fei had been the victim of a judicial error; he had, however, already spent twenty months or so in prison).
26 ASF 'Reggenza' 210 and 738.
27 ASF, 'Reggenza' 357 (18 Jan 1764) and 866, no. 9.
28 ASF, 'Regia consulta' 293 (29 July 1748).
29 BNF, II, III, 457 (6 Sept 1752, 29 Nov 1752, 3 November 1764). *Descrizione dei deliquenti stati condannati a morte in Firenze cominciando dal 1328 fino al presente anno . . .* (Florence, 1801), p. 32.
30 See pp. 150ff and 167.
31 A typical example, concerning an affair of contraband discovered in Pisa, is in ASF, 'Reggenza' 357 (2 May 1749 and 3 April 1750).
32 L. Cantini, *Legislazione toscana*, XXVI (Florence, 1806), p. 109; ASF, 'Reggenza', 357 (31 Octr 1748). The issue was all the more delicate in that the *fedecommessi* had already been the subject of a very controversial law in 1747.
33 ASF, 'Reggenza' 357 (margin notes in a report from the Council of Vienna of 24 Jan 1748).
34 Ibid. (notes added to reports of 2 May 1749 and 3 April 1750).
35 Ibid. (margin notes in the report of 2 May 1749).
36 Ibid. (margin notes in the report of 3 April 1750: '*Sansa la justis soufriret trop en Tosquan*').
37 Milan, Ambrosian Library, X 134 inf., fo. 158ᵛ (to Botta-Adorno, 6 Dec 1759).
38 Ibid., X 207 inf., 14 Sept 1758 (Baron Pfütschner to Botta-Adorno). ·
39 A. Wandruszka, 'Le "Istruzioni" di Francesco di Lorena al figlio Leopoldo', *Archivio storico italiano*, 115 (1957), p. 490.
40 Ibid., p. 489.
41 H. de Viel-Castel, *Marie-Antoinette et la Révolution française: recherches historiques . . . suivies des instructions morales remises par l'impératrice Marie-Thérrèse à la reine Marie-Antoinette lors de son départ pour la France en 1770 et publiées d'après le manuscrit inédit de l'Empereur François son père* (Paris, 1859), p. lxxii.
42 Ibid., p.vi.
43 Ibid., p. xviii.

44 Wandruszka, 'Le "Istruzioni" di Francesco di Lorena al figlio Leopoldo', p. 489.

45 Ibid., p. 492.

46 A. Wandruszka, 'Die Religiosität Franz Stephans von Lothringen: ein Beitrag zur Geschichte der *Pietas Austriaca* und zur Vorgeschichte des Josephinismus in Osterreich', *Mitteilungen des österreichischen Staatsarchiv*, 12 (1959), p. 165.

47 Wandruszka, 'Le "Istruzioni" di Francesco di Lorena al figlio Leopoldo', p. 492.

48 ASF, 'Reggenza' 357 (margin notes in the Council of Vienna report of 24 Jan 1748).

49 Wandruszka, 'Die Religiosität Franz Stephans von Lothringen', p. 171.

50 See J. Delumeau, *Le péché et la peur: la culpabilisation en Occident (XIIIe–XVIIIe siècle)* (Paris, 1983).

51 Wandruszka, 'Die Religiosität Franz Stephans von Lothringen', p. 169.

52 Father Lemoyne, *De l'art de régner* (Paris, 1665), pp. 109, 279, 424.

53 J. J. Duguet, *Institution d'un prince, ou traité des vertus et des devoirs d'un souverain* (London, 1739), pp. 11, 141, 148, 150–1, 243, 246, 257, etc.

54 I have discussed this aspect of the issue in various articles: 'La toscane après la paix de Vienne (1737–1765): prépondérance autrichienne ou absolutisme lorrain?', *Revue d'histoire diplomatique*, 93 (1979), pp. 202–22; 'Tra principato e Lumi: lo spazio della Reggenza nella Toscana del Settecento', *Società e storia*, 6 (1983), pp. 39–49.

55 It also seems that Richecourt dealt kindly with the Alberti brothers (see in ASF, 'Miscellanea di Finanza' B, 'Abbondanza' 15, their letter dated 15 Sept 1747 to the minister: Richecourt apparently helped the brothers to draw up their petitions to the emperor. One of them, Giovanni Vincenzo, then became a member of the council of Vienna, and married there in 1758 a woman of the town).

56 I have already mentioned these issues in various studies: see *Mélanges de l'Ecole française de Rome (Moyen Age et Temps Modernes)*, 89 (1977), pp. 983-1027; *Revue d'histoire moderne et contemporaine*, 25 (1978), pp. 513–29; *La fiscalité et ses implications sociales en Italie et en France aux XVIIe et XVIIIe siècles* (Rome, 1980), pp. 75–94.

57 See chapter 2.

58 Milan, Ambrosian Library, X 141 inf., fo. 28, 80ᵛ, 108ᵛ (Botta-Adorno to the emperor, 4 March, 25 April and 11 Nov 1758).
59 ASF, 'Reggenza' 184 (17 Nov 1750).
60 ASF, 'Reggenza' 357 (10 Sept 1759).
61 ASF 'Reggenza' 219 (10 Jan 1744).
62 ASF, 'Finanze' 282, file 'Amministrazione della regia cassa di Lorena in Nancy'.
63 P. L. Rovito, *Respublica dei togati: giuristi e società nella Napoli del Seicento*, 1: Le garanzie giuridiche (Naples, 1981).

THE FRAGILITY OF THE STATE

1 For the sixteenth century, various affairs of corruption in E. Fasano-Guarini, 'Città soggette e contadi nel dominio fiorentino tra quattro e cinquecento: il caso pisano', *Ricerche di storia moderna*, ed. M. Mirri, I (Pisa, 1976), p. 52; 'La Maremma senese nel Granducato Mediceo (dalle "visite" e memorie del tardo cinquecento)'. *Contadini e proprietari nella Toscana moderna*, I (Florence, 1979), pp. 424–5; 'Considerazioni su giustizia, stato e società nel ducato di toscana del Cinquecento', *Florence and Venice: comparisons and relations*, II: Cinquecento (Florence, 1980), pp. 159–60.
2 We are also far less informed about corrupters than corruption: sources in general tell us nothing – or almost nothing – on the social origins, motivations, etc., of people who corrupted the representatives of public authority. For the historian, this opens up another field of study, riddled with difficulties.

Index

'Abbondanza' affair
  arrests, 29–31
  auditors, 113
  Cosimo's attitude to fraud, 167
  defence of fraud, 126
  discovery of fraud, 30–1
  duration of fraud, 65
  effects of fraud, 36–7
  emperor's influence, 172–5,
    177–8, 183–4
  function of 'Abbondanza', 27–
    8, 57
  methods of fraud, 31–6, 108–
    11, 115–16
  other embezzlements from
    'Abbondanza', 40, 41
  personnel, 28–9, 67, 75–6, 107
  trial, 155, 168–75, 183–4
account books, 114–16
Accursio, Mariangelo, 134
Africa
  civil service corruption, 60
  value systems, 8–9, 13
Agata, Antonio Dell', 33
Alamanni, Adamo, 113
Alamanni, Bishop (of Pistoia),
  139

Alamanni, Carlo, 113
Alamanni, Marquis, 169
Alberti, Braccio Degli
  'Abbondanza' fraud, 29–33
  amount of fraud, 31–2, 33, 35
  audit, 113
  death, 173
  finances, 75
  letters, 116–17, 168–9
  pleas, 168–9
  testimony concerning, 109–10
  trial, 169–71, 173
Alberti, Muzio, 57
Alberti family, 168
Alembert, Jean le Rond d', 90
Alessandri, Alessandro Degli
  amount of fraud, 40, 65
  family, 43, 155, 162
  peasants, 68
  pleas, 154
  sanctuary, 38, 154
Ambrogi (treasurer), 40
Amiconi, Raffaello, 41, 43, 152
ancien régime, 1–2, 11–13, 16,
  100, 142–3
Antinori, Amerigo, 69
Antinori, Antonio, 155

Antinori, G., 156
Antinori, Marquis Niccolò
    Francesco, 105
Antoine, Paul Gabriel, 138
Antoninus, Emperor, 131, 134
Archi, Bartolommeo, 51
aristocracy, 74–8, 83, 112, 152–4,
    183–5, 187
Aristotle, 86–7, 89, 100
'Arte della Seta' (silk guild), 44,
    72
Artz, Geri, 47
Ascanio Sanminiati bank, 54
Austrian Succession, War of, 183
authority, transfer of, 72–4
Azerbaidjan, corruption in, 98,
    100

Bacon, Francis, 13
Baratti, Alessandro, 57
Bardi, Count, 169
Barker, Thomas, 8
Bartolini (*cavaliere*), 77, 155
Bati, Giovanni, 42, 65
Beaumont, John, 13, 146
Becalli (*custode*), 111
Becattini, Allegro, 47
Bechi (accountant), 29, 32
Bellarmine, Robert Francis
    Romulus, 89
Bellini (attorney), 48–9
Benedetto XIII, 138
Benini, Bartolommeo, 24–5, 51,
    67, 76, 115, 151–2
Benson, G. C. S., 8
Benzoni (corporal of police), 45,
    176
Berart y Gassol, G., 86, 119, 124
Berretti (baker), 32
Berti, Francesco, 46
Besançon, A., 99

Bettazzi (governor of Prato flour
    tax office), 41, 162–3
Bettazzi, Domenico Agapito, 162
Betti, Pier Antonio, 108
Bianchi, Giovanni Battista, 111
Bindi, Francesco Matteo, 40, 65
Boaistuau, Pierre, 88
Bonazzini, 156
Boniface VIII, Pope, 29
Bonifacio, J., 119, 124, 130, 163
Bonsi-Bucetti, Lorenzo, 42, 43
Borgherini, Pier Francesco, 28
Borgherini, Vincenzo Gaspero
    'Abbondanza' fraud, 28–33,
        108, 115
    amount of fraud, 31–2, 33, 35
    beneficiaries, 67
    defence, 153, 168–70
    lies, 107
    punishment, 170–1, 173, 175
    servants, 110–11
    successor, 68
Borghigiani, Vincenzo, 69
Borgo San Sepolcro, 41, 152
Botta-Adorno, Marquis, 79,
    169n., 175
Bottari, Giovanni Gaetano, 164–
    5
Bourdaloue, Louis, 88
Brezhnev, Leonid, 100
bribery, 44–5, 73–4, 93, 106,
    129–33
Bricchieri-Colombi (*auditore
    fiscale*), 175
Bronzuoli (*stimatore*), 52–3, 73,
    151
Buattini (doctor), 150
Buonaventuri, Tommaso, 23–6,
    41, 51, 75, 108, 115
Buoninsegni, Francesco, 57
Buono, Del (of 'Zecca'), 151

bureaucracy, rational, 4–5, 7–10
Burzichelli, 68
Busenbaum, Hermann, 139
Bussotti, Filippo, 41

Caccia, *cavaliere* Del, 33
Campana (judge), 14
Campbell, John, 106
Capei (*camerlengo*), 41
'Capitani di Parte', 80
Capponi, Ferrante, 149
Capponi family, 68
Cappuccini (Borgherini's
  secretary), 111
Caramelli, Lorenzo, 154
Casa, Aldieri Della, 56
cashiers, 125
Castillo, Don Luis de, 12
casuistry, 122–3, 126–9, 139–42,
  192
Catignani (*camerlengo*), 40
Cavallo (*auditore*), 115
Cavallo, P., 124, 136, 152
Chabod, Federico, 3, 13, 60
Charles V, Emperor
  criminal ordinances, 122
  Gonzaga case, 10, 104, 109,
    145
  Kingdom of Naples, 147
  rules for ministers, 12–14
  servants' wages, 59–60
Charles VI, Emperor, 14
Chiavani (master of the mint), 40
Chiavistelli (porter), 111
Chiti, Bartolommeo, 42, 50, 51,
  65
Choiseul, Etienne François, Duke
  de, 188
Christianity, 15, 87, 89, 100, 120–
  1, 140
Ciacchi (Alberti's secretary), 33,
  109–10

Cianfi (at mint), 70
civil servants, 4
clemency, 165–7, 168, 182, 187
Clement XII, Pope, 23
Colbert, Jean-Baptiste, 2, 146
Coletti (at mint), 70
Colle, 'Monte Pio', 53, 151
Compagni, Niccolò, 112
conscience, 121–2, 187, 192
'Consulta', 48
Conti, Giacomo
  on bribery, 129
  death tax calculation, 73
  Decisiones Florentinae, 101
  function, 57, 106–7
  on inequality, 153
  Strozzi case, 48–9, 101–2, 106
Corpa, Marquis, 77
corruption
  dealing with, 92–4
  definitions, 3–4, 5, 88–92
  functions, 59–63, 82–4
  views of, 85–96, 119–20
Corsini, Cardinal, 168–9
Corsini family, 23
Cortigiani, Gaetano, 47
Cortigiani, Giovanni, 46, 47
Cosimo I, Grand Duke of
  Tuscany, 28, 48, 93, 112
Cosimo III, Grand Duke of
  Tuscany
  'Abbondanza' storehouse, 27
  ambassador's observations, 14
  attitude to corruption, 176
  clemency, 164–5, 167
  council, 76–7
  funeral speech, 164–5
  Gondi's relationship with, 46,
    47
  legislation, 94
  Malegonelle affair, 161
court dignitaries, 3

Cozzini (of the war department), 44

Cranfield, Lionel, 13

Craon, Prince de, 169n.

Cremoni, Enrico Maria, 42, 65, 155

Crusca Academy, 88

customs officers, 3, 61–2, 92

Dazzi, Abbot Francesco, 46

'Decime', 44, 68

'Decime ecclesiastiche', 41, 42

defalcation, 123–4

democracy, 4, 11

'Depositeria general', 42

despotism, 4, 11

Diana, Antonio, 122, 127–9, 131–2, 136

Dictionnaire de l'Académie, 88

Diderot, Denis, 90

dishonour, 104

'Dogana', 38, 40, 42, 152, 159–60

Donnini (*camerlengo*), 32

Dragomanni (senator), 67

Ducci (of the 'Dogana'), 159

Duguet, Jacques Joseph, 182

Durazzi, Anton Francesco, 52, 67, 76, 108, 111, 176

dysfunction, concept of, 20

Elci, Cardinal d', 169

embezzlement, 38–44, 93, 123–6

England

impeachments, 13, 146

Puritanism, 189

Stuart monarchy, 6

Victorian values, 10–11

Escobar y Mendoza, Antonio de, 120, 122, 127–9, 136

esculenta, 130, 133–5

Eugene, Prince, 14

Fabbroni (of the 'Decime'), 44

falsifying accounts, 114–16

family

obligations, 75

property, 154–5, 177

Farinacci, Prospero, 133

fedecommesso, 154–5, 177

Fénelon, François de Salignac de la Mothe-, 181

Feo, Carlo Del, 41, 70, 175, 177

Feo, Francesca Maria Del, 70

financial politics, 185–6

Fioravanti, Bernardino, 42

Foggini, Giovanni Battista, 27

food and drink, gifts of, 130, 133–5

Fortini, Agostino, 81–2

Fortunati, Giovanni Maria, 51

Fossi (baker), 32

Foucault, Michel, 207

Fouquet, Nicolas, 146

France

ancien régime, 1–2

condemnation of laxism, 138

embezzlement legislation, 13, 126

Francis I, Grand Duke of Tuscany, 93

Francis Stephen, Emperor, Grand Duke of Tuscany

advisers, 14, 79

approach to clemency, 167, 172–4

approach to noble criminals, 158, 178–9

regime, 170–88

Richecourt's reports, 17–18

titles, 169n.

French Revolution, 8, 86

Fritelli, Giovanni, 47

function, concept of, 20

Gabbrielli (copyist), 50, 51

Gabbrielli, Pier Antonio, 33
'Gabella', 41, 167
'Gabella dei Contratti', 43, 46–50, 65, 72
Gaetani, Francesco
  'Abbondanza' fraud, 28–32
  amount of fraud, 31–2, 67
  audit position, 113
  family, 28–9, 169, 171
  finances, 75–6
  punishment, 173–5
  trial, 170–1
Galilei (of the 'Dogana'), 159
Galli (clerk), 31, 35
gambling, 67, 76
Gelasius II, Pope, 28–9
Genet, François, 138, 139
Gherardesca, Count Della, 68
Gherardi ('Monte Pio' master), 53, 115, 156–7
Gherardini, Antonio Maria
  embezzlement, 41, 66, 159–60, 161–2
  family, 43, 155
  love affair, 66, 68
Ghezzi (at Siena pawn-office), 40
Gian Gastone, Grand Duke of Tuscany, 25–6, 109, 167
gifts, 129–35
Ginori, 183
Giovanni Carlo, Prince, 106
'Giubbe', 114
Gondi, Francesco Maria, 46–7, 57, 65, 72, 73, 106
Gonzaga, Ferrante, 10, 104, 145–6
Gori, Girolamo, 56
Granvelle, Nicolas Perrenot de, 145
'Grascia', 42, 67, 116
Grassi, Francesco, 104

Great Soviet Encyclopedia, 99
Grifoni, Jacopo, 41, 152
Guadagni, Filippo, 72, 78–82, 169
Guidetti, Orazio, 161–2
Guidetti, Tommaso, 162
Guyot, Joseph Nicolas, 86

Habsburg family, 79, 148
Heidenheimer, Arnold, 12
honour, 104, 106
Hugo, second Duke of Gaeta, 28
Huntington, Samuel P., 61
Hurstfield, Joël, 15, 59

Incontri, Archbishop (of Florence), 139
integrity, 4, 7, 13, 15, 195–6
interest rates, 24, 55
Irish emigrants, 8

Jerson, 120
Jesuits, 122, 127, 136, 139
Joseph I, Emperor, 14
Joseph II, Emperor, 10, 188
Jousse, Daniel, 119, 123, 126, 130
judges
  casuistry, 102, 141
  corruption as sin, 120–1
  crimes of lese-majesty, 13
  dictionary definitions, 88
  early modern view, 89
  jurists' debate, 130–5
  Neapolitan, 148
  private enterprise, 3
  probabilism, 138, 141

Lagomarsini, Father, 139
Lamayène, Monsieur de, 77
Lamberg, Count, 14
Landini (judge), 48

Landriano, Urbano da, 109
Lari, 45
Lavisse, Ernest, 12
law, role of, 95–6, 97, 121, 191
laxism, 138–40, 192
Laymann, Paul, 127
Leghorn
  embezzlement cases, 38, 40–3, 50–1, 65, 155, 162
  Florentine grain purchase, 36–7
Lemoyne, Father, 181
Lessius (Leonard Leys), 127, 132, 136
Libri, Lorenzo
  'Abbondanza' fraud, 29–30
  amount of fraud, 33
  beneficiaries of fraud, 32, 67
  punishment, 105, 173–5
  trial, 169–70
lies, 107, 117–18, 141–2, 192
Lope de Soria, 14
Lorraine dynasty
  customs stations, 92
  embezzlement cases, 39
  loyalty claims, 117
  Malegonelle case, 161
  mint, 70–1
  new attitudes, 17–18, 177, 183–6
Louis XIV, King, 12, 14
Loyseau, Charles, 123
Lucatelli, Tommaso, 44, 176, 177
Luci (*auditore*), 160
Luigi, Lorenzo de', 42
Luri, Giuseppe, 57
Lyncker, J. P., 119, 130, 136

Machiavelli, Niccolò, 91
magistracies, 69–70, 147
magistrates, 130, 132–3

'Magona', 40, 43, 65, 69
Malegonelle, Antonio Maria
  amount of fraud, 40, 64
  consequences of fraud, 159–60, 161–2
  customs station embezzlement, 38, 40–1
  debts, 75
  family, 43
Malegonelle, Francesco Maria
  amount of fraud, 41, 64–5
  audit failure, 113–15
  concern for reputation, 106
  debts, 75
  family, 43
  military bank embezzlement, 41, 152
  possessions, 154
Mancini, Orazio Maria, 42
Manelli (*cavaliere*), 49
Manetti, Francesco, 112
Mannucci, Lorenzo, 44
Maona (secretary to governor of Milan), 59
Maria Theresa, Empress, 10, 14, 17
Marini, Jacopo, 176
Masetti, Father, 52
Mastrillo, Garcia, 119, 124
Mearelli, Giovanni Paolo, 41
Medici, Alexander de', 77
Medici, Prince Ferdinando de, 160
Medici, Cardinal Francesco Maria dei, 54
Medici, Gian Carlo dei, 154
Medici family
  end of era, 17–18
  level of corruption, 39
  Malegonelle affair, 161
  mint, 70

Medici family – *cont.*
  position, 134
  treatment of corruption, 159, 163–4, 172, 178, 183–5
Melari, Armanio, 56
Melati, Prior, 67
Menochio, J., 124–5, 126, 129, 130, 136
Mercianti, Luigi, 38, 162–3
Merton, Robert, 16, 20–2
middle class, 76, 78
Milan, 10, 12, 60, 104, 109, 145
mint, 40, 70–2
modernization, 7
Molina, Lodovico, 122, 131–3
monarchy, 4, 5–6, 96, 102–3
'Monte Comune', 40
'Monte dei Paschi', 159
'Monte del Sale', 54
'Monte di Pietà'
  Florence, 42, 52, 73, 108, 151, 176
  Grand Duke's intervention, 162
  role, 50
'Monte Pio'
  Colle, 151
  Leghorn, 38, 42, 50–1, 65, 155, 162
  Pistoia, 115, 156–7
  Siena, 41, 55–7
'Monte redimibile'
  account books, 115
  auditors, 112
  Benini's position, 23–5, 51, 67, 76, 151
  Buonaventuri's position, 23–5, 75, 108
  scandal, 23–5
Montesquieu, Charles de Secondat, baron de la Brède et de, 91

'Monti', 50–7
moral code, 4, 7
moralization, 142
Mori-Ubaldini, Tommaso, 108
Mormorai, 23
Mousnier, R., 1
Mozzarelli, Cesare, 10, 13
Muratori, Ludovico Antonio, 136, 138, 181

Naples, Kingdom of, 13, 14, 104–5, 147–8, 189, 194
Nelli, Francesco, 69
Nelli, Lorenzo, 69
Nelli, Vittorio, 43, 64, 69, 162
Nencini, Giovanni, 33
Nero, Baron Del, 169
Niccolini, Averardo, 113
Niccolini, Domenico Maria, 113
Niccolini, Ippolito, 65, 69
Nigeria, value systems, 8–9, 15, 98
Nobili, de', family, 106
Nobili, Francesco de', 47
Nobili, Canon Giuseppe de', 47
Nobili-Valori, Filippo de', 158–9, 164
nobility *see* aristocracy
'Nove', 155, 158, 162

oligarchic republics, 4, 5–6
Orsi, Father, 139
ostentation, 67–8, 74–5, 85

Pandolfini, Giovanni Battista, 40, 161
Paoletti, 68
Paoli, Giovanni Petro, 70
Paoli, Zanobi, 41, 70–2
Paravicini, W., 59
Parlement of Paris, 1
Parrini, Antonio, 149–50, 155
'Parte', 72, 79–82, 113

partite infognite, 52
Pascal, Blaise, 120, 136
pawn frauds, 53
Pecorini, Abbott, 110
Pergolini da Galeata, Abbot, 150
Peter-Leopold, Grand Duke of
    Tuscany, 79, 81–2, 162, 179,
    180, 189
Petra, Carlo, 104
Petrucci, Commander, 159
Pfütscher, Baron, 14
Philip II, King, 12
Philip IV, King, 147
Piedmont, 134
Pieri, Girolamo, 33
Pierino, 68
Pietrasanta, 40
Pietrozzi (deputy cashier), 115
Pisa
    contraband, 178
    customs station, 40, 113
    Dominican monks, 52
    fortress, 188
    Lari police force, 45
Pistano, 115
Pistoia
    'Monte Pio', 53, 157
    probabilist debate, 139
    Treasury, 42
Pitti (of 'Monte del Sale'), 54, 150,
    159
Pitti, Giovanni, 113
Pitti, Luca di Roberto, 113
Pitti, Ruberto, 156
poculenta, 130, 133–5
Poirot, Joseph-Charles de, 188
police force, 8, 45
Ponte Vecchio affair, 81–2
Portoferraio, 41, 70, 175
'Possessioni', 43, 65, 105, 154
power
    balance of, 72–4

display of, 67–8
Prato, 41
Prié, Marquis of, 14
privy council, 1
probabilism, 136–41, 192
Pugliese, Tommaso Del, 40
punishment for corruption, 93–
    4, 150–2, 158–64, 180–1,
    192
'Pupilli' magistracy, 45

Rautvich (commander of Pisa
    fortress), 188
regulations, 73
reputation, 105–6
Riccardi family, 74
Richecourt, Count
    'Abbondanza' affair, 36–7,
        108, 117, 168, 170–5, 183–4
    analysis of corruption, 92–3,
        98, 109, 156
    regency, 17, 169n., 183–4
    reports to emperor, 17–18, 68,
        79, 156
Roebuck, Julian, 8
Roman Empire, 98
Roman law, 122–3, 126
Rome, 134
Roncalli (*cancelliere*), 54–5, 67, 76,
    149–51, 155, 156
Rossi, Aretafila De', 66
Rossi, Isidoro De', 66
Rossi, Lorenzo
    'Abbondanza' fraud, 29–36,
        107–11, 115
    debtors, 67
    punishment, 173
    statement on Alberti, 75
    trial, 170
Rosso, Del (bailiff), 169
Rovito, P. L., 59
Rustici, Lorenzo, 41

Saint-Marthe, 88
salaries, 59–60, 62, 65–6, 82
Salm, Prince of, 14
salt tax office, 41, 66, 67, 76,
    149–50, 159
Salviati, Duke, 169
Sanchez, Tomas, 137
Santo Stefano, knights of, 66, 74,
    82, 159, 170, 173
Santucci (judge), 155, 170–1
Sarassoro, Hyacinthe, 9, 15
Savelli, M. A.
    on bribes, 129–30
    on corruption, 119
    on embezzlement, 123, 125
    on gifts, 133–5
    on justice, 85
    on probabilism, 137
    on sentencing, 153, 162–3
Scott, James, 5–6, 61
Segneri, Father, 139
'Segreteria di Finanze', 44, 186
Serristori (farmer-general), 81
Serselli, *cavaliere*, 33
Sestino, 152
Sicilian Inquisition, 131
Sicuri, Silvestro, 57
Siena
    depositario, 42
    embezzlers, 43, 159
    'Monte Pio', 41, 55–7
    pawn-office, 40, 41
    punishments for
        embezzlement, 94
silk guild *see* 'Arte della Seta'
Simis, Constantin, 99
Simkins, Edgar, 8, 15, 98
sin, 87, 88–9, 95, 120–1, 128–9
'Sindaci del Monte', 112–14
Slich, Baron, 14
social mobility, 60, 62, 82–3

Sollazzino, 68
Somerset, Robert Carr, Earl of,
    146
'Soprassindaci', 112–14
Soviet Union, 98–100
Spanish legislation, 148
Spinelli (senator), 67
Spinetti, Giovanni Cammillo, 45
Squarcialupi, A., 26, 67
Stainville, Marquis de, 188
Strozzi, Count, 169
Strozzi, Filippo, 48
Strozzi, Monsignor Leone, 48
Strozzi, Prince, 46, 48–9, 101,
    106
Strozzi family, 33, 48
Stuart monarchy, 6

Tanner, Adam, 129, 132
'Tassa del Macinato', 65
taxes, 73, 185–6
Tempi, Francesco, 69
Teri, Ascanio
    customs office fraud, 113, 115
    punishment, 152, 154, 160–1,
        162
Teri, Lodovico, 67, 105
Teri brothers, 40, 43, 64
theft, 123–5, 128–9
Thomas Aquinas, Saint, 88–9
Tiraqueau, André, 153
Torricelli (baker), 32
Torrigiani, Marquis, 29, 110
Torrigiani, Monsignor, 169
Toussaint, Baron, 79, 188
Toussaint, Felix-Yves de, 188
Toussaint, Joseph de, 188
Traversagnoli (at mint), 70
Trent, Council of, 122
tribal loyalty, 8–9
Turco, Luigi Del, 42

Tuscany, Grand Duchy of, 17

Ubaldini, Giovanni, 65, 105–6, 154
Ubaldini, Lorenzo, 112
Uguccioni ('Parte' pay clerk), 81
Uguccioni (senator), 44, 72, 176, 177
United States
  democracy, 11
  early twentieth century, 7–8
  'machine politics', 16, 20–2

Van Klaveren, Jakob, 3–7, 11–12, 15, 17
Vanni (of 'Monte del Sale'), 54, 150, 159
Varrochi, Simone, 176
Vasquez, Gabriel, 136
Venice, 105, 176
Venturi, Father, 139
Venturi-Gallerani, 42

Verdi, Giuseppe, 69, 155
Vergili, Giuseppe, 110
Verrazzano, Neri-Maria Da, 57
Vespucci family, 156
Veyne, P., 98
Vienna, court of, 14, 24, 105, 172
Vinci (procurator), 49
Violante de Bavaria, Princess, 160
violence, 61
Virgili, Giuseppe, 33
Vivai (*cancelliere*), 29

Washington, George, 7
Weber, Max, 4–5
Wraith, Ronald, 8, 15, 98
Wratislaw, Count, 14

Zampogni (accountants), 40
'Zecca', 40, 151
Zemtsov, Ilja, 98–100
Zeti, archpriest of Prato, 52